DEATH AND AFTERLIFE

DEATH AND AFTERLIFE

Perspectives of World Religions

EDITED BY
Hiroshi Obayashi

PRAEGER

Westport, Connecticut
London

Library of Congress Cataloging-in-Publication Data

Death and afterlife : perspectives of world religions / edited by
Hiroshi Obayashi.
p. cm.
Includes bibliographical references and index.
ISBN 0-275-94104-3 (pbk. : alk. paper)
1. Death—Religious aspects—Comparative studies. 2. Future life—
Comparative studies. I. Obayashi, Hiroshi.
BL504.D33 1992
291.2'3—dc20 91-3876

British Library Cataloguing in Publication Data is available.

A hardcover edition of *Death and Afterlife* is available from the Greenwood Press imprint of Greenwood Publishing Group, Inc. (Contributions to the Study of Religion, Number 33; ISBN: 0-313-27906-3)

Library of Congress Catalog Number: 91-3876
ISBN: 0-275-94104-3

First published in 1992

Praeger Publishers, 88 Post Road West, Westport, CT 06881
An imprint of Greenwood Publishing Group, Inc.

Printed in the United States of America

The paper used in this book complies with the Permanent Paper Standard issued by the National Information Standards Organization (Z39.48-1984).

20 19 18 17 16 15

Copyright Acknowledgments

The author and publisher gratefully acknowledge permission to use the following:

Watson, Burton, ed. and trans., *Chuang Tzu, Basic Writings*. Copyright © 1964 Columbia University Press. Used by permission.

Pritchard, James B., ed., *Ancient Near Eastern Texts Relating to the Old Testament*, 3d ed., with supplement. Copyright © 1969 by Princeton University Press. Reprinted by permission of Princeton University Press.

Contents

Preface

This book offers a historical and cross-cultural survey of the varieties of perceptions regarding death and hopes for survival beyond death found in different religiocultural settings. Major religious traditions of the world, past and present, contain perspectives of perennial importance on the topic of death and afterlife; this is especially evident in their mythical patterns and doctrinal teachings. These myths and doctrines are not only directly reflected in mortuary and funerary practices, but also inform patterns of beliefs and rituals that shape human lifestyles. It may not be too difficult to explore the understandings of death and afterlife in various cultures by simply isolating and discussing relevant teachings and narratives from their religious traditions. But issues such as these concern more than sacred texts; they affect the innermost core of the human psyche and constitute the very fabric of human existence. For this reason they can be explored adequately only by a comprehensive understanding of a given religious system rooted in an overall culture. For example, the Christian concept of death and resurrection is certainly misunderstood when it is uprooted from the context of a particular biblical framework and the subsequent evolution of Christian theology. The same can be said of Hindu concepts of reincarnation and the Taoist cult of immortality. Only those who have a comprehensive historicocultural familiarity with such traditions can provide a proper focus for these issues and help us come to a true understanding of them. No single scholar can master all the cultural blocs and religious traditions necessary for a thorough comprehension and penetration of the manifold conceptions of death and afterlife. Thus one must rely on experts in each field.

Although the thirteen chapters that constitute this volume share a common objective of offering an outline of the beliefs, myths, and practices, reflecting the views of respective religions on death and afterlife, the way in which they are presented varies. Some follow the history of the religion to see either the significant changes that have taken place in its views of death and afterlife or the persistent patterns that have survived through time; others select certain regional practices that might well illustrate basic patterns of belief concerning death and afterlife. Naturally, the enormous wealth of religious beliefs demands a selective approach. The method of study also varies from the sociological, such as is evident in the opening chapter, to the archaeological, historical, literary critical, theological, as well as the so-called history of religion approach. The particular method of approach is determined by the nature of the material in the respective chapters. The nonliterate cultures, such as are the main subject matter of chapter 1, call for anthropological expertise to fully unravel the beliefs and expectations behind ritual behaviors. The highly literary and theatrical genre of ancient Greek tragedies demands the literary critical method to yield successful results, bringing into relief distinctive ancient Greek attitudes toward death and afterlife. Similarly, religions that find the very foundations of their beliefs about death and afterlife in key events in their own history require historical or theological approaches. Thus it is the strength of this volume that the reader is introduced to each religious perspective by the method most appropriate to it. With death and afterlife as the common focus, this group of scholars has brought to bear its diverse expertise in anthropology, classics, archaeology, biblical studies, history, theology, and "history of religions." We hope that this book provides some suggestions as to how the reader can understand peoples' thoughts and expectations, past and present, near and far.

This book was born out of a lecture series conducted during the academic year 1987–88 at Rutgers University under the sponsorship of the Anna I. Morgan Fund of its department of religion, in cooperation with the Voorhees Assembly Board and the dean's office, both of Douglass College of Rutgers University. Without their generous support, this project would not have been possible.

From its inception as an idea through the lecture series itself and to the completion of the book, I have been indebted to many people for their assistance. It was the immeasurable help of many of my colleagues in the department that enabled me to carry the project through to its conclusion. Of special note is the generous cooperation I received from Professors Henry W. Bowden, Chun-fang Yu, and Alberto Green of Rutgers University.

To Cecelia Nodine and Grace Ahmed I owe my most heartfelt thanks for their untiring secretarial assistance, without which I could not have succeeded in this endeavor. I thank also my son Hal and my daughter-in-law, Leslie, for their many hours of capable editorial assistance, without which I would have been totally helpless, my wife, Kimiko, and my daughter, Anna, for being the inexhaustible source of encouragement, even amid tragedy. Last, but by no means the least, I thank my second son, Seiya John Obayashi (1965–1990), who in his short life taught me the meaning of suffering and even in death left vibrating the echoes of love and caring.

Introduction

Hiroshi Obayashi

A historian once recalled the day he went to hear the German theologian Karl Barth, one of the greatest thinkers of our century, who visited America in 1962. Thrilled to have heard him in person, and greatly impressed, no doubt, by the lecture itself, he told a fellow graduate student back at his apartment about his intellectually uplifting experience. The other graduate student, who happened to be a scientist, responded, "Well, is he right?" Most of us who have been educated in modern society tend to think of things in clear dichotomies of right or wrong, and true or false. The scientific mind does not tolerate two varying answers to a single question. Questions about death and afterlife, then, seem thoroughly futile because there are no criteria and no empirical evidence on which to assess the relative merits of the variety of ideas held to be true by people of various cultures.

The life sciences have been advancing the frontiers of our knowledge ever closer to the truth about the mystery of life through researches in biology and chemistry. But the human life that we live is more than a biological process, though no doubt firmly based on it. As to human life, there are various ways to live it, and a large majority of those ways may very well be valid and acceptable. There are just as many ways to observe, interpret, and evaluate the human life we live as there are ways to live it. Should it be considered futile to raise serious questions as to how to live a human life or how to view it simply because it is known in advance that there is no single true answer? Although, as a biological organism, a human being has only one way to be alive (i.e., we do not have a choice about needing oxygen to breathe), there are various ways to live humanly, endeavoring to fulfill the authentic image of humanity that people uphold. Questions about human life need not have a single true answer to be intellectually worthwhile and stimulating. Neither do they have to be scientific (about biological organisms, for example) to be able to claim their legitimate place in the domain of academic inquiry. Literature, art, philosophy, and religion are the areas in which these questions are raised, and a multitude of paths pursued in tackling such questions.

By the same token, questions about death are bound to produce a wide range of answers and viewpoints, many of which may be equally valid and acceptable, and which warrant our serious attention. On the other hand, we should recognize that although thoughts about human life have experiential bases, the same cannot be said about death. The human imagination about death and afterlife often is not only an extension of human thoughts about life (sharing the same experiential foundation), but also the source of novel insights that shed new light on our understanding of life itself. Our collective journeys into the meanings of life and death are deeply intertwined and mutually illuminating. It seems as if they almost anticipate or reinforce one another. A profound understanding of life often is accompanied by the seriousness with which death is considered. Overly euphoric views of life that take no account of human finitude and mortality can only be thoughtless and irresponsible.

The human being has a threefold structure with regard to his life: the organic-biological life, the social-cultural life, and the transcendent-ideal dimension of life. First, a human being has an organic substratum in which he shares with all living creatures common vital processes. The animal is one with life. From the moment it is born its ''life'' dictates its destiny until it dies. The only direction in which the animal can act is toward the life, that is, toward its prolongation, enhancement, and perpetuation. The animal has no freedom concerning life. No animal is capable of suicide, for this is a conscious taking of one's own life with some knowledge of the consequences.

In coming into this world the human being also is unfree. Neither the human being nor the animal is capable of going behind its own existence to choose its own coming into being. But the human being is known to be the only animal capable of taking its own life, consciously choosing death for whatever reasons—altruistic sacrifice, egotistical preservation of honor, or simple inability to undergo prolonged suffering. This proves the human being's relative ability to handle or control her own life. She has a measure of detachment from her own life. Although an altruistic sacrifice or preservation of honor may not apply to animals, prolonged pain and agony are certainly conditions the animal may encounter. The animal, however, does not have a choice of acting against its own life to opt for death to shorten or terminate the pain. So, although the human being is one with her own life in coming into life, in life she is no longer completely one with her own life.

This detachment or transcendence in rudimentary form the human being gained over his life is reflected in the simple fact of his being conscious of it. When one is at one with life, one cannot even be conscious of it. Life is now the object of conscious awareness. Animism, which E. B. Tylor proposed a century ago as an anthropological theory about the pervasive primitive tendency to view the world as permeated by life, attests to early people's awareness of, and hence their rudimentary transcendence over, their own lives.

Over the foundation of the organic substratum the human being has built a uniquely human life of which she has been increasingly aware throughout her own evolution. It is only when she became conscious of being alive that she crossed the threshold to become a human being, and this was made possible by a new horizon called society. To be human is the gift of society. It does not take functionalist, structuralist sociology to acknowledge the role of society in the formation of human consciousness. Life lived at the human level is now what is conferred on her by society. George Bond's chapter on African religions, which appears first in this book, graphically illustrates this point. Studying the native tribal funerary cult, the author makes a perceptive observation:

> Though the Yombe recognize a newborn infant as a living creature, the infant is not considered to be a social person entitled to an appropriate burial. It is still too close to nature and the organic properties of its birth. It is not of society, and if it should die, it is buried in a shallow grave in the bush or the wild, or, in the olden days, tossed on the rubbish heap. The act of being born does not establish humanity.

Thus, each society recreates through a series of rites of passage the life offered by nature into a human life, that is, a social person.

Although, as a social being, he is now aware of both life and death, being aware of something, and understanding and comprehending it are not the same. We are not fully in control of our own lives; neither do we comprehend the complexity and wondrous workings of our own destinies. But at least we are familiar with the mundane reality of our day-to-day lives. We even learn how to live it and how to cope with life's difficulties, thanks to the accumulated wisdom of social convention. That must have been the case with early people as well. With death we have no such prima facie empirical familiarity. When challenged by this awesome and unavoidable fact, we, like early people, find ourselves with neither an empirical basis nor the conceptual tools needed to penetrate the veil. Therefore, we have no choice but to deal with it as yet another form of life—afterlife. We use all the familiar features extrapolated from our own lives in an attempt to understand and comprehend death by inference.

Death is not only deeply tragic to people as the negation of life of a dear one; it also is disruptive to the ongoing rhythm of the society. If life is a socially created reality, then so much more should death be tackled as a devastation to social life. Thus the socially disruptive effect of death is sought to be softened by proper funerals and ensuing rituals by translating death itself into a continued form of life. In the Yombe's case that Bond examines, the dead person undergoes a transformation into an ancestor, and as such becomes reintegrated into the ongoing societal process of the living. Ancestors are as much a part of the community as the living descendants; they function as the source and support of the moral order. Just as society ritually recreates the (mere) biological individual into a social person, it is now clear that it tackles organic death by taking the deceased and ritually turning him into an ancestor.

Thomas Hopkins's chapter on Hinduism and Judith Berling's on Chinese religions confirm the foregoing interpretation concerning the ancestor. In Hinduism, unlike later and more developed varieties, such as the Upaniṣadic and the bhakti (devotional) religions, which aim at the ultimate release from reincarnation, the earliest Vedic religion was geared to maintaining continuity in the ancient Hindu caste society. The Vedic rituals are believed to prepare the deceased for their journey to the World of the Fathers. "Afterlife in the Vedic ritual tradition," Hopkins explains, "is a corporate family concern. Only a married householder can perform the required rituals for himself and his ancestors, and only a continuing family line can secure the welfare of the departed." Berling's discussion of ancestor worship in traditional China, echoing the Yombe tribal beliefs and rituals, brings to the fore the point that the ancestor is made "a continuing presence in family business, an ongoing participant in the life of the clan."

Scholars are in general agreement that early people were unable to understand death and invariably believed in some form of immortality after the biological death. Some argue that this is due to early people's perception of the world as replete with the rhythm of life pulsating in everything, animate and inanimate (primitive panvitalism and animism). Others maintain that the early people's average life expectancy, which hardly exceeded eighteen years, did not allow anyone to live out the full course of natural life to enable one to realize the intrinsic mortality. Death always came about by accident or disease. It always was a premature and abrupt interruption of life. People did not die but always were killed, no doubt leaving survivors wondering how long the victim might have lived were it not for the interruption. Thus the inability to see through to a natural end left people with a belief in immortality.

These and other arguments may have something to contribute to our understanding of the pervasive presence of the belief in an afterlife among primal human beings, but only by serving to supplement the more basic thesis that afterlife is predominantly a social requirement, as many of the authors in this book maintain.

Having crossed over the threshold from animal to human being, the human being is now a fully social, cultural being. Both life and death are social realities. Death is the transition from one form of life to another, and society is responsible for ensuring a smooth transition for the deceased. The idea of a postmortem destiny displaying both similarity and continuity with the present life is best exemplified by the beliefs of the ancient Egyptians, whereas that marked by a radical discontinuity is best illustrated by the ancient Mesopotamians. Ancient Egyptians visualized their afterlife with unusually colorful vividness. The extent to which they invested their time, energy, and imagination in preserving the bodies, constructing enormous tombs to house them, and building mortuary temples to offer prayers and gifts to maintain some form of ties is indicative of a belief in the aforementioned continuity. In discussing this bond between the living and the dead, William Murnane says in his chapter on ancient Egypt, "No distinction seems to be made in these scenes between family members who were living at the time of the funeral and those who already were dead. The implication is that the extended family transcends the boundary of death. Indeed, the liturgical calendars of ancient Egypt regularly included the dead in the celebrations of the living."

The basic continuity between this and the other side of the river of death is amply supported by the general optimism with which the ancient Egyptians viewed their world. It was an ordered cosmos, with the sun and the Nile playing the most prominent roles in its annual rotation. Human life was firmly embedded in a structured universe whose order was centripetally personified in the divine authority of the pharaoh.

Such was not the case with the ancient Babylonians. Their world was perceived as plagued by irregularities. The tenuous order of the cosmos was seen to be the product of a fragile compromise worked out among clashing wills of the celestial bodies, subject to constant revisions and rearrangements. Much has been made of the climatic, geographical, and topographical differences between two of the greatest cradles of human civilization, Egypt and Mesopotamia, as possible explanations for such diametrically opposed attitudes and perceptions. But the fundamental difference in world views, which goes deep into the mythic consciousness of the two civilizations, cannot be completely ascribed to such external conditions. There must have been a deep-seated general pessimism on the part of the ancient Mesopotamians that was in stark contrast to ancient Egyptian optimism. The difference ultimately can be ascribed only to the structures in the depths of their respective psyches.

Reflecting his anxiety-laden psyche, the ancient Mesopotamian has a relatively low self-estimation, ranking himself the lowest in the order of beings in his tension-filled universe. The human being perceives his own life to be but a fragile existence with little or no value to boast of in this world. This world, including heaven and earth, belongs to gods; gods reside in heaven but own the earth. The proper home of the human creature, quite in contrast, is the underworld. The liminal figure, the human being, spends his brief life "hovering at the threshold of the netherworld," which was believed to lie beneath the thin layer of the earth's crust. And this netherworld acted as the great leveler of all distinction that existed among people in this life. "Former rulers," says Jerrold Cooper in his chapter, "eat dust and clay themselves, but serve real food and drink to the gods. . . . Life there is a dim shadow of earthly existence, and certainly nothing to anticipate with any enthusiasm."

It is not entirely a coincidence that the same idea of a shadowy underworld resonates in ancient Israel, for it was the common Amorite heritage that made itself known in both Babylonian and ancient Israelite beliefs of the underworld. Sheol, as it was called by the ancient Israelites, is the land of no return, lying below the cosmic ocean, to which all, the mighty and the weak, travel in the ghostly form they assume after death, known as Raphaim. There the dead have no experience of either joy or pain, perceiving no light, feeling no movement. That is to say, it is a dismal place when it comes to the events that the ancient Israelites were only so thoroughly acquainted with in the arena of history. Not even the blessing of God reaches down into Sheol. On the other hand, as delightless as it may be, it is, at least, a place where "the wicked cease from troubling, and there the weary are at rest. There the prisoners are at ease together; they hear not the voice of the taskmaster. The small and the great are there, and the slave is free from his master" (Job 3:17–19). Samuel, an exemplary citizen of ancient Israel, now a resident of this underworld, proclaims to Saul, who has fallen out of God's favor, that he will join him in Sheol tomorrow. He who deserves blessing and he who deserves only punishment find themselves together in the same Sheol.

Note that Sheol is not yet differentiated into realms of reward and punishment. The function of the underworld as the great leveler prominent in ancient Mesopotamia is clearly retained in ancient Israelite thought regarding the afterlife. The Israelites seem to have been content with this undifferentiated, hence undeveloped, notion of the shadowy realm because they were more deeply concerned with the survival of their peoplehood on this earth directly under the covenantal guidance of Yahweh, the God of Israel. The idea of a corporate personality surviving through time gave them solace and encouragement, though people might fall away into this shadowy underworld. No people was more concerned, more obsessed with the perpetuation of the group identity—with all the religious and emotional energy invested into the dynamics of social continuity—than the ancient Israelites. The social survival has been particularly difficult and maintained only at inordinate cost to the Jews throughout their long history.

The examination of the ancient Israelite view of the afterlife offers George Mendenhall an ideal opportunity to bring into the open the long, arduous struggle between the ancient Near Eastern political paganism and the concern for justice with full covenantal rigor, championed by many a Hebrew prophet. The cult of the dead, necromancy, is vividly dramatized in the episode of "the witch of Endor." Saul, the waning king of Israel, trembling before his inevitable defeat at the hands of the Philistines, resorts to mediumship to appeal to the ghost of Samuel for his support and advice. Mediumism, the practice of consultation with deceased forebears, represents the cult of the royal ancestors in this biblical example. "What the cult of the ancestors really involved was the appeal to the past as an authoritative justification and legitimation of the present," Mendenhall observes.

When the Exodus nation of Israel established itself as a kingdom of Yahweh, it did do away with thirty-one Canaanite kings, as recorded in Joshua 12. That signified its refusal to accept pagan political necromancy. Historical and political decisions ought to have been made in the spirit of justice clearly laid down in the covenantal stipulation. The nation's conduct was never to be fashioned by the political cult of the ancestors. "You shall make no graven image" is the prohibition of this political and moral necromancy. Saul, in his moment of weakness, had reverted to such political paganism.

What is perceptive of Mendenhall is that he views the whole history of Israel as the story of the struggle between persistent paganism in the form of political necromancy and a covenantal cry for justice. Saul's deranged appeal to necromancy is not an isolated incident. Mendenhall points out that throughout much of ancient Israelite history the political necromancy of obedience to precedent and the dead convention preserved by a ritualized, arcane cult was so firmly built into the machinery of the king's government that there was no room for the genuine ethical consideration based on the covenant that calls fervently for justice. It is all too familiar to us that in political processes, ancient as well as modern, moral considerations often fall before expedience. This persistent call of the prophets for justice, despite abuses and harassments by the royal political necromancers, provided the needed springboard for a great religion to break into the consciousness of humankind.

The ancient Israelite vision of reality was "historical," as opposed to being "cosmological," with the covenantal promise of Yahweh as the *terminus a quo,* and its fulfillment as the *terminus ad quem.* But when the Jerusalemite theocracy turned David and Zion into the final fulfillment of the promise, the historical vista was closed and sealed. No longer did anything have to happen in the drama of their history. Thus the story of David and Zion became something of a permanent and fixed pattern, and began to function as a cosmological myth, much like those of the ancient Egyptian and Mesopotamian imperial institutions. It took the relentless and cumulative efforts of the major prophets such as Amos, Hosea, Isaiah, Jeremiah, and Deutero Isaiah to break the logjam of complacency and reopen the dynamics of the covenantal history. They thus restored the historical vista so vital to the Hebraic consciousness, and in so doing, the prophets of ancient Israel signaled something quite remarkable in the history of human consciousness. They ushered in, in the Semitic world, what cultural historians call the "axial period." During this span in antiquity a profound change took place in human consciousness. This period saw a real turning point (axis) in human history and a change so profound that it altered the human sense of value. (Axiology means "theory of values". Socrates and other great philosophers of ancient Greece, Buddha of India, Zoroaster of Persia, and Confucius and Lao Tzu of China all left their permanent imprints in human civilization during this axial period, with Jesus and Muhammad concluding the vibrant impulses of this unspeakably creative period. Today's great religions of the world are the results, directly or indirectly, of the creative inspirations of these great thinkers and visionaries of the axial period.)

The covenant religion of ancient Israel had devolved through centuries of cultic practice into a heavy casuistry of both the moral and ritual kind, into matters of rituals, liturgies, and legalism of conduct—no longer a matter of the heart. It was the major task of these prophets to redefine the covenantal religion into one of faith, justice, and love. Israel, as a chosen people, had failed to live up to its covenantal obligations, and hence had to be handed over to the enemy to be destroyed. They saw in this catastrophe Yahweh's rejection of Israel's cultic religion, and thereby rejection of its entire past. The proclamation of a new faith and a new hope that hinged on the remnants of Israel was the axial prophets' response to national catastrophe. They reminted the once collective tradition of Israel into an individual piety; a once external cultic practice into an inner relationship of loyalty to God; and a covenant once written on stone tablets into one inscribed in the human heart. What the people of Israel failed to fulfill Jeremiah took upon himself to bring to fruition. In his own personal life of rejection and torment he saw the meaning of God's chosen vessel being disclosed. Deutero Isaiah carries even further the meaning of the suffering of an individual who bears the burden of God's chosen vehicle—a burden the people of Israel had failed to carry.

Through these vicarious experiences of the axial prophets an irreversible shift took place in the locus of religious faith, that is, from the collectivity of peoplehood to the personhood of the individual. This trend was carried even further during the time of the Maccabees. Though the basic character of Hebraic thinking was collectivity and, for the most part, remained such (even in the time of national catastrophe the hope was for the restoration of peoplehood out of the remnants of the scattered nation), the suffering during the Maccabean period became the most serious challenge to the old Israelite thinking. This time it was not the shared suffering of all the Jews, but only those who remained loyal to the Torah who suffered and died. Thus the ancient belief of Sheol, the underworld, which summarized the common fate of all the Jews, proved no longer satisfactory. The logic of salvation that focused only on corporate or collective survival was no longer sufficient. The fate of the individual who perished for the faith had to be addressed. It was through this situation that the idea of resurrection, which Robert Goldenberg calls "the most individualistic of all religious conceptions," was introduced into Judaism. Goldenberg's chapter on Judaism traces the changes that occurred in the postbiblical and rabbinic history of Judaism about death and afterlife—changes necessitated by the axial revolution that came as a response to and as an interpretation of the national experience. Resurrection and apocalypticism were the Judaic answer to changing times.

The importance of the axial discovery of the personal and the individual in ancient Israel can be matched only by that of the establishment of the soul by the Athenian philosophers, such as Socrates and Plato, as the central core of human selfhood. The human soul (psyche), which had been regarded by the pre-Socratic nature philosophers "as material consisting of whatever primeval element—such as air or fire—they thought to be the basis of all that exists," or, at best, as "the vehicle of passion, emotion, fear, anxiety, hope, or desire," as evidenced by the tragedies, is now seen by Socrates as the seat of intellectual and moral activity.

Helen North guides us through the development of the ancient Greek idea of the soul from the tragedies through Orphic and Pythagorean cults to its height in Socrates and Plato. The soul is the dynamic center of the self that is nourished by dialogues with itself, with other selves, and, most important, with the eternal reality called "the Good." The essence of a human being's selfhood lies in the soul, which contains the divine spark of ultimate goodness. Death is the liberation of this noble soul from its bodily prison. To achieve a clean and effective departure from this corporeal world and return to its proper home of the eternal bliss in the world of the Good, the soul must prepare itself.

Thus the "care of the soul" becomes, for Socrates and Plato, the most important activity in which human beings can engage. Philosophy as "the care of the soul," whose essential need is intellectual and moral, prepares it for its proper intellectual salvation, separation from the flesh. If death is the final liberation of the soul from the prison of the body, then preparation must mean its training in the body as if out of the body. Philosophy as the art of training the soul intellectually can thus be considered rehearsal for death by lifting the soul ascetically out of the environment of the body while still in the body.

With Socrates and Plato, the human being has discovered in his own self the dimension of a mystery that cannot be explained away in organic and physical terms or controlled by social and cultural conventions—a mystery that clears a path to the ultimate. For this is the mystery of participation—the participation of the soul in the ultimate Goodness. The soul in and by itself apart from the ultimate Goodness cannot be good. Neither is it the actualization of Goodness in temporal reality. But by participation the soul shares in the ultimate Goodness that is beyond the bounds of temporal and ephemeral reality. Only by participation does the soul bear in itself the spark of the ultimate. Though that spark does not make the soul a completely realized goodness, it does make the soul seek the ultimate realization of the Good. The mystery of participation thus enables the soul to realize both that it is far removed from the ultimate and that nonetheless it desires to attain the perfection of the ultimate Goodness and is capable of doing so. From the viewpoint of the evolution of consciousness, this conceptual development signals a monumental accomplishment, that is, the discovery of the ideal self. The human being is born with an organic biological self. It was made over by society into a sociocultural self. Now the self has to strive to achieve its own goal of the ideal. The ideal self is not a given. It is what the human being chooses and aspires to attain. If the organic-biological self represents a human being's past tying him to his animal origin, and if the sociocultural self represents his current reality, then the ideal self can be said to represent his futurity, the self yet to be realized.

It is in the discovery of the ideal self that the great religions of the world have their origins. The axial period also is the period during which Buddha, Confucius, Lao Tzu, Zoroaster, and the authors of the Upaniṣads, in different parts of the world and in different historical and cultural conditions, gained new visions of reality. Their discovery was preceeded by the axial impulses of many Hebrew prophets and followed by the Athenian philosophers mentioned earlier. It was an uncannily creative period in the development of the human mind that virtually set the course for the rest of human history. When Jesus and Muhammad appeared on the scene later to universalize the contributions of the axial visionaries, they were already very much awash in the dynamic flow of the axial religions. Thus in the rest of this book are chapters dealing with death and afterlife encompassing the major religious traditions of the world, East and West: Leander Keck on the New Testament, Hiroshi Obayashi on Christianity, William Chittick on Islam, Thomas Hopkins on Hinduism, Frank Reynolds on Buddhism, Elisabeth Benard on Tibetan Tantrism, and Judith Berling on Chinese religions.

The vision of reality shared by the Semitic religions, Judaism, Christianity, and Islam, is essentially personalistic and historical. The ultimate center of value is found in the dimension of the personal; hence the ultimate reality is committed to a personalistic symbol of God, regardless of the name by which he is addressed, such as Yahweh or Allah. Then the world of reality is essentially perceived as the realm in which the personal expresses itself through its life activity. The creation of meaning is the self-expression of the personal being. It is true that even under the most favorable conditions, such as peace, affluence, and freedom, human beings can waste their lives by being most uncreative of meaning. Conversely, even under the most adverse conditions of dehumanization, such as in a concentration camp, people have tenaciously strived to live creatively and meaningfully because such is the essence of human life—to create meaning.

History is the stage on which the personal being, individually or collectively, engages in the continuous activity of creating meaning. And only when something utterly new is brought into being, *ex nihilo,* as it were, can it be called creation, and this happens only in the creation of meaning, both aesthetic and moral. Everything else is just a recombination or rearrangement of the same old ingredients in the material world. Thus creation is a term most correctly applied to the creation of moral and aesthetic values called meaning, which is the exclusive prerogative of the personal being. That is why creation is the most fundamental metaphor in these personalistic and historical religions of Semitic origin (not because of any belief in creation as opposed to evolution as a biological theory—a contemporary debate most misplaced and pointless).

Given such a vision of reality, how do the Semitic religions approach the question of death and afterlife? We can reasonably anticipate the correlation of death and afterlife. Though these Semitic religions are as thoroughly aware as Indian religions of death as being intrinsic to the natural constitution of human existence, they nevertheless connect it to a most value-laden condition known as sinfulness. Death and mortality are not merely matters of nature, but religious and theological problems. "If God is the author of life, why must everything that lives die?" Leander Keck formulates the problem as seen by the New Testament. The New Testament brings the question of death and afterlife to the center of the domain of value and meaning. Death is life lived meaninglessly. Death is no longer just a natural process, but the destruction of life's meaning, and afterlife in the New Testament now means the overcoming of death through the creation of meaning. It is thus understandable why Paul stressed death as being the wage of sin. He could not leave death free of moral implications. Similarly, neither is afterlife a simple matter of the prolongation of life. It is now connected to salvation, the final establishment or affirmation of the meaning of life.

It is through meaning that the finite material life of the human being is bound to the eternal. So through the creation of meaning a finite life can transcend its limitations. Whether it is called the breaking in of the eternal into the temporal or the transcending of the temporal to the eternal, what happens is that the personal life overcomes the nay-saying of death by creating a meaning that defeats the disintegrating effect of death, or by reaffirming the fact that life is meaningful. The ultimate victory and establishment of meaning over meaninglessness, variously symbolized as salvation, beatitude, or blissfulness, and committed to the mythological language of heaven, kingdom of God, or paradise, are thus presented by these Semitic religions as lying ahead in the future, beyond the reach of death.

The finite life that is snuffed out by death may seem meaningless because it is so fragile and transient. But if that brief episode called life is rooted in a larger context of meaning, it would be possible to keep that life from ending in despair. It is in meaning that the all-too-short life of a human being finds itself part of a larger context. The finite life of a person can be given a meaning that goes beyond spatio-temporal boundaries. So, if death is now defined as the wage of sin (i.e., dissolution and negation of meaning), then afterlife is as salvation (i.e., establishment and affirmation of meaning).

In the New Testament this establishment of meaning is possible only by God, the initial author of life. Human beings cannot attain it by themselves or possess the ability as a natural asset. It has to come from God. Afterlife does not stem from any innate immortality, but must be conferred by God by his gratuitous act of raising humanity out of death, that is, resurrection. Resurrection is "real transformation, not simply resuscitation," emphasizes Keck, a transformation of life devoid of meaning into one bestowed with eternal meaning, of life lived without God into one lived in proper relation to God.

Turning now to the East, we see that the vision of reality shared by religions of Indian origin, Hinduism and Buddhism, is basically nonpersonalistic. Though since ancient times the Hindu world has never lacked gods and deities, none of these countless gods developed into a monotheistic God. This is because personhood is not the basic paradigm for the Hindu vision of reality. The world of reality is far more comprehensive than what the personalistic category can encompass. Personhood is only one of many modes and categories of being, and is too specific and confining to be the basic paradigm to understand the totality of reality. The person, the individual is found in a vast complex of reality, which is forever in flux. Hindu thought, represented by the Upaniṣadic thinkers, seeks to identify the permanent and unchanging ground common to all things, which are themselves transient and impermanent, and of which personhood is merely an instance. The cosmic reality, the One Being, that underlies all particular beings in space and time must transcend all determinations and particularities. That One Being, called Brahman, underlies and permeates all forms of existence. "As gold is the underlying reality of all objects made of gold," Thomas Hopkins explains, "and clay of all objects made of clay, *Brahman* is the underlying reality and essence of the phenomenal world." It is the all-encompassing, overarching, and comprehensive reality that transcends and penetrates the totality of existence.

It is obvious that it is we, the personal beings, who seek to discover this nonpersonal Brahman. Therefore, some kind of connection has to be established between the personal and the nonpersonal dimensions. The Upaniṣadic thinkers found the needed connection where the personal, which is necessarily "individual," is rooted in the universal consciousness. Thus Hopkins explains that the same impersonal Brahman, at the same time, "is the 'self,' or *ātman,* the conscious Being that underlies each person and remains unchanging in the midst of activity and change."

Buddhism does not share the same confidence with Hinduism about an ultimate, all-encompassing reality, or its being amenable to metaphysical comprehension and conceptualization, such as in terms of Brahman. Buddhism is more reserved in its metaphysical enterprise and more daring in its ontological skepticism. So instead of investing the whole of religious energy in a finalized concept of Brahman, Buddhism leaves the vista open with the seemingly negativistic concept of nothingness or void *(Sunyata).* The ultimate is the nothingness, and its attainment is not a union with Brahman, but extinction. There is such a crucial difference, to be sure, but they share the same nonpersonalistic and cosmic vision of reality, which is echoed in the Taoist vision of reality, one of the important streams of ancient Chinese thought.

In the Indian vision of reality the personal thus is a category that must be seen within a larger flow of beings and, ultimately, within the unchanging and permanent absolute. The personal, which is the most important category in the Semitic vision of reality, was displaced from the center and relegated to the periphery. In other words, when the ideal self was discovered by the Indian axial philosophers, it was found transcending not only the concrete, individual self, but also the personal as the category of being. The ideal self, *ātman,* is found identical with Brahman, the cosmic nonperson.

It is only a small step from this to the idea of transmigration or reincarnation of the personal soul. The Semitic religions are barred from these ideas (except for some rare instances, such as in the cabalistic tradition of Judaism) because of the sanctity and ultimacy they attach to the category of the personal. Not only do the Semitic religions believe "that only God is eternal and that nothing created is co-eternal," but they believe that "the idea of transmigration of eternal souls undermines both the uniqueness of the self and the ultimate consequences of this life." The religions of Indian origin see no contradiction in the personal enduring many rounds of births and rebirths because the personal is exactly what has to be transcended and found rooted in a larger cosmic totality. This is the way the East combats and overcomes death.

Death as the termination of the once-and-for-all life may be unspeakably tragic, but death as the end of one of many lives may not be as tragic. What Hopkins, speaking from the Hindu viewpoint, means when he says, "It is not coincidence that there are no massive monuments to the dead in Hinduism, no tombs, sarcophagi, or pyramids to mark the final resting place of the dead, because death is not in any sense a final stopping point," is echoed by Reynolds when he observes that the Buddhist preparations for death "do not involve—as the preparation for death commonly does in the West—a process of achieving, through memory and confession, a kind of personal 'integrity' that has about it the ring of summation and finality. On the contrary, [they] prepare for death by undertaking present-oriented activities that are aimed at achieving psychic detachment from the life they have lived in the past, and at intensifying the practice of the religious path that will lead to the attainment of a more favorable rebirth in their next life and beyond." Thus the importance of the idea of reincarnation can scarcely be overemphasized.

This should not lead us to think that the Eastern religions attach ultimate significance to transmigration or multiple rebirths. It is true that the rounds of births and rebirths do soften the blow of death, placing life and death in proper perspective, and the possibility of rebirth enables one who is facing death to hope for another and better chance of reliving one's life. But that is not exactly the way the East combats the threat of death in the final sense. If that were the case, then that would only be an evasion of the problem altogether. Rebirths simply point us beyond the obsessive attachment to or preoccupation with this single life and toward the larger context of reality. This is the way in which Chuang Tzu, an ancient Taoist sage, is represented by Berling as having dealt with the death of his wife by placing life and death in the larger context of the creative processes of nature. This larger context of reality does not mean merely that there are many lives ahead, but that there is liberation from the very process of reincarnation itself. The possibility of reincarnation or rebirth first frees one from the immediate horror of facing death by removing its crushing finality. More important, the same series of births and rebirths directs one to the ultimate release from the whole process. The ultimate goal of Hindu and Buddhist strivings is not a better reincarnation, but final release from the cycle of rebirths. Hinduism conceives of this ultimate state of release in positive terms as the final unity with Brahman, the state called *Moksha;* Buddhism refers to this state in negative terms as the final extinction, called *Nirvana,* which also can be considered realizing *Sunyata* (nothingness). In this context Reynolds presents a cogent argument for the Buddhist death as an achievement. In those celebrated cases of saints *(arhats),* including the Buddha himself, they attain conquest of death by achieving enlightenment in the height of their lives, thereby transcending and attaining final release from the process of rebirth. They now turn the tables against death to bring it under their conscious control. Discussing the practice of early Chinese Buddhist monks, Berling reports that many of those saints decided "to choose the time and manner of their deaths (thereby defeating death's negation of human will)." By achieving what is to be achieved in life, that is, release from life, they rob death of its threat and turn it into an occasion of triumph.

It has now become clear how the Eastern vision of reality dictated the Easterners' approach to death. The reader is introduced to the full range of approaches within the Eastern vision of reality, from Vedic Hindu to Taoist Chinese views and practices. The authors have succeeded in offering us the spectrum of human attitudes toward death and afterlife of both the preaxial and axial religions, and the contrasts are indeed fascinating.

On the whole, the Eastern attitudes, particularly Hindu and Buddhist, lead us out of our transient world. Release from this impermanent world is the basic pattern of the Eastern recommendation. This is in keeping with the Eastern nonpersonalistic vision of reality. In contrast to this, the Western or Semitic attitudes are overwhelmingly historical, nudging us back into the world of events and engagements. Salvation is not out of the world, but into the kingdom of God, which only means "living" under God.

This is not to say that there are no exceptions to this general difference. One can see, for example, a pull toward the other world in the Christian tradition, and conversely, the Mahayana branch of Buddhism is known to equate Nirvana with Samsara, that is, "release" with the world of impermanence.

Despite such a notable gulf between East and West, and considerable varieties within each bloc, there is a strong undercurrent that seems to bring all religions, scattered so widely by time and geography, back together in a common fold. That is the consistent emphasis made by the authors in this book, that salvation—which in mythological language is located in the hereafter or in the idealized future—is attainable now, in this life. Both Hinduism and Buddhism are represented here as claiming the possibility of ultimate release in the midst of this life. The New Testament faith as presented by Keck and the theological development of Christianity surveyed by Obayashi bring home the point that immortality is not "more life after death," but the realization of life in proper relation with God, the center of value, right here in this life. The reader will be struck by the amazing degree of consensus found in these faiths that are otherwise so much apart from one another. But that is, after all, precisely the essence of cross-cultural overview among these, the axial religions, that has enriched human experience down through the centuries.

I

DEATH AND AFTERLIFE IN NONLITERATE AND ANCIENT RELIGIONS

1

LIVING WITH SPIRITS: DEATH AND AFTERLIFE IN AFRICAN RELIGIONS

George C. Bond

INTRODUCTION

Sub-Saharan Africa is marked by its great diversity. Its 415 million people do not share nor have been united by a common history. There are differences in environment, population density, technology, economic activity, history, political systems, social and cultural arrangements, and languages. There are literally hundreds of different ethnic populations with their own religious beliefs and practices and customs related to death and burial. No one body of indigenous religious texts or iconic presentations provides a common and shared religious order. There are, however, broad currents or intellectual streams surrounding birth, death, and notions of an afterlife. These streams relate culture to nature and provide the basis for ritual configurations, including beliefs and practices about death. Death is an idea, a social experience, and a concrete biological reality. It is here that the play of culture with nature may begin to take on meaning.

Before exploring the interplay of culture and nature one must look to the scale or magnitude of death. Scholars tend to forget about the realities and the magnitude of death, especially anthropologists working in rural Africa. For this reason throughout this chapter I attempt to retain some of the reality; it is the death of human beings that is being discussed.

Death is not uncommon in Africa. It has taken on monumental proportions. Infant mortality ranges from the high of 210 per 1,000 in Chad to the low of 13.9 in the Seychelles. The figures for Canada and the United States are 8.5 and 10.9, respectively. The statistics for Africa do not always include the consequences of drought, famine, and disease. About a million Ethiopians will die of starvation over the next decade. The World Health Organization estimated that by mid-1989, at least half the people infected with the human immunodeficiency virus, 3 to 4 million people, were in sub-Saharan Africa.[1] Thus, in the next decade, millions of Africans are expected to die of AIDS. This magnitude of death will impose a heavy strain not only on medical facilities but also on customary religious and medical systems, geared to localized, parochial misfortunes. A different order of explanation will no doubt be required. I do not make these assertions without some experience. I have lived through a severe epidemic in which the sheer number of organic deaths tested the order of religious explanation related to death and burial practices. The death rate in Africa is on a steady upward rise.

I have indicated the range of diversity in Africa to make two points. The first point is that there is no one major religious tradition in black Africa with a body of texts that one may turn to or that Africans themselves refer to as a guide. The traditions are parochial and not written, but part of the lived-in domain of human activity. There are a multiplicity of religions and notions of death.

Anthropologists have derived most of their knowledge of a particular religion from observations, the accounts of informants, and any available written materials. The best data come from the actual observation of several events and discussions with numerous informants. But as we know, people do not die at our convenience, that is, unless we take an active part in bringing the situation about. Thus many anthropologists have never traced a life from illness to death nor observed the burial practices. They rely on the accounts of informants. Others have attended a large number of funerals and are able to describe the subtle variations in performance from one to the next. The problem always is to make sense of what one has observed and been told.

The second point is that given the variety of beliefs and practices in Africa, I have concentrated on only one population, the Yombe of northern Zambia. I do so for two primary reasons. The first reason is that I know them best, since I have studied them for twenty-five years and participated in their funeral rites. The second reason is that the Yombe have ancestor cults, a form of religious belief and practice that is widespread in African societies. It is common among many agricultural populations but not usually among hunters and gatherers. The afterlife of the biologically dead is as ancestors. There is the notion of social persistence, and thus the social persona of the deceased remains part of the world of the living, concerned with human affairs. As a form of religion, the ancestor cult is oriented toward this world and helps to maintain and secure an enduring social order. The ancestors are a moral, temporal force, a projection of the past into the present and the future. There is the marked notion of continuity of social life through death, and death is a moment not only of disruption but also of renewal and reaffirmation. The afterlife is of this world, and the ancestors help to shape it.

The purpose of this chapter, then, is, through the exploration of Yombe religious beliefs and practices surrounding birth and death, to see how rituals negate organic realities of birth and death and transform them into the social collective. According to French sociologist Emile Durkheim, the social order creates the social person by negating the individual. The ancestor is the social person par excellence, and yet even he may be accorded some degree of idiosyncrasy. The afterlife is nought but the ideological construction of this world, part of the series of illusions by which we govern ourselves.

The Yombe and most other Africans with ancestor cults fully recognize the biological properties of birth and death but attempt to constrain the full implications of the two. The organic individual is born and dies, but the social order is thought to endure. Death is recognized as disruptive; rituals, however, constrain the disruption and make it part of the social construction. Thus there may be two parts to the funeral ceremonies; the first entails the immediate disposal of the corpse and the second, involving a more complex set of issues, entails securing the social order by freeing the living from mourning and by removing the spirit of the deceased to the place where the spirits reside. The rites performed to the ancestors are a constant reminder of their power and authority and of social continuity. In many African societies ancestors may be associated with special places or locations, such as shrines and villages, secret associations, and kinship groupings. Among the Yombe of Zambia the ancestors are related to kin groups and, at times, to a territory.

THE HADZA: HUNTERS AND GATHERERS

As part of the exposition and for comparative purposes I begin with a brief description of beliefs and practices in which there is limited recognition of death, burial rites, and an afterlife. This situation is most pronounced among the hunting and gathering populations of Africa. These populations are organized into small camps with little property and few, if any, positions of authority. The division of labor is based on sex and age, and movement is frequent in pursuit of game and the gathering of plants.

In a chapter titled "Social Dimensions of Death in Four African Hunting and Gathering Societies," J. Woodburn provides an insightful exposition of burial practices and views of the dead. He also provides a useful set of guides for examining these matters, guides that we may use in looking at the Yombe.

Woodburn studied the Hadza of northern Tanzania, and it is they whom I take as my principal example of a hunting and gathering population. Woodburn is careful to make the point that during his four years of fieldwork among the Hadza, the only death was that of a two-day-old infant. He says that his "knowledge of what actually happens when somebody dies is based not on observation but on a mixture of accounts, often somewhat contradictory."[2] Thus even a long stay among people does not guarantee a personal knowledge of burial rites.

For the Hadza, human death is marked by its ritual simplicity and the absence of complicated beliefs. As Woodburn observes, "there is no real corpus of doctrine or of formal practice."[3] Death is taken as a matter of course, the burial rites are simple, and beliefs of an afterlife are almost nonexistent.

When a person dies he is immediately buried in a shallow grave. The men dig, and inter the corpse on its side. They dampen and stamp the clay soil, which hardens, preventing scavengers from digging up the corpse and eating it. During the interment the women cry and wail. Once the burial is accomplished those assembled resume their regular activities. There is no period of pollution and mourning. The deceased is, however, remembered in the near future in the performance of the *epeme* dance. The dance is performed at night once a month to promote general well-being, good health, and successful hunting. The dancer is believed to be *epeme,* a powerful sacred being. The Hadza do not believe that the dead are dangerous to the living or may affect them, and thus the dance dedicated to the deceased is merely an act of remembrance. The dance is an act intended neither to placate the spirit of the dead nor to remove it into the land of the dead. Valuable items such as gourds are broken and left on the grave. The site of the grave is neither marked nor visited.

The Hadza do not have a clear belief in an afterlife. They believe that the corpse rots in the ground and that is the end of the person. The relatives are not constrained by beliefs in pollution. There is no period of mourning involving a second phase of rites, and the deceased's possessions are immediately shared out without ceremony. Because the Hadza believe that people die naturally, they are not concerned with establishing the cause. There is thus no intensive search for the reasons and agents of death. Death is thought to have neither social nor supernatural consequences for the living. It occurs, and that is pretty much the end of it. The entire process of death and burial is simple, without elaborate rituals and beliefs in an afterlife. The social and spiritual existence of the person ends with the burial of the corpse.

Woodburn postulates that hunters and gatherers with simple death beliefs and practices are those with immediate-return economies, social organization, and values.[4] The main feature of an immediate-return system is that stress is laid on present-oriented activity, the use of labor to gain food and other resources for immediate consumption and purposes and a minimum of long-term investment in artifacts and social relations. Sharing with an ad hoc local community is emphasized. The Hadza, with their simple notions of death, burial, and afterlife, exemplify this type of hunting and gathering society based on an immediate-return system.

THE YOMBE: DEATH AND BURIAL

The Yombe of northern Zambia provide an example of an African population with a far more complex and intricate set of beliefs and practices surrounding death, burial, and afterlife than is found among the hunters and gatherers described by Woodburn.[5] Before discussing Yombe notions of death and burial practices, some comments about them and their religious organization are in order. There are distinctions between the organic properties of the individual, the social person (singular, *muntu;* plural, *bantu*), and the ancestor (singular, *ciwanda;* plural, *viwanda*). The Yombe notions of the biological, social, and spiritual dimension of the individual represent facets of their beliefs, which at times provide for interesting inconsistencies and contradictions. The beliefs also may provide rationalizations and justifications for social patterns of inequality. The notions and practices surrounding birth, death, burial, and afterlife may enunciate these inequalities. For example, though the Yombe recognize a newborn infant as a living creature, the infant is not considered to be a social person entitled to an appropriate burial. It is still too close to nature and the organic properties of its birth. It is not of society, and if it should die, it is buried in a shallow grave in the bush or the wild or, in the olden days, tossed on the rubbish heap. The act of being born does not establish humanity.

Historical Perspective

Yombe beliefs and practices related to birth, death, and afterlife (the ancestors) may best be apprehended within the context of their parochial or regional history. Three phases may be distinguished, with each phase retaining properties of the previous one. Before the 1800s the area that became Uyombe was populated by small, autonomous, self-sufficient agnatic groups, practicing swidden millet cultivation, gradually moving across a sparsely inhabited landscape. The core group of men claimed descent through the male line from an ancestor whose kin had once occupied a particular territory. Today the notion of this territory exists more as a direction and an ephemeral location than as a concrete land to which an agnatic group is entitled. It was the ancestral land but not quite the land of the ancestors. Women who married into the agnatic cluster were subject to the authority of their husbands and their husbands' male agnates. They were ritual and jural minors, a situation that obtains still in Uyombe.

Agnatic clusters formed the basic units of worship, a situation that obtains today, even though agnates have ceased to form residential units. The ancestor cult was intimately associated with the structure, organization, and the moral code of the kinship system based on agnatic descent. There was a marked order of hierarchy of ritual entitlement. Only the senior men of a descent group were entitled to pray and make offerings to the spirits of dead members, the ancestors. A junior agnate was not supposed to approach them. According to Yombe religious belief, even if he or a member of his family were experiencing a misfortune, if he approached the ancestors himself, they would not listen to him and would punish him for failing to adhere to the structure of lineage authority. Thus the domestic ancestor cult was based on the agnatic descent group and its structure of ritual authority.

During the 1800s a form of centralized territorial rulership, chieftainship, was imposed on the Yombe, regulating the movement of the autonomous kin clusters, their access to land, their residential pattern, and their productive activities. The territorial framework provided the basis for the localized political and ritual systems.

The domain of spirits and the scope of rituals increased with the change in political scale. Through the spirits of dead chiefs the chief had ritual control of the land. Seasonal rites followed the structure of territorial authority and regulated the agricultural cycle. The chief and his headmen made annual offerings to their ancestors for the well-being of the chiefdom and its villages. Once the chiefdom rites had been performed, the headmen were entitled to perform rites to their ancestors, and finally the heads of descent groups made their offerings. The order of ritual performance reflected the domains of the ancestor spirits. The chiefdom ancestor cult was based in territory, anchored in locality, and restricted in jurisdiction.

Within the context of the ancestor cult, God, *Leza,*[6] was thought to be distant and removed from human affairs, and it was only under exceptional conditions of crisis that misfortunes were attributed to him. Only then were the ancestors expected to approach him. God, *Leza,* the supreme being, was believed to control natural forces, since he himself is such a manifestation, lightning, thunder, elements associated with the sky, rain, and fertility.

Important properties of this religious order remain as essential features of Yombe society. The domestic and territorial ancestor cults were part and parcel of the same religious order; they were, after all, based on the same set of principles. It also should be clear that the world of the ancestors, the afterlife, was the world of the living. The spirits of the dead were believed to be intimately involved in human affairs.

The final phase occurred during the early decades of the twentieth century with the gradual expansion of mission Christianity, British commercial activities, and colonial rule. Uyombe and the northern provinces of what is today Zambia and Malawi were transformed into centers of Christian and Western activity and brought into the domain of British colonial authority. Presbyterian mission stations and missionaries have played a critical role in shaping village life and preparing the Yombe to enter the colonial order and the one being created by the independent Zambia state.

Though most Yombe are now Christians, they also belong to ancestor cults. The belief in the ancestors remains a strong and active spiritual and moral force in the daily lives of the Yombe; the ancestors are thought to intervene in the affairs of the living. They are an intimate part of Yombe explanations of events, of their notions of temporal progressions, and of misfortunes. They support the moral order of the collectivity and impose it on the individual. Witchcraft represents a nonspiritual counterforce in that it represents the power of the individual acting against the moral order. Death may be attributed to ancestors or witches.

A central question is how does a person become an ancestor? For me the answer is both remarkably simple and complex; it is through ritual. The rituals of birth and death establish a world that includes the living and the spirits of the dead. The afterlife is this world. The rituals negate and constrain the organic properties of the individual, transforming him from nature into the social idiom of culture. The rituals of birth make the individual into a social person, and the rites of burial provide the conditions for the social person to become an ancestor.

Rites of Birth

The vital and active forces of biological and social reproduction are contained within the cultural notions of substances such as blood and semen and essences such as breath and wind. They are the principal properties from which people are made as organic natural creatures. Through ritual the force of natural substances is contained and the living creature transformed into a social person.

The rituals of birth are an essential aspect of this process. The Yombe fully understand biological reproduction. But they also assign symbolic significance to biological parts. A woman's womb, *Nthumbo,* often is referred to as a house, *nyumba.* When I first attended court cases involving adultery or illegitimacy, it took me some time to grasp the full meaning of the expression "he entered another man's house." The embryo grows in the mother's womb (or house) and is born in the house of its father. The natural substances of blood, afterbirth, and a portion of the umbilical cord are buried beneath a false fig tree, *musolo.* Great care is taken in this ritual because failure to perform it properly is believed to close the woman's womb and to render her and her child infertile. The woman and child are cleansed and purified by water and smoke. Social recognition is not accorded to the infant until it is ritually brought from the house and presented to the ancestors and the community. The father takes the infant to the doorway and directs its face toward the clan territory, informing the ancestors of the birth. Then he blows water onto the infant and passes it through smoke, carrying it outside into the domesticated world of the village. If the infant dies before these rites, it does not receive a funeral, since it has not been recognized as a living social being, a person. The rites establish the infant in the domestic unit, the lineage, the community, and the ancestor cult, including both its living and its dead members. As a social person the infant occupies a social position and enters into a world of corporately based relations regulated by the ritual, legal, political, and economic systems.

Rites of Burial

I unfortunately have attended many Yombe burials, and the description that follows is based on those observations as well as the accounts of numerous informants.

The rites of burial illustrate the strength of the Yombe notion of person and the negation of the natural and organic by the cultural and spiritual. Death is a simple yet dramatic affair involving the community and the relatives of the deceased. A person's death is announced by a particular beat delivered on the public drum. Burial is supposed to occur only during the daylight hours, since night and the dark are associated with the activities of witches and their familiars, such as hyenas, *bacimbwe*. Thus if a person dies in the evening, his relatives must spend the night preventing rigor mortis from setting in by moving the limbs. The corpse is washed, clothed, and often wrapped in a white cloth; it often is put into a coffin.

In the early morning most men leave the village and go to the cemetery to dig the grave. The cemetery is removed from the village, and to reach it one must pass through the bush, *ntengere*. It is not a neatly cleared area, but itself seems as if it were part of the bush. The graves are overgrown with secondary growth and appear to be arranged in no particular order; most are unmarked. Mounds of earth rising to different elevations indicate the placement and age of the grave. The cemetery is like a village that has been left to fall into disrepair and return to nature.

The corpse of a social person is buried in a well-constructed grave. The term used to describe the grave as it is being dug, before the interment of the corpse, is house, *nyumba,* and as a house, it has rooms. A bedroom may be dug either at the bottom of the grave or in the side of the wall.

The men who dig the grave are known as hyenas, *bacimbwe*.[7] Any man is entitled to participate in the digging, and there is a constant flow of men in and out of the grave as the rectangular hole deepens to the expected four to five feet. As the men move in and out of the grave they joke, laugh, and recount amusing experiences. Once they have dug, they rejoin small clusters of other men awaiting the completion of the grave. Conversation flows easily, but it is not about the corpse or the burial.

Once the grave is finished, the sleeping area is prepared. Four logs of the false fig (or *musolo*) tree are placed at the bottom and then covered by a strong mat. A senior man comes forward, peers into the grave, carefully inspecting it, and then utters the phrase ''nyumba yamara'' (the house is finished). While the grave was being completed, other men had prepared a bier and already started back to the village to tell the mourners that the house was ready. All along the women had engaged in crying and wailing; with the approach of the men the intensity of such demonstrations of grief markedly increases. The men enter the house. As they bring the corpse from the house through the doorway a gun may be fired, accompanied by an upsurge of women crying and close relatives wailing and exclaiming their loss. There are limits on the expression of grief, and older women may tell a mourner to moderate her crying. There is a social and esthetic component to grief and the manner of its expression. Older men may tell women when they may cry and wail, and older women instruct younger ones and children. The strength of the crying often is related to the order of relationship to the deceased.

The men, carrying the corpse securely strapped to the bier, lead the way to the grave, followed by a stream of women, often singing hymns. When they reach the grave site the *bacimbwe,* hyenas, inter the corpse. The corpse is lowered through the grave onto its carefully prepared bed. A senior agnate inspects the corpse and with great care directs its face and eyes toward the clan's territory of origin, so that the corpse's spirit may find its way safely home to the ancestors. Senior villagers and relatives may say a few words. If the deceased belonged to a church, a senior member also might make a statement and offer a prayer to *Chiuta,* the term used within the Christian religious context to refer to God.

Once the services have been performed, the bottom of the grave is covered with heavy logs and a mat, creating a small chamber. The *bacimbwe* begin to fill the grave with dirt, and when it is almost full the close relatives of the deceased throw handfuls of soil and pebbles into the grave. The remaining soil is piled on, pounded, and shaped into a smooth oval form. The grave is carefully swept by a senior agnate, and the perimeters are sealed symbolically with an axe. There is an important reason for the careful sweeping and the sealing of the grave with an axe. Both acts are attempts to discover the cause of death and to safeguard the person and the corpse from being disinterred and consumed by a witch or one of its familiars, such as a hyena.

After the burial the mourners go to a nearby stream and wash their legs, arms, and faces and rinse their mouths, either spitting or blowing out the water. These are acts of cleansing and ridding oneself of the polluting aspects of disposing of the corpse. The mourners return to the village, leaving the corpse to rot in the grave, and the grave, as an uninhabited house, is left to fall into disrepair, that is, to return to the order of nature. The immediate relatives of the deceased remain in seclusion for several days. The Yombe recognize the grief of individuals, and thus the mourners are not left alone. They are constantly visited and brought food to eat. Villagers fear that the most intimate relatives of the deceased might harm themselves, and thus fellow villagers sit with them. The conversation is constantly directed away from death or troubling topics to inconsequential matters. There is the appearance of joviality and yet there remains the persistent undercurrent of grief, sorrow, anxiety, and fear.

For the first few days after the death a man may remain secluded in his house for much of the day but spend the night and morning hours outside with his friends. Women remain close to the house. The friends of a man watch him and make sure that he is never alone. They fear that his grief may drive him into the bush where he will literally and metaphorically lose his way and become insane, a creature of the wild. In this condition of impurity he might hurt himself, open himself to witchcraft, or fall to the spirit of the dead person who has not as yet been transformed into an ancestor. The village is believed to provide a marginal sanctuary from the wild; the bush provides none. The mourner is thought to be of danger to himself and in danger. Friends provide him with protection from himself and the activities of witches and unsettled spirits. It was not uncommon that in the morning, men would find the spoor of animals associated with witchcraft. A subtle cultural drama was being played out related to the relation of culture and nature and the domesticated and the wild. The mourner was at the edge, and his grief could draw him into the abyss. His grief could drive him insane and, thus, into the wild. He would return to the order of nature. Villagers struggled against this possibility, and at night, as he slept in the open, they kept the fire burning brightly. They were of the domesticated contending against the forces of the bush. The as yet unclaimed spirit of the deceased was thought to be especially powerful in the bush and much less so in the village. For the Yombe the drama had a degree of reality that at first escaped me. I saw only men sitting by a fire and women sitting in the house mourning their loss of a relative. There was much more to the situation than that.

At the end of this period of mourning the women sweep the house thoroughly and carefully throw the rubbish into the bush. The rite, known as *Kutaya chikungu,* involves removing the polluting elements of the death from the domain of domestic dwellings into the domain of the wild, of nature. Members of the family shave and wash, and the hair is hidden in the bush. There is a meal, and the family reenters the community. If the deceased was a married man, the wife (or wives) remains in semiseclusion until the final burial ceremony is performed several months later. She stays in the house with her husband's valued personal property, such as his axe and spears. She is the keeper, if not the temporary guardian, of these personal items.

In former times iron was scarce and a form of wealth. Objects made from iron were highly valued, especially arm rings, axes, hoes, and spears. Arm rings were used in the rites of marriage and as part of the gifts a man gave to his bride. The iron axe was an essential implement used for domesticating the bush as, for example, in preparing fields for cultivating. Hoes were used to cultivate, and spears were deadly weapons of protection and fighting. More than these other items, the axe was the personal property of a man; it was of him and symbolized his person. The wife of the deceased held his personal property in trust until it was inherited at the second phase of the burial rites, the *yipupalo.* The last rites would end her mourning and allow her to reenter the life of the community. The spirit of the dead also would be removed to the land of the ancestors, and he, too, would enter the community of the living as an ancestor.

Cause of Death

During the period between the first and second burial rites the relatives would attempt to establish the cause and agency of death. The Yombe fully recognize that people die of natural causes, but they also seek the social or cultural reasons. The relatives attempt to discover why a person died at this time and under these conditions. The explanations sought often are more cultural than biological. If an old person dies under socially acceptable conditions of natural causes, death is attributed to old age; otherwise, an explanation is sought.

Like many African peoples, part of the mortuary rites is for a person's relatives to discover the cause of the death. The reasons lie within the social and cultural order, and may relate to failures in social relations and be attributed to witches and ancestors.

The process of discovering the agent responsible for the death begins at sunrise of the day after burial. A small party of agnates returns to the grave to inspect it for any signs of disturbance. They look especially for the spoors of those wild animals, such as hyenas and owls, associated with witches and witchcraft. The Yombe fear that the deceased may have been killed by a witch, who returns at night to exhume and eat the corpse. Any major disturbance of the grave will confirm suspicions of foul play.

In any event, the agnates of the deceased meet to review the death and establish the cause. They do so through divination. A man is sent to hunt a small antelope. If he fails to kill one after three nightly attempts, suspicion is removed from the deceased's relatives. If he should kill a male antelope, the cause is thought to stem from the male kin, and if a female, from the female kin of the deceased's relatives. By offering only two alternatives each time, the range gradually is narrowed. The inquiry may come to an abrupt and yet unsatisfactory conclusion if the direction points to the very people responsible for making the inquiry. The assumption is that one of them is a witch and responsible for the death.

The Yombe believe that witchcraft is not the only cause of death; death also may stem from the ancestors. They believe that the ancestors take an active interest in the affairs of the living and expect to be consulted on most private and public matters by the appropriate people. If a person neglects his ancestors, and fails to fulfill his obligations toward his relatives, and there are serious disputes among kin, the ancestors may decide to punish the person or group by taking a life. Ritual beer, *fingah,* is prepared to the ancestors to establish the cause and reason for the death. One also may consult a diviner or a prophet, who may narrow the range of ancestors. Only in rare instances, such as a major epidemic, are deaths attributed to *Leza* or *Chiuta* (God). The full range of the explanatory system may be brought into play as death increases in its magnitude of scale. Explanations that involve witches and ancestors are related more to individual deaths, whereas *Leza* and *Chiuta* explain the deaths of many. The progression is from human agency to ancestor spirits to local and universal spiritual forces.

Mortuary Rites and Afterlife

The second burial ceremony, *yipupalo,* occurs several months after the corpse has been interred. The last rites are directed toward preserving the notion of an enduring social order. The rites involve the living and the dead. The ceremony is attended by relatives of the deceased and villagers; the scale depends on the importance of the deceased and his kin group. A number of activities occur that involve different categories of persons. An aspect of the occasion is to end the mourning, to repay those who helped to bury the corpse, and to demonstrate appreciation for services rendered by fellow villagers. Another feature is directly involved with the transmission of rights in people, property, and status. The relatives often go to the grave and address the dead person's spirit. There usually is some crying and wailing.

The practical matters of inheritance and succession occur after this order of discourse with the spirit. Once the personal items, axes, spears, and hoes, of the deceased have been purified by water, smoke, and the appropriate medicines, the male agnates of the same generation as the deceased line up before his wife. She takes her late husband's axe and selects his replacement from this line. In some instances she gives the axe to her eldest son, who assumes his late father's social position but not his sexual rights and responsibilities. Valuable property is then transferred to the appropriate heir, who assumes responsibility for it on behalf of the descent group. It is he who may distribute less valuable items. He is the one who will administer the rights of the lineage in the property and in people. Ritual beer, *fingah,* has been made as an offering to the ancestors, and prayers are offered to them in public. The wife and other mourners are shaved and washed, removing the last vestiges of pollution. The ceremony turns into a festive occasion of drinking beer. All conflict is supposed to have been removed, thus integrating the disruption caused by death in the fabric of social relations and reaffirming the image of an enduring social order.

One important final ritual act is performed, if it has not been done already. The rite involves bringing the spirit into the house, and it is one that may be performed a few days after the interment of the corpse. A small party of agnates go to the grave of the deceased, and a senior man hits it with a switch of the *musolo,* or false fig tree. The Yombe believe that the spirit of the dead person enters the switch and is taken to the house. There the spirit is placed in an object of value, an axe, a hoe, or a coin. The spirit is now of the world of the living, preserving the social persona of the deceased. The body is left to rot in the ground and return to nature and is of no concern to the living. This notion of the body is in marked contrast to the burial practices of the Merina and other Madagascar populations, who constantly are involved in wrapping and placing the dead.[8] The Yombe preserve the social person and forget about the body.

A notion of this type may obtain even among people without ancestor cults. The Nuer of the southern Sudan are such a people. They are cultivators and cattle keepers, and their religious beliefs include a complex world of spirits with a central God, *Kwoth.* Though the Nuer believe that men and women have souls, they do not believe in ancestors. They distinguish between biological and social death, a distinction that may have profound consequences for a person's rights, duties, and privileges. In his book *Nuer Religion* Evans-Pritchard describes the plight of a man who experienced social death. The man had been away for some time, and his relatives, hearing of his death, performed mortuary rites. He was not in fact dead, but when he returned home he was treated as a "living ghost."[9] His soul, "the essential part of him, had gone and with it his social personality."[10] A Nuer said of him "his flesh alone remains standing." Though the man was fed by his relatives, he had lost such "privileges of kinship as pertains to the living and not to the dead."[11] He was an example of the living dead: biologically he was alive but socially he was dead. Among the Nuer and the Yombe life and death are social constructions. Increasingly, computer errors have made us aware of similar situations in our own society. Such situations often provide the plots for television sit-coms and serious drama. The social person is expunged or killed off while the biological person remains alive, or the biological person dies while greedy employees keep the social person alive.

Whereas the Nuer attempt to forget about the dead, the Yombe bring them back as ancestors and give them moral authority. The ancestors are treated as a moral force within this world, and the Yombe believe that they act directly on it. Ritual is here essential in regulating the activities and relations of both the living and the dead and the nature of the interactions between them.

When a Yombe experiences a misfortune he seeks the cause, usually by divination or through the assistance of a ritual practitioner, a diviner *(ng'anga),* or a prophet *(ncimi).* In the first instance he may prepare ritual beer, *fingah,* to the ancestors, inquiring as to the reason for the misfortune. He also may consult a diviner, who, through the manipulation of ritual paraphernalia, may establish the identity of the particular ancestor and the reason he has sent the misfortune. An offering of beer is immediately made to the specific ancestor, whose name may be given to the afflicted or a young agnate. In this way the ancestor is believed to secure his perpetuity from one generation to the next, the tie being particularly strong between alternate generations. The ancestors are thus merely an extension of the living. As a man grows old he gradually relinquishes his worldly authority to his eldest son, who becomes a quasi-father to his own siblings. An old man gains in spiritual authority and becomes a quasi-grandfather to his own children. Biological death does not end the steady progression, and through the final mortuary rites the person is transformed into an ancestor and the enduring properties of the social order are reaffirmed. Thus the inevitable properties of the human condition, biological death, are confounded by ritual; the spirit of the person predominates over the natural facts of human existence. The person triumphs over the realities of nature through the belief in the enduring qualities of the ancestors.

THE MENDE: MODES OF DEATH

The Mende of Sierra Leone may provide a final example and serve as a contrast of both Hadza and Yombe beliefs and practices related to death, burial, and afterlife. I take them because of the complexity of their social arrangements in that they provide for death as part of an orderly progression through life,

and have a more developed set of notions of an afterlife than do either the Nuer or the Merina.

The Mende are part of the West Atlantic Poro Complex. This means simply that they have secret associations, the most important of which are the Poro for boys and the Bundu or Sande for girls. The Mende live in large, compact villages that are divided into wards. The villages are organized into chiefdoms under chiefs. Though descent is in the male line, considerable recognition is given to relations through women. The Mende cultivate rice, and in the past they were warriors as well as farmers. They believe in a high God, *Ngewo,* numerous lesser spirits, and their ancestors.

For the Mende death is a social construction, and occurs, as a social condition, at least twice in a person's life. The first time is as an initiate into the primary male and female secret associations, the Poro and Sande, respectively, and the second, when one experiences biological death. Again at issue is the making of the social person. Social recognition does not begin with birth. Because an infant being introduced to the community is part of an extended process that eventually leads to adult status. The child must die and enter the world of spirits before achieving full recognition as a social person. Boys must go into the sacred grove of the Poro and girls, that of the Sande. The young male initiate is thought to be "swallowed" by the Poro spirit when he enters the sacred grove, and the separation from the community and his relatives signifies his death.[12] The initiate is now thought to be dead; he is a spirit living in the world of spirits. At the end of several months of training the initiates are "reborn" by the Poro spirit. They emerge from their grueling experience as men, full social persons, with the full social entitlement of manhood. Girls undergo a similar experience in the Sande and emerge as women.

The second major transition occurs when a person actually dies. The rites are remarkably similar to those of the Yombe. The grave is considered a house, and through the appropriate rituals the social person becomes an ancestor concerned with the affairs of the living. The funeral rites enable the spirit to "cross the water" to the new land. Though the notions of an afterlife are vague, they picture a clean village. The spirit joins his dead relatives and, some say, takes up activities similar to the ones he left. There are, however, more complex beliefs. According to Hofstra, some Mende believe that after being created by God, "people begin their lives in the sky. When they die there, they are reborn on earth. When they die on earth, they go to a place under the earth."[13] The process of being born, dying, and moving to a lower level of earth continues through ten lives.

The spirits of the dead are believed to retain their social persona and an interest in their living relatives. As among the Yombe, they may be the source of misfortunes and may be appeased by ritual offerings. Children who have fallen ill often are named for them, thereby preserving them as part of the social order. The Mende believe that ancestors may appear in dreams or as humans clad, or painted, in white. The last are thought to be harmful and avoided at all cost. Death may come from witchcraft and the ancestors. God is remote and usually does not interfere in the affairs of the living.

For me the remarkable feature is the basic similarity of principles of Mende and Yombe beliefs and practices. It is a similarity that is found among most African peoples with ancestor cults. The most pronounced difference lies in the belief that death occurs twice, once through the initiation rites into Poro, when the initiate is believed to be eaten by the Poro spirit, and again at the occurrence of biological death. The burial and mortuary rituals remove the spirit of the dead person to the land of the dead and into the world of the living.

CONCLUSION

I have attempted to set out some of the properties of a widespread religious form, the ancestor cult, found among many African peoples. There is, however, a wide range of religious diversity in Africa that extends even to those populations with ancestor cults. The diversity lies in the particulars of custom and not so much at the level of social and cultural principles.

From the Hadza we were able to see a population with rudimentary beliefs and practices surrounding death, burial, and afterlife. There was not the marked distinction between the biological and social properties of a person with an accompanying body of rituals. The Hadza provide the dead with a simple burial and quickly forget about them. The progression of a person through life is not marked by rituals. The situation is typical of hunters and gatherers with an immediate reciprocity system. It is one in which the population is strongly oriented toward neither the present nor the future.

This order of social and temporal immediacy is much less pronounced in African societies characterized by delayed reciprocity systems and a political order based on patterns of what German social theorist Max Weber described as traditional authority. In this type of society there is an emphasis on precedent and the enduring attributes of the social order. The religious ideology of the ancestor cult emphasizes persistence, continuity, and regularity, all properties that relate to establishing notions of precedent and a social order based on particularistic relations. This form of religious ideology obscures processes of radical change, since it is based on notions of social endurance and regularities in social reproduction.

The ancestor cult assigns primacy to things social and cultural and diminishes the organic realities of existence. Its rituals constrain the dangerous biological properties of nature. The rituals of birth remove an infant from its natural organic condition and transform it into a social person. They reduce but do not eliminate the constant tension between the organic and the social properties of human beings. Death and the burial and mortuary rituals are necessary to achieving this end. The corpse is left in the ground to rot while the social person is brought back into the community of the living and into the house of its relatives as a spirit, ancestor. The ancestor transcends the temporal organic order of the body, and being so released it becomes as breath and wind. Because the ancestors are spirits created through rituals, they are of a fundamentally different order of spirit than is either the Mende or the Yombe notion of God. God is not created but creates. The ancestors are of people, whereas God is external to creation. They are of this world and close to the living. The Yombe believe that the afterlife of the ancestors lies in this world and that they are a spiritual and moral force within it. The ancestors are thus a local, parochial social construction, lacking universal properties. They are the spirits of people and not of Gods.

NOTES

1. A. Akeroyd, "Sociological Aspects of AIDS in Africa." Unpublished paper presented at the Conference on AIDS in Africa and the Caribbean, New York, Columbia University, 1990.

2. J. Woodburn, "Social Dimensions of Death in Four African Hunting and Gathering Societies," in M. Bloch and J. Parry, eds., *Death and the Regeneration of Life* (New York: Cambridge University Press, 1982), 188.

3. Ibid., 188.

4. Ibid., 205.

5. George C. Bond, *The Politics of Change in a Zambian Community* (Chicago: University of Chicago Press, 1976); "A Prophecy That Failed: The Lumpa Church of Uyombe," in G. Bond et al., eds., *African Christianity* (New York: Academic Press, 1979); "Ancestor and Protestants," *American Ethnologist* 14, no. 1 (1987).

6. *Leza* is the term Yombe use for God in the context of the ancestor cults. *Chiuta* is the term they use within the Christian context.

7. Among the Yombe, hyenas are associated with dead animals. The grave diggers are thus called hyenas. I do not intend to explore the symbolism here.

8. See Maurice Bloch, *Placing the Dead* (New York: Seminar Press, 1971), and M. Bloch, "Death, Women and Power," in Bloch and Parry, *Death and the Regeneration of Life*.

9. Edward E. Evans-Pritchard, *Nuer Religion* (Oxford: Oxford University Press, 1956), 152–53.

10. Ibid., 153.

11. Ibid.

12. Kenneth L. Little, *The Mende of Sierra Leone* (London: Routledge & Kegan Paul, 1951), 118–25.

13. S. Hofstra, "The Ancestral Spirits of the Mende," in *Internationales Archiv für Ethnographie* 34, Heft 1–4:187.

2

The Fate of Mankind: Death and Afterlife in Ancient Mesopotamia

Jerrold S. Cooper

INTRODUCTION

Some deaths in Mesopotamia have had earth-shaking consequences. The martyrdom of the imam Husein at Karbalah in A.D. 680 fuels the fires of revolutionary Shiʿism even today. The course of history might have been quite different if Alexander had not died prematurely at Babylon in 323 B.C., leaving his empire to crumble and be divided among his squabbling generals. To the Assyriologist both of these events are recent history. The Mesopotamia described in this chapter is pre-Islamic and preclassic; it has its origins in the first climax of Sumerian civilization, around 3000 B.C., and comes to an end when the Achaemenid Persian king Cyrus marches victoriously into Babylon in 539 B.C.[1]

The Babylonian king defeated by Cyrus was Nabonidus. When the mother of Nabonidus had died at the ripe old age of 104, she was memorialized in an inscription that ends as follows:

> She died a natural death in the 9th year of Nabonidus, king of Babylon. Nabonidus, king of Babylon, the son whom she bore, laid her body to rest wrapped in fine wool garments and shining white linen. He deposited her body in a hidden tomb with splendid ornaments of gold set with beautiful stones. . . . He slaughtered fat rams and assembled into his presence the inhabitants of Babylon and Borsippa together with people from far off provinces, he summoned even kings, princes and governors from the borders of Egypt on the Upper Sea, to the Lower Sea, for the mourning . . . and they made a great lament, scattered dust on their heads. For seven days and seven nights they walked about, heads hung low, dust strewn, stripped of their attire. On the seventh day . . . all the people of the country shaved and cleaned themselves.[2]

The people were then presented with new clothes and an elaborate feast, and sent home. They were fortunate. Had they lived 2,000 years earlier, their fate might have been quite different. Sir Leonard Woolley, excavator of the ancient Sumerian city of Ur, the biblical "Ur of the Chaldees," reconstructed a royal burial of 2500 B.C. as follows:

> The royal body was carried down the sloping passage and laid in the chamber . . . inside a wooden coffin. . . . Three or four of the personal attendants of the dead had their place with him or her in the tomb-chamber. . . . These attendants must have been killed, or drugged into insensibility, before the door of the tomb-chamber was walled up. . . . When the door had been blocked . . . down into the open pit . . . comes a procession of people, the members of the dead ruler's court, soldiers, men-servants, and women . . . in all their finery . . . with the insignia of their rank, musicians bearing harps or lyres, and . . . chariots drawn by oxen . . . and finally a guard of soldiers forms up at the entrance. Each man and woman brought a little cup of clay or stone or metal . . . then each of them drank from their cups a potion . . . and they lay down and composed themselves for death.[3]

Royal burial with retainers is attested both at Ur and at the more northerly city of Kish around 2500 B.C. but must have been abandoned shortly after, since no further traces of it have been found and there is no mention of it in any surviving Sumerian text.[4]

Despite the radical difference in royal burial customs, the scribes of mid–third-millennium B.C. Ur wrote in a cuneiform that the scribes of Nabonidus 2,000 years later would have been able to read and understand. And the moon-god, whose cult was central in Ur already at the time of Woolley's burials, is the same moon-god whose worship Nabonidus passionately promoted above that of all others. Ancient Mesopotamia knew extraordinary cultural continuity, continuity that often disguises the many profound changes that occur from period to period. Ideally the subject of this chapter would be presented diachronically, with both changes and similarities of belief and practice over time detailed. Unfortunately the evidence for Mesopotamian notions of death and afterlife is unevenly scattered over 2,500 years of history. Rarely, as in the case of burial with retainers, change can confidently be noted. More frequently there is just no way to know if something documented in one period is valid in another.

Writing and urbanism were developed by the Sumerians, a people of unknown affinities who were settled in what is now southern Iraq by at least the mid–fourth millennium B.C. and probably earlier. Soon after the invention of cuneiform writing, around 3000 B.C., Semitic-speaking peoples began to settle in Sumer and the area just to the north of it, and by 2500 B.C. were so integrated into the Sumerian cultural milieu that some of them were writing Sumerian literary texts. At the same time, cuneiform was spreading into the solidly Semitic territories of northwestern Syria, as the spectacular archives found by the Italians at Ebla attest.[5]

But whereas the scribes of Ebla were writing in a combination of Sumerian and their own Semitic language, Semitic-speaking scribes in southern Mesopotamia would continue to write almost exclusively in Sumerian for another 150 years. When the cuneiform writing system was adapted to write the Semitic Akkadian language of southern Mesopotamia, the same scribes who wrote Akkadian would continue to write Sumerian as well, and even after Sumerian's extinction as a spoken language, it continued to be studied and written as a prestige language of literary, religious, and legal texts, much as was Latin in the European Middle Ages. What developed in Mesopotamia was a Sumero-Akkadian cultural sphere in which the interaction of the two linguistic communities was so close that it usually is impossible to label any particular early Mesopotamian institution or belief Sumerian or Semitic.

In the third millennium on into the early second millennium Babylonia, that is, southern Mesopotamia, most commonly consisted of a number of vying city-states. Strong central powers arose to exercise hegemony over Babylonia and often beyond: the kingdom of Kish before 2500 B.C., the dynasty of Sargon of Agade around 2350 B.C., the third dynasty of Ur from 2100 to 2000 B.C., and the empire of Hammurabi of Babylon, who came to power around 1800 B.C. But none lasted for more than a century before falling prey to external pressures, the centrifugal force of decentralization, or a combination of the two.

After the middle of the second millennium Babylonia is, ideally, a united area, although local rebellion and breakaway entities, particularly in the far south, are not uncommon. More important, Assyria in northern Mesopotamia grows into a major power, and there is frequent conflict between the two. But even when Assyria was dominant, as it often was, Babylonia was perceived as culturally superior. Just as it was difficult to distinguish earlier between Sumerian and Akkadian institutions and beliefs, so, too, is it hard to separate distinctively Assyrian practices from a shared Assyro-Babylonian culture.

In the early first millennium Assyria created a relatively stable empire that at times reached from Iran to Egypt. This is the period of the great Assyrian kings who struck fear into the biblical writers' hearts: Tiglath-pileser III, Shalmaneser V, Sargon II, Sennacherib, Ashurbanipal. When Assyria fell to the combined armies of the Medes and the resurgent Babylonians in the late seventh century, the western portions of the Assyrian empire passed to the Babylonians, whose best-known ruler was Nebuchadnezzar II, the same Nebuchadnezzar who destroyed Jerusalem and exiled the Judeans. The Babylonians, in turn, were conquered by Cyrus in 539 B.C., and what had been the Assyrian and then the Babylonian empire became the western part of the Persian empire until it was conquered, two centuries later, by Alexander.

ATTITUDES TOWARD DEATH

To the Mesopotamians death was the inevitable lot of humankind.[6] The most common euphemism for dying was "to go to one's fate." When the epic hero

Gilgamesh refuses to accept this destiny and travels to the ends of the earth to learn the secret of immortality, he is told by the barmaid Siduri:

> Gilgamesh, whither rovest thou?
> The life thou pursuest thou shalt not find.
> When the gods created mankind,
> Death for mankind they set aside,
> Life in their own hands retaining.[7]

Only metaphorical immortality, living on through the remembrance of great deeds and accomplishments, was possible, and indeed sought after by the many rulers whose inscriptions enjoin the attention of future generations. This figurative immortality was Gilgamesh's objective too when early in the Gilgamesh epic he urges his companion, Enkidu, to join him on an expedition against Huwawa, the monster guardian of the cedar forest:

> Who, my friend, can scale heaven?
> Only the gods live forever under the sun.
> As for mankind, numbered are their days;
> Whatever they achieve is but the wind!
> Even here thou art afraid of death.
> What of thy heroic might?
> Let me go then before thee,
> Let thy mouth call to me, "Advance, fear not!"
> Should I fall, I shall have made me a name:
> "Gilgamesh"—they will say—"against fierce Huwawa
> Has joined battle!"[8]

Real-life kings, unlike Gilgamesh, accepted their mortality, although they were hardly eager to hurry things up. The seventh-century Assyrian ruler Esarhaddon was notoriously superstitious, or rather excruciatingly attentive to anything that might portend ill for him and his regime. Much royal time and energy were consumed carrying out the ritual and behavioral instructions of his divination experts and astrologers to counteract those ill portents, that is, to prolong the royal life. The most extreme countermeasure, the ceremony of the substitute king, in which the actual king disguised himself as a peasant and a substitute was enthroned (and eventually executed) so that the portended evil would strike him and not the true king, is best documented from his reign.[9]

Esarhaddon seems to be an exception; his obsession with portents and rituals probably derived from his failing health. But there is evidence that his father, Sennacherib, as well as other kings of the dynasty, also received regular reports and instructions designed to postpone the king's demise (unfortunately these did not prevent Sennacherib's assassination by one of his own sons).[10] Yet Sennacherib, in one of the few preserved royal tomb inscriptions, seems to accept death with equanimity:

Palace of sleep,
Tomb of repose,
Eternal residence,
Stable family dwelling
Of Sennacherib, the great king,
The mighty king, king of the universe, king of Assyria.[11]

Death, then, is sleeplike repose, eternal, and maintains familial ties. True enough, if the rituals of death are properly managed, as shall be seen later.

Gilgamesh, too, saw death as a kind of sleep, asking his newly dead friend Enkidu, "What, now is this sleep that has laid hold on thee?"[12] But more definitive physical symptoms were noted too:

He touched his heart, but it beat not at all,
He veiled his friend's face like a bride's.
. . . .
"Enkidu, whom I loved dearly,
Who with me underwent all hardships—
Has now gone to the fate of mankind!
Day and night I have wept over him—
I would not give him up for burial—
In case my friend should rise at my plaint—
Seven days and seven nights,
Until a worm fell out of his nose."[13]

Later in the epic the ghost of Enkidu, returned from the dead, compares his body to a vermin-ridden old garment. The cessation of bodily functions and corruption of the flesh were the obvious consequences of death. For him who has died "suddenly there is nothing."[14]

BURIAL, FUNERAL RITES, AND MOURNING

Most burials from ancient Mesopotamia have been found under the floors of houses, but because these are never plentiful enough to account for the number of deaths that should occur in a given household during the period for which the house was occupied, it is assumed that cemetery burial was common as well.[15] Because excavations usually are confined to the artificial mounds called "tells" that are built up through long periods of human settlement, cemeteries outside town limits normally would not be uncovered, and in fact, few Mesopotamian cemeteries have been found.

Corpses were wrapped in reed mats or set in wood or clay coffins, lying on their sides with limbs flexed. Royal and other important personages could have more elaborate burials. The royal tombs from Ur have already been mentioned. In Uruk crypts for the royal family were found under an early–second-millennium palace, and in Assyria kings were buried in stone sarcophagi in crypts at the old royal palace in Assur, long after Assur had ceased to be the capital. In general, relatively few elaborate burials have been recovered, and there is little textual information on burial practices of any kind. The inscription about Nabonidus's mother cited earlier is one. Another dates to the time of Esarhaddon or Ashurbanipal.[16] In this poorly preserved text the king is laid to rest in oil (possibly to preserve the body) in a stone sarcophagus within the royal tomb, together with his personal valuables and offerings for the gods of the netherworld. The fragmentary elegaic end of the text describes the lamenting of the landscape, vegetation, and architecture—presumably people, too, were mourning in the lost sections.

Grave goods, as the text makes clear, were intended both for the deceased's personal use and for sacrifice to the deities that control the world he is about to enter. This also is true in two late third-millennium literary descriptions of royal burials and entry into the netherworld: the Sumerian composition about the death of Gilgamesh, and a text recounting the death of the first king of the third dynasty of Ur, Urnammu, who ruled around 2100 B.C.[17] The portions in each describing the actual funeral are poorly preserved, and the texts focus more on laments for the dead and the entry of the dead into the netherworld. A letter to the Assyrian king Esarhaddon reports succinctly on the funeral of the just-executed substitute king: "He and his queen have been decorated, treated, displayed, buried and lamented."[18]

Lamentation is typical mourning procedure, and could be conducted by specialists, who, it is presumed, followed set texts or patterns, and those close to the deceased, such as Urnammu's wife in the Urnammu text, whose laments would be specific and spontaneous. Two remarkable literary laments for a dead father and wife of a private person have been preserved from the early second millennium.[19] But what the professional lamenters recited for a dead person is unknown.

Mourning lasted for seven days, according to the Nabonidus text cited earlier, and this is supported by another record from the reign of Nabonidus that tells of a seven-day mourning period for the king's wife.[20] In addition to wailing, mourning behavior included scratching and tearing at the body and hair and wearing dirty, matted hair and a dirty, ragged garment.[21]

AFTERLIFE AND THE NETHERWORLD

Once buried, the dead, or rather the ghosts of the dead (see later), set out for the netherworld, "the land of no return."[22] The entrance to this subterranean realm was on the western horizon, where the sun set in the evening. The new arrival passed through seven gates guarded by seven fierce porters. Once inside, offerings were made to the gods of the netherworld, presided over by the netherworld queen, Ereshkigal, and her consort, Nergal. The ghost was then judged and, if acceptable, assigned its appropriate station. This judgment does not seem to be concerned with earthly deeds or piety, but is rather a vetting of the ghost's credentials. Only those spirits who are properly interred and cared for are entitled to refuge in the netherworld.

By most accounts, it's a grim refuge indeed! When Enkidu recounted to Gilgamesh a dream about the netherworld presaging his death, he painted a sorry picture:

> To the house which none leave who have entered it,
> On the road from which there is no way back,
> To the house wherein the dwellers are bereft of light,
> Where dust is their fare and clay their food.
> They are clothed like birds, with wings for garments,
> And see no light, residing in darkness.
> In the House of Dust, which I entered,
> I looked at collected crowns,
> And heard the wearers of crowns who in days of old had ruled the land,
> Who now were serving meat roasts to the gods Anu and Enlil,
> They were serving baked goods and pouring cool water from waterskins.[23]

That is, former rulers eat dust and clay themselves, but serve real food and drink to the gods. The served have become the servers. Some visions are more kindly; the dead king Urnammu is provided with a retinue of dead warriors and executed criminals in the netherworld.[24] But life there is a dim shadow of earthly existence, and certainly nothing to anticipate with any enthusiasm. Although kings, priests, and notables are recognizable as such there, they enjoy none of the earthly perquisites of their positions, or, at best, only a pale reflection of such. Kinship relations may be maintained, but no emotions may be expressed toward spouse or children.[25]

There is one exception to this grim picture. A Sumerian poem known as ''Gilgamesh, Enkidu and the Netherworld'' tells the story of Enkidu's effort to retrieve the ball and stick of Gilgamesh, which had fallen into the netherworld.[26] Part of this tale was translated into Akkadian and appended to the Gilgamesh epic as its twelfth tablet.[27] The netherworld was a dangerous place for the living, and so Gilgamesh gave Enkidu elaborate instructions to enable him to get in and out unscathed. True to story patterns the world over, Enkidu disobeyed the instructions and was ''seized'' by the netherworld; that is, he was treated as if he were dead and would not be allowed to return to the surface of the earth. (It should be obvious by now why the translation of this poem is considered an appendage to the Akkadian Gilgamesh epic. There, Enkidu dies in a quite different way already in tablet seven, and tablets eight through eleven concern Gilgamesh's efforts to come to terms with both Enkidu's death and his own mortality.)

In the Sumerian story Gilgamesh, distraught over his friend's demise, petitions the gods to help him rescue Enkidu, and a hole is opened up through which Enkidu rises ''like a phantom.'' Gilgamesh proceeds to question him about the "order of the Netherworld," asking him about the fate of various categories of people. Enkidu replies, "If I tell you the order of the netherworld which I saw, sit down and lament! I, too, will sit down and lament!"[28] But despite this negative overall assessment, which corresponds to everything else known from Mesopotamian tradition, some of the denizens of the netherworld have a not unpleasant situation there.[29] For example, those with small families exist on bread and water, whereas the man with seven sons "as a companion of the gods sits on a chair and listens to music."[30] The woman who never had children "gives no man joy," the young man and woman who died without knowing connubial pleasures "weep," the man who disrespected his parents is afflicted with unquenchable thirst, but the slain warrior is comforted by his mourning family.

Curiously, the grandest arrangements have been made for those who had untimely deaths: he who died prematurely "lies on the bed of the gods"; stillborn babies "play at a table of gold and silver, laden with ghee and honey"; and a person set on fire didn't descend to the netherworld at all, but rather "his ghost does not exist, it went up with the smoke to heaven." And here the composition ends.

There certainly seems to be some kind of moral judgment at work here: the valorous in battle has the comfort of his family, whereas the disrespectful son is made uncomfortable. But many of the situations seem to depend on human reproduction: having no children or few children results in discomfort in the netherworld; having many leads to rewards. This is because the memorial rites that ensure that one is properly cared for after death are the responsibility of one's children. The three final cases that close the composition are puzzling. The stillborn, who never lived at all, and those who die in their prime and hence don't complete a normal life cycle are the most comfortable of all the inhabitants of the netherworld, with the exception perhaps of the man with seven sons. And the person consumed by fire—cremation was *not* practiced in Mesopotamia—escapes altogether.

The most convincing interpretation of these lines has been offered by Bendt Alster:

> Life as such is not to be desired. In our text life and death are viewed as an eternal cycle: Men must have children who can provide them with funeral offerings after their death, and they must also have children, and so forth. Our lines contain the poet's thought: Is the cycle something good or bad? He certainly gives the second answer. In the very last phrase he asks: Would it be possible to stop the cycle at all? He can think of one possibility: The total annihilation of both body and soul in fire, but since we can hardly believe that he would take the full consequence of this idea and burn himself, we are rather left with a humorous acceptance of the present tragic state of things.[31]

Whether a humorous or just a pessimistic view, the notion of a highly differentiated existence in the netherworld that depended on accidents of the ghost's former life is heterodox and confined to this one composition. The orthodox vision of the netherworld and existence there can be expressed in a single word: gloom.

BODY AND SOUL

When the flesh perishes two entities remain: bones and ghost.[32] The Akkadian word *eṭemmu*[33] is translated "ghost," and not "spirit" or "soul," intentionally. Living beings do not have one; the word is used only in connection with the dead. The origin of this ghost is described in a myth written down in the seventeenth century B.C. When the gods set out to create man, Enki, god of wisdom, orders that a god be slaughtered and clay be mixed from his flesh and blood:

> Let god and man
> Be mixed together in the clay.
> Let us hear the "drum" for the rest of time,
> Let there be a ghost from the flesh of the god,
> Let it proclaim the living (man) as its sign,
> So that he/it not be allowed to be forgotten, let there be a ghost.[34]

This passage has generated an enormous amount of commentary.[35] It is perfectly preserved, and neither the words nor the syntax is difficult. It is highly ambiguous, however, and its imagery is far from clear. Is the "drum" an actual drum, or is it the human heartbeat? Does the "drum" or the ghost do the proclaiming? Is "living (man)" what is not to be forgotten, or the ghost, or the drum, or perhaps the act of creation? What is a "sign" of what?

Part of the answer is to be found with Bottéro ("La création de l'homme") in the recognition that only the dead have ghosts.[36] But the ghosts in fact represent the former living. And, as can be seen later, these ghosts are dangerous precisely when those former living have not been properly memorialized. Because the ghost is just that part of a person that lives on eternally, it is said to derive specifically from the "flesh" of the normally immortal god. And the ghost's function is to ensure that the memory of the dead man is not forgotten, that is, that his memorial rites *(kispu)* are not allowed to lapse, because if they do lapse, the ghost will haunt those family members responsible for carrying out the rites.

But before memorial rites can be properly performed, the corpse must be properly buried. Here is where the bones are important. The memorial rites usually were performed in proximity to the place of interment; if the bones of the dead have been disturbed, the rites can't be performed. Thus both deprivation of burial and disruption of burial can result in the ghost haunting the living, and an enormous exorcistic literature is devoted to symbolically burying or reburying these errant spirits. The following is a catalogue of malefactors being conjured by the exorcist:

> Whether you are one who has been abandoned in the wilderness and not covered with earth,
>
> . . . .
>
> Or one who has slipped off a palm tree,
> Or one who has fallen into the water from a boat,
> Or an unburied ghost,
> Or a ghost who has no one to care for it,
> Or a ghost who has no one to perform its memorial rites,
> Or a ghost who has no one to libate water to it,
> Or a ghost who has no one to recite his name.[37]

Two examples illustrate the importance of ancestral bones to the living.[38] When Ashurbanipal of Assyria captured the Susa, capital of the perennial enemy Elam in 646, he wrote: "I tore down, demolished and exposed the tombs of their ancient and recent kings who did not revere Ishtar, my queen. I took their bones to the city of Assur, inflicting unrest upon their ghosts and depriving them of memorial rites and libations."

More than a half century earlier, in 700 B.C., Ashurbanipal's grandfather, Sennacherib, defeated the Babylonian rebel Merodachbaladan. The latter "loaded onto ships the gods of his entire land, together with the bones of his ancestors which he had gathered from their tombs, and his family, and crossed to . . . the other side of the Bitter Sea (Persian Gulf)." In the first instance, by bringing the bones of Elamite kings to Assur, Ashurbanipal inflicted eternal punishment on surviving members of the Elamite royal family, who would be forever haunted by the uncared for ghosts. It was just this fate that Merodachbaladan tried to avoid by bringing the bones of his ancestors with him into exile.

Although both of these examples are relatively recent, the complex of beliefs they represent can be traced back to the mid-third millennium. When, around 2400 B.C., the Sumerian ruler Enmetena of Lagash defeated an invading force from a neighboring city-state, he reports that the retreating ruler "abandoned sixty teams of asses . . . and left the bones of their personnel strewn over the plain."[39] The ignominy of defeat was augmented by the abandonment without burial of fallen soldiers. (To his credit, Enmetena himself had the enemy dead buried.)

The effects of the ghosts of the unburied or untended dead on the living are truly calamitous. In addition to haunting the living while asleep or awake, which can be unsettling in the extreme, they are the cause of numerous physical and psychological maladies.[40] But if properly cared for, ghosts can be invoked for protection.[41] For example, a sufferer being persecuted by an evil demon turns to his ancestors:

You are the ghosts of my family who have created all: my father, my grandfather, my mother, my grandmother, my brothers, my sisters, my family, my kith and kin, as many as lie in the ground. I have performed your memorial rites, libated water for you, cared for you, glorified you, and honored you. . . . Grab and bring down into the grave the evil spy-demon, the evil-doer who has attached himself to me and evilly persecuted me! May he not approach, come near or get close to me! May he not waft over to me or spy on me! May, I, your servant, live and get well![42]

Thus the carrot and the stick. The same ghost who, untended, can disrupt and ruin a person's life can, when properly cared for, be a valuable assistant against other malefactors. This ambivalent nature of ghosts, their role as both persecutor and protector, well illustrates the nearly universal ambivalence felt by the living toward the dead.[43]

MEMORIAL RITES

Caring for the dead involved the regular offering of food and libations together with the invocation of the dead person's name.[44] This first occurred at the funeral and then was repeated monthly, in certain periods on the day of the new moon.[45] The Akkadian word *kispu* refers to the food offerings for the dead, but in a broader sense it can refer to the entire ceremony. The regular performance of the memorial rites—probably at the grave—was the responsibility of the dead person's heir. A curse at the end of a contract from first-millennium Babylonia asks that the sun-god punish whoever alters the contract by taking away "the heir who will make libations for him, so that in the . . . netherworld, his ghost will be deprived of memorial rites."[46] Through the memorial rites the deceased remained integrated in the living family, and the position of the new head of family was reinforced by his performance of the rites.

Whereas the performance of memorial rites for commoners extended back only one or perhaps two generations, royal memorial rites reached back much farther, even including kings of previous dynasties. Ashurbanipal, the last great Assyrian monarch, claimed that "I (re)established the memorial rites and libations, which had been interrupted, for the ghosts of the kings who had preceded me."[47] These Assyrian memorial rites were performed at the royal mausoleum in the old capital, Assur. In other periods royal memorial rites could be performed in the palace or temple before the statues of earlier kings.

A text from eighteenth-century Mari, on the middle Euphrates near the current Syro-Iraqi border, tells of *kispu* offerings to the statues of Sargon and Naramsin of Akkade, who ruled 500 years earlier in Babylonia.[48] And from Babylonia itself in the seventeenth century a list of tribal ancestors and deceased kings of the Hammurabi dynasty concludes with the following exhortation:

The Amorite dynasty, the Hanean dynasty, the Gutian dynasty, any dynasty not recorded on this tablet, and the soldiers who died in their master's service, princes, princesses, all persons from east to west who have neither caretaker nor attendant: Come, eat this, drink this, and bless Ammisaduqa, son of Ammiditana, king of Babylon![49]

That is, in addition to the king's own ancestors, members of other dynasties and all manner of improperly cared for dead are invited to partake of the food and drink proffered by King Ammisaduqa. Unlike the individual, the king embodies the state, and his well-being and the state's coincide. Many portents—astronomical, meteorological, teratological—affect king and state, never the individual.[50] The broad range of deceased invoked in the royal memorial rites must reflect, as Bayliss has noted, "a belief in numerous forces which might affect the king's well-being."[51]

CLOSING THOUGHTS

For the Mesopotamians, a human was a liminal figure whose short life was spent hovering on the threshold of the netherworld. Occupying the surface of the earth, humankind filled the space between the divine realms of heaven and the netherworld, and served both. But a human's actual sphere was properly the netherworld; the same word in both Sumerian *(ki)* and Akkadian *(ersetu)* signifies both the earth's surface and the netherworld beneath it. Like the gods and demons of the netherworld, a human is destined to spend an eternity there; unlike them, a human has a brief opportunity to enjoy earthly pleasures.

Enjoyment of those pleasures, maximization of the opportunity, these were the ancient Mesopotamians' strategies when confronting the inevitable. After telling Gilgamesh that his quest for immortality is vain, the barmaid Siduri continued:

> Thou, Gilgamesh, let full be thy belly,
> Make thou merry by day and by night.
> Of each day make thou a feast of rejoicing,
> Day and night dance thou and play!
> Let thy garments be sparkling fresh,
> Thy head be washed; bathe thou in water.
> Pay heed to the little one that holds on to thy hand,
> Let thy spouse delight in thy bosom!
> For this is the task of mankind![52]

NOTES

1. A. Leo Oppenheim, *Ancient Mesopotamia: Portrait of a Dead Civilization,* rev. ed. (Chicago: University of Chicago Press, 1977), remains the finest introduction to ancient Mesopotamia. See, too, Samuel N. Kramer, *The Sumerians: Their History, Culture and Character* (Chicago: University of Chicago Press, 1963), for details on the Sumerians.

2. James B. Pritchard, ed., *Ancient Near Eastern Texts Relating to the Old Testa-*

ment, 3d ed. (Princeton, N.J.: Princeton University Press, 1969), 561ff. Copyright © 1969 by Princeton University Press. Reprinted by permission of Princeton University Press.

3. P. R. S. Moorey, *Ur "of the Chaldees." A Revised and Updated Edition of Sir Leonard Woolley's Excavations at Ur* (Ithaca, N.Y.: Cornell University Press, 1982), 72–76.

4. Kramer thinks the Sumerian text describing Gilgamesh's arrival in the netherworld refers to burial with retainers, but the passage is uncertain. Cf. Samuel N. Kramer, "The Death of Gilgamesh," *Bulletin of the American Schools for Oriental Research* 94 (April 1944):2–12.

5. Harvey Weiss, ed., *Ebla to Damascus: Art and Archaeology of Ancient Syria* (Washington, D.C.: Smithsonian Institution, 1985).

6. Lambert argues, not entirely convincingly, that natural death (as opposed to accidental or intentionally caused death) was not considered to be humankind's fate until the postdiluvian restructuring of the human condition. Before the Deluge, human life had no fixed end. Cf. Wilfred G. Lambert and A. R. Millard, *Atra-hasis: The Babylonian Story of the Flood* (Oxford: Oxford University Press, 1969). Bauer interprets certain Sumerian creation stories as positing a primordial human existence without sexuality or death. Cf. Josef Bauer, "Leben in der Urzeit Mesopotemiens," *Archiv für Orientforschung* Beiheft 19 (1982):377–383.

7. Pritchard, *Ancient Near Eastern Texts,* 90.

8. Ibid., 79; for similar sentiments expressed in the Sumerian forerunner to this part of the Gilgamesh epic, see Samuel N. Kramer, "Gilgamesh and the Land of the Living," *Journal of Cuneiform Studies* 3 (1947):9.

9. Some idea of the importance of divination, astrology, and apotropaic ritual can be gleaned from the letters in A. Leo Oppenheim, *Letters from Mesopotamia* (Chicago: University of Chicago Press, 1967), 160–169, but the best collection of material is to be found in Simo Parpola, *Letters from Assyrian Scholars to the Kings Esarhaddon and Assurbanipal,* Alter Orient und Altes Testament 5, 1–2 (Kevelaer, Germany: Butzon & Bercker, 1970). The substitute king ritual is discussed by him on pp. xxii–xxxii of vol. 2.

10. Parpola, *Letters from Assyrian Scholars,* vol. 2, xii.

11. Jean Bottéro, "Les inscriptions funéraires cuneiformes," in G. Gnoli and J. P. Vernant, eds., *La morts dans les sociétés anciennes* (Cambridge: Cambridge University Press, 1982), 373–406.

12. Pritchard, *Ancient Near Eastern Texts,* 88.

13. Ibid., 88–90.

14. Lambert and Millard, *Atra-hasis: The Babylonian Story of Flood,* 55.

15. Most of the material in this section, unless otherwise attributed, is from Eva Strommenger, "Grab" and "Grabbeigabe," in *Reallexikon der Assyriologie und Vorderasiatischen Archaeologie* 3 (1957–71):581–93, 605–8.

16. John McGinnis, "A Neo-Assyrian Text Describing a Royal Funeral." State Archives of Assyria Bulletin 1 (1987):1–12.

17. Samuel N. Kramer, "The Death of Ur-Nammu and His Descent to the Netherworld," *Journal of Cuneiform Studies* 21 (1969):104–125.

18. Parpola, *Letters from Ancient Assyrian Scholars,* no. 280.

19. Samuel N. Kramer, *Two Elegies on a Pushkin Museum Tablet: A New Sumerian Literary Genre* (Moscow: Oriental Literature Publishing House, 1960).

20. A. Kirk Grayson, *Assyrian and Babylonian Chronicles,* Texts from Cuneiform Sources 5 (Locust Valley, N.Y.: J. J. Augustin, 1975), 111.

21. *The Assyrian Dictionary of the Oriental Institute of the University of Chicago.* Chicago: Oriental Institute, 1956.

22. Recent discussions of afterlife and the netherworld are found in Akio Tsukimoto, *Untersuchungen zur Totenpflege im alten Mesopotamien,* Alter Orient und Altes Testament 216 (Kevelaer, Germany: Butzon & Bercker, 1985), and Jean Bottéro, *Mesopotamie* (Paris: Gallimard, 1987). See, too, the still informative discussion in Alexander Heidel, *The Gilgamesh Epic and Old Testament Parallels* (Chicago: University of Chicago Press, 1949), ch. 3.

23. Pritchard, *Ancient Near Eastern Texts,* 87.

24. Kramer, "The Death of Ur-Nammu," 119.

25. Pritchard, *Ancient Near Eastern Texts,* 97.

26. Aaron Shaffer, *Sumerian Sources of Tablet XII of the Epic of Gilgamesh.* Dissertation. University of Pennsylvania, 1963. (Ann Arbor: University Microfilm, 1963), 63–7085.

27. Jeffrey H. Tigay, *The Evolution of the Gilgamesh Epic* (Philadelphia: University of Pennsylvania Press, 1982), 105–109.

28. Pritchard, *Ancient Near Eastern Texts,* 98.

29. Shaffer, *Sumerian Sources,* 116–121.

30. "Junior Colleague" would be better than "companion." The translation "music" is uncertain; perhaps he is sitting and listening to the gods converse.

31. Bendt Alster, ed., *Death in Mesopotamia,* Mesopotamia, Copenhagen Studies in Assyriology 8 (Copenhagen: Akademisk Forlag, 1980), 59.

32. See especially Elena Cassin, "Le mort: Valeur et représentation en Mésopotamie ancienne," in Gnoli and Vernant, *La morts dans les sociétés anciennes,* 355–372; Jean Bottéro, "Les morts et l'au-delà dans les rituels en accadien contre l'action des revenants," *Zeitschrift für Assyriologie und Vorderasiatische Archaeologie* 73 (1983):153–203; Tsukimoto, *Untersuchungen zur Totenpflege.*

33. The word is borrowed from the Sumerian *gidim.*

34. Lambert and Millard, *Atra-hasis: The Babylonian Story of Flood,* 58.

35. Among the most important are William L. Moran, "The Creation of Man in Atra-hasis I, 192–248," in *Bulletin of the American Schools of Oriental Research* 200 (December 1970):48–56; Anne D. Kilmer, "The Mesopotamian Concept of Overpopulation and Its Solution as Reflected in the Mythology," in *Orientalia* 41 (1971):160–177.

36. Jean Bottéro, "La Création de l'homme et sa nature dans le poeme d'Atrahasis." *Societies and Languages of the Ancient Near East* (Warminster: Aris & Phillips, 1982), 24–32.

37. Compare Van Gennep, who sees those for whom proper funeral and mourning rites were not performed as "the most dangerous dead. . . . They lack the means to subsistence which the other dead find in their own world and consequently must obtain them, at the expense of the living." See Phyllis Palgi and Henry Abramovitch, "Death: A Cross-Cultural Perspective," *Annual Review of Anthropology* 13 (1984):390.

38. Cassin, "Le mort: Valeur et représentation en Mésopotamie ancienne," 362, 365.

39. Jerrold S. Cooper, *Sumerian and Akkadian Royal Inscriptions. I. Presargonic*

Inscriptions. American Oriental Society Translation Series 1 (New Haven, Conn.: American Oriental Society, 1986), 55.

40. Bottéro, "Les morts et l'au-delà," 161–169.

41. Ibid., 169–174; Tsukimoto, *Untersuchungen zur Totenpflege,* 159–167.

42. Walter Farber, *Beschworungsrituals an Istar und Dumuzi.* Akademie der Wissenschaften und der Literatur. Veroffentlichungen der Orientalischen Kommission. (Wiesbaden: Franz Steiner, 1977), 151–153.

43. Palgi and Abramovitch, "Death: A Cross-Cultural Perspective," 393–398.

44. This section is based on Tsukimoto, *Untersuchungen zur Totenpflege,* and Miranda Bayliss, "The Cult of Dead Kin in Assyria and Babylonia," *Iraq* 35 (1973): 115–125.

45. There also are references to a given month, which may be different from period to period, during which more elaborate royal memorial rites were performed, but these seem to have been the memorials discussed in the following paragraph.

46. Tsukimoto, *Untersuchungen zur Totenpflege,* 118ff.

47. Ibid., 110ff.

48. See the comments on this text and the relation of the kings of Akkade to Mari by D. Charpin and J. M. Durand, "Fils de Sim'al': Les origines tribales des rois de Mari." *Revue d'Assyriologie* 80 (1986):141–183.

49. See the recent interpretation of this text by Charpin and Durand, ibid., 159–170.

50. Oppenheim, *Ancient Mesopotamia: Portrait of a Dead Civilization,* 206–227.

51. Miranda Bayliss, "The Cult of the Dead Kin in Assyria and Babylonia," 122.

52. Pritchard, *Ancient Near Eastern Texts,* 90.

3

Taking It With You: The Problem of Death and Afterlife in Ancient Egypt

William J. Murnane

Make good your dwelling in the graveyard,
Make worthy your station in the West.
Given that death humbles us,
Given that life exalts us,
The house of death is for life.

"The Instruction of Hardjedef"[1]

INTRODUCTION

Fascination with death is credited to no nation more widely than it is to Egypt of the pharaohs. Alone among the peoples of the ancient Near East, the Egyptians have left us a considerable body of monuments, artifacts, and written records that attest to essentially the same view of death and the afterlife for more than 3,000 years. Preparations for death were made carefully and long in advance: tomb chapels and burial chambers were built, grave goods laid aside, and endowments set up to pay the mortuary priests who provided for the eternal well-being of the deceased's spirit. The prominent role played by mortuary arrangements in the ancient Egyptians' daily lives could suggest a gloomy preoccupation with mortality, even a morbid celebration of the inevitable end that shadowed people all their days. Such an impression would be misleading. As we shall see, the Egyptians regarded the pleasures of life highly and did not look forward to "the day of landing," as the end of life was called. A noted writer on the phenomenon of death in the Western world has discussed what he calls "tamed death"[2]—the "normalizing" of death as a necessary and expected part of the human voyage, thereby lessening its terrors. Although there is doubtless some element of this in what we may term the "mortuary industry'' in ancient Egypt, it also is clear that these provisions were not mere palliatives. The concerns of the mortuary cult throughout the long history of ancient Egypt were focused, not on the obliteration of death as a significant fact for the living (as in modern Western society), but on the expectation that everyone would one day arrive at the same crossing and would take, in consequence, a prior interest in whatever lay on the other side.[3]

The inevitability of death did not soften the dread image it presented to the ancient Egyptians. Only in the most idiosyncratic of compositions is it welcomed, and then only as an alternative to a wretched life.[4] Otherwise, death was an enemy. The decay of the body in old age was itself a painful and humiliating foretaste of approaching dissolution: ''Eyes are dim, ears deaf. Strength wanes through weariness. The mouth, silenced, speaks not. The heart, void, recalls not the past.''[5] Death, when it came, brought with it the danger of total annihilation,[6] of being snatched away into a realm of darkness[7] where the dead sank into exhausted sleep[8] or could be subjected to all sorts of perils—imprisonment, reversal of one's customary manner of existence, fear, and a full range of otherworldy torments to mock and ultimately frustrate one's hope of personal survival.[9] Not content with bringing life in this world to an end, death warped one's being by exposing the personality to a prolonged and unpleasant ''second death'' in the hereafter.

DEATH AND THE NEW LIFE

Fortunately, although death pervaded the Egyptians' universe,[10] it did not win a final victory there. On the contrary, the cycles of nature in the Nile Valley suggested that the inevitable corollary of death was new life. The sun continually rose at dawn after setting on the evening of the previous day, the moon waned and waxed without cease, and the stars—if they were not among the ''Imperishable Ones'' that never faded from the night sky—were always reborn after they had disappeared from the heavens for a time. Most immediate and dramatic of all these cyclical phenomena was the annual flood of the Nile, on which the prosperity of Egypt was built. Failure of the river to rise at its appointed time was as menacing a disruption of the natural rhythm as an eclipse, and one that the average Egyptian felt more keenly: A succession of low Niles meant famine, with its attendant evils of social and political unrest.[11] The Egyptians' concept of universal order (called *Ma'at,* a word also synonymous with ''justice'') included the regular and uninterrupted procession of all these natural cycles, and thus, too, their built-in sequences of life and death. The Egyptians' very surroundings, then, shaped their ultimate convictions on the nature of death and the afterlife, not as an end, but as a continuation of life in another state. It was to secure this immortality and to avoid the final, agonizing ''second death'' of the soul[12] that the mortuary cult was dedicated. As the practical expression of the ancient Egyptians' strategy to avoid personal extinction, the usages of this cult have much to tell us regarding their attitudes toward death and the afterlife.

The Pyramid Texts, an anthology that includes some of the oldest mortuary spells from Egypt, assured the deceased that his physical death was an illusion: "It is not in the state of being dead that you have gone away; it is being alive that you have departed."[13] The burial arrangements of the earliest Egyptians certainly conform to this assumption. Although the tomb often was no more than a deep hole dug into the desert sand, the corpse was invariably accompanied by jars of food and drink and by an assortment of personal property. That these items were intended for the deceased's use in his next life is explicitly said in an incantation that probably came down from this remote period into the Pyramid Texts: "Raise yourself up. . . . Take your head, collect your bones, gather your limbs, shake the earth from your flesh! Take your bread that rots not, (and) your beer that sours not."[14] Egyptian mortuary religion throughout antiquity retained this comforting emphasis on the similarity of the next life to that which the deceased had enjoyed in this world.

MUMMIFICATION

This similarity, once granted, imposed a number of requirements on the mortuary cult. The preservation of the body was the first and most important of these: How else could the deceased expect to enjoy the benefits of his new "life"? Excavations have shown that in the earliest burials the desert sands performed this task well, naturally removing the corrupting moisture from the corpse. This admirably simple preservative was ruled out as burials became more grand. Because the required desiccation could not take place once the body was enclosed in a coffin, an artificial method of preservation had to be found: Thus developed the arts of mummification for which the Egyptians are so famed.[15] It took some time to fully develop this process, and although the few mummies that survive from the Old and Middle Kingdoms (c. 2613–1782 B.C.) achieved a lifelike outer appearance, the bodies themselves were less successfully preserved. Although internal organs (lungs, liver, intestines, and stomach) usually were removed to be preserved separately, failure to remove the brain and the retention of other soft tissues caused some decomposition. More careful attention was given to the mummy's exterior. Sometimes it was modeled in plaster with the deceased's features; at other times the interior cavities were stuffed with linen to reproduce the plump appearance of life before the entire corpse was wrapped with bandages. Because most corpses were returned to their families in this condition for burial, it is unlikely that the inner state of their interiors attracted any notice or concern.

Only by the New Kingdom (c. 1570–1070 B.C.) did the Egyptians succeed in thoroughly preserving the body before it was encased in its outer wrappings. Essentially, as it was to be described by Herodotus (Book II, 85–88) a millennium later, the process involved the removal of all soft organs (including the brain) before the body was buried in natron, a natural combination of natrium carbonate and natrium bicarbonate that was widely available on the fringes of the Nile valley.[16] The immersion in natron, which lasted for seventy days, completed the desiccation of the corpse. It could then be packed with resin-soaked linen before being wrapped in its outer bandages. Precious amulets, placed at various points on the body and inside the wrappings at this time, gave magical protection to the corpse (and, ironically, hastened the destruction of all too many mummies at the hands of tomb-robbers). Coats of hot resin hardened the outer bandages of the mummy, and further protection could be found in a form-fitting body case made of cartonnage (linen, strengthened with plaster), which was then painted with mythological scenes and motifs. Any completely equipped mummy also would wear a funerary mask bearing an idealized portrait of the deceased's features. Many such masks were made of cartonnage, but more expensive examples in wood (not to mention the solid gold mask made for King Tutankhamen) are found as well. The finished mummy was then enclosed in its coffin.[17] People of some means were provided with wooden coffins, but more modest containers of pottery and even wickerwork also are seen. A massive stone sarcophagus completed the essential protection of the body in an affluent burial. The poor, who had to make do with the cheapest sort of mummification, did without both coffins and outer sarcophagi. Most frequently buried in pit graves, they also took advantage of ravaged, empty tombs to make their final resting places: Intrusive burials, in which mummies often are stacked like firewood, have survived in great numbers because of their poverty, whereas the more elaborate original occupancy of the tombs thus used has all but disappeared.

Thus laid out, the deceased was indeed "wrapped for eternity." But what if the corpse were destroyed by tomb-robbers or in some other catastrophe? To avert this danger, the deceased was provided with one or more "substitute bodies"—statues, displayed in the tomb chapel or kept for added security in a closed chamber that is known today as a *serdab* (Arabic for "cellar"). This was not an underground room, but one that was off the main offering chapel on the same level, from whence the statue could "see" the cult rituals through a slit in the wall. The statue thus served a double function: an alternative body for the deceased in case of need, it was more regularly a handy substitute for his person and as such received the prayers and offerings of the mortuary cult.

THE TOMB

The proper venue for this cult was the tomb.[18] Only seldom were cemeteries situated in places frequented by the living. They normally lay at some distance from the settlements they served, either in the neighboring desert or across the river—usually in the west, which already had a mortuary aura from its association with the setting sun. In the earliest tombs accommodations for the burial are far more extensive than those that served the continuing mortuary cult.

Most of the space in these structures was taken up with the burial chamber and the storerooms that held the deceased's provisions for the hereafter, whereas only the barest arrangements—a small chapel, or a niche in the dummy superstructure of the tomb—were made for the regular services on behalf of his spirit.[19] This proportion was reversed by the end of the third millennium B.C., by which time the burial chambers were much reduced in size and the chapel had become the most important medium through which were realized the tomb owner's aspirations for the life to come.

The range of activities depicted in the reliefs and paintings of Egyptian tombs reveals an entire world in miniature.[20] Peasants till the soil on the deceased's estate and present their yields. Other laborers are seen tending his flocks and aviaries, while artisans manufacture essential goods and luxuries in his workshops. Elsewhere the tomb owner is seen acting in his highest earthly dignity—supervising his subordinates, reporting before the pharaoh, and being honored in the sight of his contemporaries. The main impulse behind these vignettes was not artistic, charming though they are. One serious use was to provide a magical backup for the offerings deposited in the tomb on the day of burial: With the farming and manufacturing scenes so close at hand the deceased need not lack for anything, even if his mortuary cult ceased. Another was to establish his enduring memorial on earth. Someone with so many virtues and so high a standing might well be an "effective spirit" whom later generations would honor. To be remembered was very much in the deceased's interest, for such remembrance "caused one's name to live." It improved the likelihood of one's keeping a functional mortuary cult in the remote future, and in the most notable cases it conferred fame, itself a prized form of immortality in virtually any society.[21]

A more immediate "memory bank" is exhibited on the walls of virtually any tomb, where one is aware of not only the tomb owner, but also his wife, his children, and swarms of relatives. These people share in (or, in the case of the younger generations, give) offerings, and all together they participate in a banquet honoring the deceased. No distinction seems to be made in these scenes between family members who were living at the time of the funeral and those who already were dead. The implication is that the extended family transcends the boundary of death. Indeed, the liturgical calendars of ancient Egypt regularly included the dead in the celebrations of the living. For example, their statues took part in the festival of Sokar, a deity whose cult blended mortuary with fertility rituals.[22] A more explicit intermingling of the living with their ancestors took place annually at Thebes, in the "Festival of the Valley." During its course family members crossed over to the cemetery and opened the tomb chapels, setting out a meal to be eaten in the company of the dead. They presently were joined by priests and priestesses, bringing from the temple at Deir el-Bahari sanctified flowers, thus symbolically giving "life" to the dead (based on a pun between the words for "life" and "bouquet," both written *ʿankh*).[23] Although this celebration was held under state auspices, it could hardly have taken place without the involvement of the family. Nor can it be doubted that this institution, above all others, kept the mortuary cult going in Egypt. By maintaining such ritualized meetings between the living and the dead, and by upholding the standards of "proper" burial, even when it was clear that such buried wealth invited robbery,[24] family members vicariously looked after their own futures. This was a well-attested fact of life, at least to the man who observed on his own mortuary stela that, "as it is said from mouth to mouth, 'one acts for one who has acted.' "[25]

The tombs, then, were outfitted as alternative dwellings for the deceased, who were expected to be "at home" whenever their families sought them out there. To be sure, this happened mostly on festival days, but there were other occasions on which the tomb chapels might witness attempts at contact. Sometimes living relations who were sick or in trouble left "letters to the dead": These typically present the survivor's excuses for a fault committed in life and beg relief from some ill through the deceased's intercession.[26] Less welcome visitors also might count on finding the tombs occupied. One story of the late period describes how a high priest of Memphis, on entering an ancient burial chamber in search of a papyrus book, is confronted by the tomb owner, who strenuously objects to having his treasure removed![27] The disappearance of a tomb was catastrophic, for the "memory" of the deceased and his access to mortuary rites was thereby cut off. Another tale presents the owner of a lost tomb as "haunting" someone (not one of his relatives) until the man consents to find the tomb again.[28] Even though scenes and inscriptions on tomb walls were designed to act as magical substitutes for offerings that would surely fail if the mortuary cult ceased, the possibility that this might happen gave rise to an anxiety that the happy ending of the "ghost story" does not altogether conceal.

THE *KA* AND THE *BA*

Ultimately, the Egyptians' emphasis on the next life in the tomb is paradoxical, since no one expected the deceased to make his exclusive home in it. To be sure, some elements in the Egyptian concept of the personality (which, as a composite, fulfilled the functions of the "soul") were intimately bound to this world. The "shadow," portrayed as a dark, skeletal figure, naturally stayed close to the body. The *Ka* is another element that seems to be at home in the orbit of the tomb.[29] Coming into being with each person at birth, it was a spiritual "double" whom the person joined at death. It was the *Ka* who dwelt in the tomb owner's statue, it was to the *Ka,* rather to any other aspect of the personality, that mortuary offerings were made. Still another aspect, the *Ba,* represented the dynamic forces, both physical and psychic, of the personality.[30] Most often represented as a human-headed bird, the *Ba* symbolized the deceased's capacity to move about in the world beyond the tomb. What is most interesting about the *Ba* is that although it was equipped to perform all the corporeal functions of a living being, it also possessed the power to join the sun in the heavens. This double capacity to act in the realm of men and of the gods is shared by one other element of the personality, the *Akh*. We have already met the *Akh* as an importunate ghost, in the story mentioned earlier, and "letters to the dead" were addressed to the *Akh;* its more customary environment, however, was the next world, where it can be defined loosely as an "(illuminated) spirit."[31] The realm of the dead, then, oscillated between the tomb and other places that were not of this earth.

In a tomb of the late Old Kingdom an official boastingly states, "I am an effective spirit who knows his magic spells; and I know the spell of ascending to the Great God, the lord of heaven,"[32] meaning that he had the power to join the sun-god Re in the sky, as does the king in the Pyramid Texts. Joining the circuit of nature, whether by traveling with the solar bark across heaven and through the caverns of night, or by resting among the stars, conferred personal immortality by association with the most conspicuously "eternal" phenomena in the cosmos. One's ability to do this depended on magic—on the spells mentioned earlier or, in the king's case, on one's own divine power:

> Unas eats their magic, swallows their spirits:
> Their big ones are for his morning meal,
> Their middle ones are for his evening meal,
> Their little ones are for his night meal,
> And the oldest males and females for his fuel.
> The Great Ones in the northern sky light him fire
> For the kettles' contents with the old ones' thighs.
> For the sky-dwellers serve Unas,
> And the pots are scraped for him with their women's legs.[33]

This is an extreme. In the anthology of spells that make up the Pyramid Texts the king usually does not storm heaven in this manner, and may even seek a place there in the humble role of the sun-god's secretary:

> Unas squats before him,
> Unas opens his boxes,
> Unas unseals his decrees,
> Unas seals his dispatches,
> Unas sends his messengers who tire not,
> Unas does what Unas is told.[34]

Even for the king, it seems, the next world is an uncertain place. Mortuary literature adapted to this uncertainty by providing a number of strategies to gain entry: If brute force did not work, the way might yet be won by self-confidence, humility, or even subterfuge.

PHARAOHS AND THE MORTALS: THE TWO NOTIONS OF THE AFTERLIFE

Like master, like man. Throughout the long history of Egyptian civilization, conceptions of the afterlife originally designed for the ruler eventually were adopted by his subjects. By the later third millennium B.C. selections from the royal corpus of Pyramid Texts, extensively reworked and augmented, had found their way into private tombs, inscribed for the most part on coffins.[35] A later revision of this collection was the well-known "Chapters of Going Forth by Day," misnamed "Book of the Dead" by its first modern translators.[36] Copied onto papyri, these texts appeared as a regular part of the deceased's burial equipment as of the early new Kingdom and remained in use down to the end of paganism in Egypt. Other compositions present themselves as guides to the next world, listing the dangers and significant features that the deceased should know on his journey.[37] Starting in the fifteenth century B.C. a number of such guides—"The Book of What Is in the Underworld," "The Book of Gates," "The Book of Caverns," and others—were inscribed on the walls of the royal tombs in the Valley of the Kings at Thebes, showing all the alternative routes to the king's celestial destiny. Commoners were not slow to take a similar interest in the hereafter. Extracts from these royal guides to the next world dominated the decoration of private chapels by the later new Kingdom, even crowding out the scenes from daily life that had been the deceased's traditional "life-support systems" in the tomb. It is these compositions, as much as the tombs themselves, that best reveal the Egyptians' vision of the afterlife.

The distinction between pharaohs and mortals is immediately felt in the religion of these works. The king, after all, entered the gods' realm by right, as a divinity, even if a twinge of human anxiety occasionally is shown. Mortals had no such claims to back them up. Thus the afterlife that common men sought was not the circuit ruled by the sun-god in the Pyramid Texts. Rather, it was the underworld, in which the dead god Osiris held sway. These two theologies would mingle, and in time Re and Osiris would become complementary poles in the Egyptian conception of the next world[38]; what set the Osirian afterlife apart from the king's solar destiny was its precondition, an ethical judgment of the dead. On reaching the hall where Osiris was enthroned before his retinue, the deceased recited a lengthy "negative confession," in which he disavowed having committed a number of sins. Having established his righteousness, he was then questioned by the assembled gods, and even by the different elements of the gate before the hall: This interrogation had to do not with the deceased's purity of life, but with his knowledge of his questioners' names of power—even extending to the names of his own feet!—and it is doubtless an interjection of the more traditional funerary magic. Only when these queries were satisfied was the deceased allowed to proceed into the presence of Osiris himself. There, inside the judgment hall, the deceased's heart (the seat of intellect and emotion) was weighed in the balance against a feather, which was the symbol of Ma'at (cosmic harmony, or justice). If the heart was still weighted down by sin, its owner was lost—he was immediately thrown to a monster whose body was amalgamated from several fearsome animals. The spells in the "Book of the Dead" ensured, however, that the scales would remain evenly balanced, permitting the deceased to emerge "vindicated" and to take his place in the underworld.[39]

The destination of the blessed dead was the "Field of Rushes," where they were granted plots of land for their eternal sustenance. Vignettes illustrating this locality regularly depict the deceased working their own fields, a perfectly normal occupation in an alternative universe that paralleled the Nile valley, but not one that would appeal to the more leisured among the saved. Wealthy Egyptians were accustomed to being served in the afterlife as they had been in this world. The earliest pharaohs had buried their retainers around their tombs (perhaps even forcing these unfortunates to follow them in death). Later generations made use of models that showed people working at various occupations and even reproduced the workshops in which each task was accomplished.[40] A similar expedient, translated into the Osirian afterlife, became an indispensable part of any Egyptian's burial equipment, the "shabti"—figurine. Thousands of these objects have been found in tombs from the Middle Kingdom and later. Most of them are simple, even crude objects, but their purpose is established by the more elaborate examples, which were inscribed with a spell that ordered them to take the owner's place should he be called for any hard labor in the next world.[41] Death clearly was no leveler of rank. The order of society had to be maintained, even in the afterlife.

The range of options that Egyptian mortuary religion seems to offer hints at unresolved ambiguities in the conception of death and the afterlife. One strategy, to all appearances the oldest, centered on the continued sustenance that the dead required from the world of the living—in a real sense, "taking it with them." Its alternative involved a journey from this world to another part of the universe, where the deceased joined the circuit of nature or took up residence in the realm of Osiris. Entry into this other world was facilitated by the paraphernalia of the mortuary cult, but it is hard to see what further need the deceased would have of this magic once they had reached these blessed realms. Incompatible as these two notions of the afterlife seem to be, the fact remains that they coexisted throughout Egypt's ancient history: The otherworldly orbit of the dead was not seen as a bar to their inhabiting their tombs or participating in the feasts of the living. Most Egyptologists explain the inconsistency of these notions in terms of the conservatism of Egyptian society. Many people probably put their trust in familiar rituals without thinking too closely about them: A man who usurped another's burial to make way for his own, for example, is not likely to have been bothered by the thought that he might suffer a similar fate.[42] Factors such as the family's concern for its prestige, as well as a natural anxiety regarding the deceased's fate after death, would have been potent arguments in favor of respecting traditional forms. Who, after all, could say with certainty that any of these measures did not work?

One wonders, however, whether it is realistic to assume that the Egyptians simply could not face these problems. An alternative interpretation of the cult[43] has suggested that all mortuary practices, from mummification to the periodic commemorations at the tomb, were sacramental in character. Thus understood, they brought the deceased into another plane of existence in which all the potentialities in the universe were simultaneously active. The two modes in which the Egyptians perceived the passage of time—linear time and the cyclical procession of the seasons—merged. There was no question of choosing between the sun-god and Osiris, or among the many ways that led to the realm of the blessed: The deceased traveled along all the ways at once, and all the divine essences combined, separated, and took other forms in different locales and situations. Life in the next world, then, actually freed the personality from the limitations of time and space: It was always everywhere and existed in a timeless present. In the Coffin Texts Re declares, "I have spent millions of years [existing] between myself and the Weary-hearted one, the son of Geb [Osiris]. Now I shall dwell with him in one place. The mounds shall become cities and the cities shall become mounds: [one] mansion will desolate [the other] mansion."[44] This apocalyptic statement, in which the sun-god anticipates his own fusion with Osiris and a complete reversal of universal order, refers not to the "end of days" in a Judeo-Christian sense, but to that fusion of cyclic and linear time that is implicit in all transitions—from day to following day through the night, and from life to new life beyond death. "Yesterday is mine, and I know tomorrow—[that is,] as for yesterday, it is Osiris; as for tomorrow, it is Re."[45] In the gods' realm the deceased were always on the cusp, as it were, between Re and Osiris, and, like them, always winning through to new life.

CONCLUSION

Seen from this perspective, did the fate of the mummy and tomb actually matter? It is possible to argue that it did not, and that the Egyptians had indeed arrived at a completely spiritualized view of the afterlife. Developments in their religion seem to point in this direction, as noted earlier, and one can make a reasonable case that at least some people thought of the life after death in this way. At the same time there are good reasons for believing that traditional mortuary practices were still being carried out for their own sakes. Tombs built in the later centuries of paganism made significant advances in security devices[46]; and insofar as one can tell, most of the traditional burial customs continued to be practiced in them. If most Egyptians viewed the mortuary cult in the predominantly spiritual light that has been suggested, it is surprising that they did not acknowledge its symbolic character by drastically simplifying it (as had been done earlier, when models had replaced actual offerings and serving personnel). The fact that no major change took place suggests, to the contrary, that the burial itself continued to possess some efficacy in securing the tomb owner's fate. To all appearances, mortuary religion remained the hybrid it had been from its earliest development. Only with the eclipse of paganism would a fundamentally different notion of the afterlife take hold; but although neither Christianity nor Islam had any use for grave goods, one feature of the traditional burial could not be dislodged. Architecturally, at least, the tomb's function as an alternative dwelling for the deceased continued through the early Christian centuries and into the cemeteries of modern Egypt.

All told, the Egyptians never lost their deep-seated sense of uncertainty about any of the strategies they had developed for overcoming death. Keenly fond of life's pleasures, they were nonetheless haunted by an awareness of their own mortality. The Greek historian Herodotus alleges (Book II, 78) that guests at a banquet would pass from hand to hand a mortuary image while exhorting one another to "look here, drink and be merry; for when you die, thus will you be."[47] This morbid custom is not directly attested in any of the reliefs and inscriptions that have come down to us from ancient Egypt. A similar attitude is expressed in some examples of a poetic genre known as "Harpers' Songs," in which listeners are urged to consider the impermanence of life and all that is done in it. "I have heard the words of Imhotep and Hardjedef [two famous sages], whose sayings are recited whole," says one such singer from the Middle Kingdom. However:

> What of their places?
> Their walls have crumbled,
> Their places are gone,
> As though they had never been!
> None comes from there,
> To tell of their state,
> To tell of their needs,
> To calm our hearts,
> Until we go where they have gone!
> Hence rejoice in your heart!
> Forgetfulness profits you,
> Follow your heart as long as you live![48]

Let us allow the last word, to another Harper's Song, which implicitly repudiates such skepticism and makes a more typical avowal of faith in the beneficence of the Egyptian cosmos:

> I have heard those songs that are in the tombs of old,
> What they tell in extolling life on earth,
> In belittling the land of the dead.
> Why is this done to the land of eternity,

The right and just that has no terrors?
Strife is abhorrent to it,
No one girds himself against his fellow;
This land that has no opponent,
All our kinsmen rest in it
Since the time of the first beginning.
Those to be born to millions of millions,
All of them will come to it;
No one may linger in the land of Egypt.
There is none who does not arrive in it.
As to the time of deeds on earth,
It is the occurrence of a dream;
One says, "Welcome safe and sound,"
To him who reaches the West.[49]

NOTES

1. Miriam Lichtheim, *Ancient Egyptian Literature* I, *The Old and Middle Kingdoms* (Berkeley: University of California Press, 1973), 58.

2. Philippe Ariès, *Western Attitudes Toward Death: From the Middle Ages to the Present,* trans. Patricia M. Ranum (Baltimore: Johns Hopkins University Press, 1974), 1–25.

3. On funerary religion and practices, see A. J. Spencer, *Death in Ancient Egypt* (Harmondsworth: Penguin Books, 1982). This book supersedes in every way Sir E. A. Wallis Budge's *The Mummy* (New York: Causeway Books, 1974), which first appeared in 1893.

4. "The Dispute Between a Man and His Ba," sometimes described as the "Dialogue of the Suicide with His Soul;" for competing translations of this controversial work see Lichtheim, *Ancient Egyptian Literature* I, 163–69; J. A. Wilson, in James B. Pritchard, ed., *Ancient Near Eastern Texts Relating to the Old Testament,* 3rd ed. (Princeton, N.J.: Princeton University Press, 1969), 405–407; Raymond O. Faulkner, in William Kelly Simpson, ed., *The Literature of Ancient Egypt* (New Haven, Conn.: Yale University Press, 1973), 201–209; and cf. Ronald J. Williams's interpretive article "Reflections on the *Lebensmuede,*" *Journal of Egyptian Archaeology* 48 (1962):49–56.

5. Lichtheim, *Ancient Egyptian Literature* I, 63 (from the "Instruction of Ptahhotep"); cf. J. Zandee, *Death as an Enemy,* Studies in the History of Religion, Supplements to *Numen* 5 (Leiden: E. J. Brill, 1960), 10–13, 56–66.

6. Zandee, *Death as an Enemy,* 45–52.

7. Ibid., 85–91.

8. Ibid., 81–85.

9. Ibid., 73–81, 109–92.

10. Even the gods, to the extent that they were part of the created order of the universe, were not exempt from death; see Siegfried Morenz, *Egyptian Religion,* trans. Ann E. Keep (Ithaca, N.Y.: Cornell University Press, 1960), 24–25, 186.

11. See Barbara Bell, "The Dark Ages in Ancient History. I. The First Dark Age in Egypt," *American Journal of Archaeology* 75 (1971):1–26.

12. Although a sense that the body's death inflicts a complementary danger on the soul is commonplace in world religions, the Egyptians' tendency to view the world in

terms of dualities can only have sharpened their anxiety on this score; on this see, in general, Eberhard Otto, "Dualismus," in *Lexikon der Aegyptologie* I (Wiesbaden: Otto Harrassowitz, 1975), cols. 1147–1150; and cf. Erik Hornung, *Conceptions of God in Ancient Egypt: The One and the Many,* trans. John Baines (Ithaca, N.Y.: Cornell University Press, 1982), 240–41.

13. Cf. R. O. Faulkner, *The Ancient Egyptian Pyramid Texts* I (Oxford: Clarendon Press, 1969), 40 (Utterance 213); the translation used in the text is mine.

14. Faulkner, *Pyramid Texts,* 123; Lichtheim, *Ancient Egyptian Literature* I, 41 (Utterance 373).

15. See, in general, Spencer, *Death in Ancient Egypt,* 29–44, 112–38; and Barbara Adams, *Egyptian Mummies,* Shire Egyptology I (Aylesbury, Bucks: Shire Publications, 1984).

16. Alfred Lucas, *Ancient Egyptian Materials and Industries,* 4th ed., rev. J. R. Harris (London: Edward Arnold, 1962), 281–303, 493.

17. Spencer, *Death in Ancient Egypt,* 164–94.

18. In general, see ibid., 45–73, 214–42.

19. An apparent exception was the royal tomb, which seems to have possessed a separate cult enclosure elsewhere in the necropolis; see Barry J. Kemp, "Abydos and the Royal Tombs of the First Dynasty," *Journal of Egyptian Archaeology* 52 (1966): 13–22; idem, "The Egyptian 1st Dynasty Royal Cemetery," *Antiquity* 41 (1967):22–32.

20. This applies to the tombs of the more affluent classes. The decorative program in royal tombs is more limited and deals almost exclusively with the hereafter, since the king was regarded as a divine being; on this see briefly Barry J. Kemp, in Bruce Trigger et al., eds., *Ancient Egypt: A Social History* (Cambridge: Cambridge University Press, 1983), 71–76.

21. The great personalities "lived on" as heroes of fiction even when their monuments had disappeared, and authors "made heirs for themselves of the writings and the books of instructions which they made" (Spencer, *Death in Ancient Egypt,* 70–72).

22. See Edward Brovarski, "Sokar," in *Lexikon der Aegyptologie* V, cols. 1056–1066; G. A. Gaballa and K. A. Kitchen, "The Festival of Sokar," *Orientalia* 38 (1969): 1–76.

23. Morenz, *Egyptian Religion,* 94.

24. On security measures in the tombs, see Spencer, *Death in Ancient Egypt,* 74–111.

25. Eberhard Otto, *Die Biographischen Inschriften der aegyptischen Spaetzeit, Probleme der Aegyptologie 2* (Leiden: E. J. Brill, 1954), 190.

26. A. H. Gardiner and Kurt Sethe, *Egyptian Letters to the Dead* (London: Egypt Exploration Society, 1928).

27. "Setne Khamwas and Naneferkaptah," in Lichtheim, *Ancient Egyptian Literature* III (Berkeley: University of California Press, 1980), 127–38.

28. "A Ghost Story," in Simpson, *The Literature of Ancient Egypt,* 137–41.

29. No comprehensive monograph on the *Ka* exists in English. See the remarks of Spencer, *Death in Ancient Egypt,* 58–61; cf. the well-documented article by Peter Kaplony, "Ka," in *Lexikon der Aegyptologie* III, cols. 275–82.

30. See Louis V. Zabkar, *A Study of the Ba Concept in Ancient Egyptian Texts,* Studies in Ancient Oriental Civilization 34 (Chicago: University of Chicago Press, 1968); and idem, "Ba," in *Lexikon der Aegyptologie* I, cols. 588–90.

31. Gertie Englund, *Akh—Une notion religieuse dans l'Egypte pharaonique,* Boreas: Uppsala Studies in Ancient Mediterranean and Near Eastern Civilizations 11 (Uppsala: University of Uppsala, 1978); cf. Florence Friedman, "The Root Meaning of 3b, Effectiveness or Luminosity," *Serapis* 8 (1985):39–46.

32. Labib Habachi, "Identification of Heqaib and Sabni with Owners of Tombs in Qubbet el-Hawa and Their Relationship with Nubia," in *Sixteen Studies on Lower Nubia,* Supplement aux Annales du Service des Antiquites de l'Egypte 23 (Cairo: Institut Francais d'Archeologie Orientale, 1981), 20–21.

33. Lichtheim, *Ancient Egyptian Literature* I, 37 (Utterances 273–74).

34. Ibid., 39 (Utterance 309).

35. R. O. Faulkner, *The Ancient Egyptian Coffin Texts* (Warminster: Aris & Phillips, 1973–78).

36. R. O. Faulkner, trans., *The Ancient Egyptian Book of the Dead,* ed. Carol Andrews (London: British Museum Publications, 1985).

37. For one such work that is found in private burials of the Middle Kingdom, see Leonard H. Lesko, *The Ancient Egyptian Book of the Two Ways* (Berkeley: University of California Press, 1972); see Spencer, *Death in Ancient Egypt,* 147–54, for the "guidebooks" in the New Kingdom royal tombs at Thebes.

38. Edward F. Wente, "Funerary Beliefs of the Ancient Egyptians: An Interpretation of the Burials and Texts," *Expedition* 24, no. 4 (Winter 1982):22–25.

39. Faulkner, *Book of the Dead,* 27–34, 55–56 (Spells 30, 125).

40. Spencer, *Death in Ancient Egypt,* 67–68, 216–17.

41. Ibid., 68–69.

42. Ibid., 109–12.

43. For what follows see Wente, "Funerary Beliefs," 17–28.

44. Coffin Texts Spell 1130 (cf. Faulkner, *Coffin Texts* III, 168; Lichtheim, *Ancient Egyptian Literature* I, 132).

45. Coffin Texts Spell 335 (cf. Faulkner, *Coffin Texts* I, 262).

46. Spencer, *Death in Ancient Egypt,* 106–108.

47. Morenz, *Egyptian Religion,* 195–96.

48. Lichtheim, *Ancient Egyptian Literature* I, 196.

49. Ibid., II, 115–16.

4

Death and Afterlife in Greek Tragedy and Plato

Helen F. North

INTRODUCTION

The Greeks had a variety of ideas about the fate of the soul after death, and we have no reason to believe that there was any universally accepted set of beliefs. What we learn from literature and archaeology suggests that the following beliefs were familiar to most of the Greeks of the classical period and thus could be drawn on by the tragic poets and the philosophers.

1. Something of the human personality survives the death of the body. This often is called the *psyche* (roughly "soul," but not really equivalent to our word at any period; sometimes "shade" is a less confusing translation). In Homer, the psyche seems to be the "breath-soul" or the "life-source" that leaves the body at the moment of death. Another term is the post-Homeric *daimon* ("spirit"), associated with Pythagoreanism.[1]
2. Whatever survives, whether the body has been cremated or buried, continues its existence in a location often thought of as within the tomb, or beneath the earth, but sometimes far away at the ends of the known world, usually the far West.
3. This existence for most shades is a dim, pallid reflection of their life on earth. The shades are themselves shadowy, without flesh, blood, or sinews, yet retaining a recognizable semblance of their earthly appearance.
4. The realm of the dead is ruled by a brother of Zeus called Hades (sometimes Pluto) and his wife, Persephone. This realm is known as the House of Hades, but ultimately itself comes to be called Hades, though not in the classical period. Separate from the House of Hades are the Isles of the Blessed, where certain heroes go and lead a pleasant existence under the rule of Kronos, father of Zeus, or Rhadamanthys, one of his sons. The only judge mentioned in *Odyssey* XI,

Homer's most detailed picture of the afterlife, is Minos, another son of Zeus. He does not determine anyone's fate, but merely settles disputes among the dead. Later we hear of judges who punish misdeeds; "another Zeus,"[2] a "great Hades, chastiser of mankind,"[3] Minos himself (in Plato).

5. Funeral rites are necessary if the person is to enter the land of the dead, and these rites, even if only in brief, symbolic form, must be offered. Otherwise, the gods are offended and punish those responsible.

6. If the shade lingers in the tomb, the living can communicate with it there. They may propitiate it with offerings (food, drink, a lock of hair), and gain its assistance or prevent it from doing them harm.

No one source contains all these elements, but most are found in the earliest epic poetry, that of Homer and Hesiod.[4]

To summarize one poetic account known to virtually all Greeks and presupposed by tragedy and Plato, Odysseus, in Book XI of Homer's *Odyssey,* visits the realm of the dead while still alive to consult the famous seer Teiresias, from whom he hopes to find out how he may return to his home in Ithaca after the Trojan War. To do so, he sails from the island of Circe to the far west, goes ashore, and digs a trench over which he sacrifices sheep and into which he pours libations of honey mixed with milk, water, and wine. He allows the shades that gather around him to drink the blood of the sacrificed animals, thus enabling them to speak with him. Without drinking the blood they can only squeak like bats. Although Odysseus is not at first underground or actually within the House of Hades, later in the book we are told what it is like in there—a meadow of asphodel, where Odysseus meets the shades of the heroes Agamemnon, Achilles, and Ajax. Still later he sees a place where the shades of notorious sinners undergo punishment, while the shades of other heroes continue the activities—such as hunting—that they had pursued in life. The shade of Achilles tells Odysseus that he would rather be the serf of a poor tenant farmer on earth than king among the dead. But elsewhere in the *Odyssey* other references to the condition of the dead include a description of the Elysian fields, to which Menelaus is to go because he is the husband of Helen, thus the son-in-law of Zeus (not because he is particularly virtuous or heroic).

These, and other passages in the *Iliad* and *Odyssey* referring to the moment of death and the fate of the dead, provided the Greeks with a common picture on which poets could elaborate if they wished to do so, adding details, even major changes, that might come from cult practices, local rituals at the tomb, the mystery religions, and other sources with which we are imperfectly acquainted. Our task is to see how death and the afterlife are depicted in tragedy and Plato, always with the realization that each writer chose from available material what would best suit his needs. A word of caution: Each treats the material with great freedom. There was no dogma to which he was obliged to conform, and because beliefs varied so widely (although actual rites seem to have been quite uniform), each writer could select what would enhance his poetic or philosophical purpose.

TRAGEDY

What, then, does tragedy make of traditional beliefs about death and the afterlife? I have chosen a few instances that illustrate not only different aspects of Greek belief, but also methods of treatment that I consider typical of the individual poet in each case.

Let us begin with Aeschylus. It need hardly be emphasized that, given the nature of Greek tragedy, which Aristotle in the fourth century analyzed as involving *pathos,* suffering, and preferably the transition of the principal character from good to bad fortune, and given the basic fact that most known examples of Greek tragedy are taken from the great cycles of mythology in which heroes and heroines face mortal danger and death, the tragic poet often focuses on plots that involve death and its aftermath. Aeschylus is particularly fond of spectacular visual effects. Of his seven surviving plays, two bring on stage ghosts of the dead, and a third emphasizes the lurking presence of the dead hero in his tomb; three lead up to the death of one or more characters offstage. I shall discuss two of these plays, the *Persians,* the earliest extant example of Greek tragedy (produced in 473/2 B.C.), and the *Libation-Bearers,* the second play in the only surviving complete trilogy, the *Oresteia,* produced in 458 B.C.

The *Persians,* the only surviving tragedy based on historical, rather than mythical, material, uses the disastrous defeat of the Persian fleet in the Battle of Salamis in 480 B.C. as an occasion to demonstrate in dramatic fashion the danger of pride, what the Greeks called *hubris,* in this case the hubris of the Persians, who violated many of the moral and geographical boundaries imposed by the gods in their attack on the Greek cities. Instead of presenting the failure of the Persian campaign from the point of view of the triumphant Greeks, the poet invites us to share the reactions of the defeated Persians. The drama takes place in the Persian capital, Susa, and the characters are exclusively Persian: the queen mother, Atossa; the messenger who brings the news of Salamis; Xerxes himself; the defeated king, represented as weak and hubristic; and the ghost of his father, the wise Darius. The tomb of the late king is visible in the orchestra, and when the queen hears of the destruction of her son's army, she offers propitiatory libations there: milk, honey, lustral water, wine, olive oil. She bids the Chorus of elderly Persian nobles call up the *daimon* of Darius, his shade; they duly pray to Earth, Hermes, and the King of the Dead to send forth to the light the psyche of Darius, in case he knows of a remedy for the Persians' troubles. At once Darius appears, responding to a ritual intended to make possible necromancy, the consultation of the dead.[5]

The theater of Dionysus in Athens does not have what several later Greek theaters did, a tunnel leading from behind the stage building to a trapdoor at the center of the orchestra, enabling an actor to rise from beneath the earth. This device is known as Charon's Steps, and its prevalence in Greek theaters suggests how frequent scenes of necromancy must have been. In Athens there must have been some kind of structure that could be identified as the tomb, and from this Darius emerges. He does not know why he has been summoned; Atossa must inform him of the disaster that has destroyed the power of Persia. When the Chorus repeats its plea for counsel, the old king utters a solemn warning against attacking the land of the Hellenes, and prophesies a second defeat (at Plataea), where the penalty for hubris will be exacted. The *daimon* is familiar with oracles that foretell the defeat of Xerxes; he also knows that Xerxes has rent his garments and will need clothing when he returns, a bit of information probably included for dramatic reasons, since Xerxes does indeed appear in just this condition. With a sententious reminder that Zeus punishes the proud and that the living should, even in the midst of trouble, take pleasure in the joys of life, the ghost descends once more into the tomb.

What does Aeschylus accomplish with this spectacular scene? Several things, among them the following: He electrifies his audience with an eerie, supernatural event; he focuses attention on the message put into the mouth of Darius, which would have been less effective delivered by a mortal; he underlines the hubris of Xerxes by contrasting it with the moderation and wisdom of his father (however unhistorical this characterization may be); and he finds a way to incorporate into the play a number of sage pronouncements, the gnomic wisdom so rife in Aeschylean tragedy, and to endow them with renewed authority because of the awe and reverence accorded the ghostly visitor. (Shakespeare's use of Hamlet's father's ghost is analogous.)

A very different, but equally impressive effect is secured by the other great tomb scene in Aeschylean tragedy. This scene occupies the entire first half of the *Libation-Bearers,* the second play of the trilogy about the killing of Agamemnon by his faithless wife, Clytemnestra, and of Clytemnestra in turn by their son Orestes, and the ultimate release of Orestes from the curse on his dynasty, through the intervention of the first jury-court in Athenian history, the Areopagus. Orestes, returning from exile, visits the tomb of his father to make the traditional offering of a lock of his hair. Electra, his elder sister, who saved his life when he was a baby by sending him away from his murderous mother, visits the tomb and finds the lock with other signs that her brother has returned. They recognize each other and plot the murder of their mother, which they accomplish in the second half of the play, set, not at the tomb, but at the palace. The scene at the tomb is the necessary spiritual forerunner of what takes place physically at the palace. Only after invoking the spirit of their dead father can his children nerve themselves to commit the horrible, but necessary crime of killing their mother. Unlike Darius, Agamemnon does not rise from the tomb or become visible either to his children or to the audience, but his spirit somehow enters into them. That is why Aeschylus sets the scene at the tomb.

Only there can Orestes and Electra make direct contact with the hero, who still inhabits the place where he is buried.

The Chorus of captive women who accompany Electra to the tomb speak of how under the earth dead men hold a grudge against their slayers. They have been sent by Clytemnestra to offer libations at the tomb because she has had an ominous dream, in which she gave birth to a serpent that bit her breast as she tried to nurse it. The libations are meant to pacify Agamemnon. Orestes, in the first word of the play, invokes Hermes, lord of the dead, to become his savior and ally. Electra, too, invokes Hermes *chthonius,* and bids him carry her prayers to the daimons below ground and to Earth. In the great choral song *(kommos)* shared by Orestes, Electra, and the Chorus, the children pray to their father, the Chorus maintains that the murdered man shows his wrath in the afterlife, and finally the children seek some way to bring their father to them.[6] They call on all the powers of the world below, including the Furies, whose function it is to avenge deeds of blood within the family. At the climax of the scene[7] Orestes asks his father to emerge, and at that moment, although we see no ghost, we feel the spirit of the dead man entering into his children. What happens thereafter is the visible working out of what has already happened in spirit at the tomb.

The third play of the trilogy, the *Eumenides,* contains a brief, but extraordinarily thrilling scene in which the ghost of Clytemnestra appears and arouses the sleeping Furies—her Furies now, not those of Agamemnon. By falling asleep in the temple of Apollo at Delphi they have allowed Orestes to escape. Clytemnestra reproaches them for neglecting their duty and reminds them of the sacrifices she has offered them in the past. From her speech we learn that among the dead she is shunned because of the murders she has committed (Agamemnon and his paramour, Cassandra), despite the fact that she in turn has suffered death at the hands of her own son. She bids the Furies behold her wounds, implying that the ghost still bears the marks that the body bore. All this, including the visibility of the ghost to the audience, must be accepted as part of the dramatic apparatus of the play. What is useful to the poet is, once again, the belief that something of the personality survives the death of the body, is indignant over what it suffered in life, and tries to take vengeance on its enemies. This ghost, by the way, unlike that of Agamemnon (or Darius), is not confined to the region of its tomb, but has been able to follow Orestes and the Furies from Argos to Delphi.

Neither Sophocles nor Euripides (at least in the extant tragedies) makes such spectacular use of ghosts and apparitions, but each of them refers to beliefs about the afterlife in ways important for plot and characterization. Sophocles, in his two earliest surviving plays, the *Ajax* and *Antigone* (produced in the late forties of the fifth century B.C.), uses popular belief about the obligation of the living to bury the dead for precisely these two purposes, to establish his plot and to define his characters. As nearly everyone knows, the fatal clash between

Antigone, daughter of Oedipus, and her uncle, the tyrant Creon, is caused by his arbitrary decree forbidding the burial of her brother Polyneices because he has led a group of attackers (the famous Seven against Thebes) in an attempt to wrest the kingship from his brother Eteocles. The two brothers have killed each other in single combat. Their uncle Creon becomes king and forbids the burial of the traitor Polyneices. Antigone determines to provide burial rites for him because the unwritten laws of the gods demand it. In fact, she performs these rites twice, scattering earth on the corpse and, when the earth has been brushed away, doing so a second time (this is the time she is caught and arrested). She also pours a triple libation to the dead.[8] By these symbolic actions she consecrates the corpse to the gods below.[9] Her stubborn repetition of the rites (which performed once would have been valid, no matter what happened later) is a strong indication of her character, as is her courageous defiance of Creon.

But most interesting for our current concern (and definitive for the characterization of Antigone) are the reasons she gives for defying the tyrant's decree. She never says that the dead, if unburied, will be unable to enter Hades, a notion familiar to the Greeks at least since Homer, in whose *Iliad* the shade of Patroclus asked Achilles to bury him for this very reason.[10] At different times Antigone justifies her decision by saying that she will be among the dead for ever,[11] that the unwritten laws required it[12] and to disobey them would be to risk paying a penalty to the gods,[13] that she will win glory for her deed,[14] that Hades requires the rites,[15] that she hopes to be welcomed by her parents and her brother when she arrives in the realm of the dead,[16] and (a surprising admission) that she would not have performed the rites for a dead husband or child, either of whom could theoretically have been replaced, but only for a brother, since her parents were dead and she could have no more brothers.[17]

This admission, made just before Antigone is led away to the tomb in which she is to be walled up alive, has puzzled critics, some of whom in the past have gone so far as to excise the speech as inconsistent with Antigone's noble character, but today it is accepted as authentic, and is seen as a crucial indicator of her nature, not unyielding and impervious to normal feeling, but far more interesting and more tragic. By having Antigone's sister, Ismene, who has the same responsibility to her dead brother, shrink from joining in the burial, out of fear of Creon based on a realistic assessment of the weakness of women in the Greek world, Sophocles—who often makes use of the foil character—enables us to see the heroic strength and stubbornness of Antigone's nature. Likewise, he demonstrates the narrowness and inflexibility of Creon's nature by his refusal of the customary rites to Polyneices, and his fatal pride by his elevation of his own arbitrary decree over reverence for the will of the gods. When the unburied corpse pollutes the land and causes sacrifices to the gods to become corrupted, Creon at last yields, but too late to prevent the downfall of his dynasty.

So, too, in the slightly earlier play, *Ajax,* Sophocles focuses attention in the second half of the tragedy on the burial of the hero, who committed suicide after a failed attempt to kill the leaders of the Greek expedition against Troy. His brother Teucer is determined to bury him, the offended generals, Menelaus and Agamemnon, are determined to prevent the burial, and the outcome is decided by Odysseus, whom Ajax had tried to torture and kill, but who is sufficiently magnanimous to recognize the humanity he shares with Ajax, and therefore refuses to carry enmity beyond the grave. How important the issue is we realize when we observe that in both of these plays, Sophocles uses as the very hinge of his plot and the definitive indicator of character the requirement that the dead receive proper burial, even in the case of enemies of the state or personal enemies. It is as if the poet had looked for a simple, universally understood, and deeply felt religious norm that would illuminate the difference between the will of man and the will of the gods. In the *Ajax,* as in the *Antigone,* the anger of the gods at the violation of their laws is the penalty to be feared, not the vengeance of the dead man himself.

If we had more time, it would be interesting to explore Sophocles's dramatic exploitation of Greek beliefs about the nature of the hero (in the technical sense of the word)—the extraordinary person who is destined to acquire divine status in death. He shows us such a figure in the *Women of Trachis,* which culminates in the death of Herakles on the funeral pyre that burns away all that is mortal and releases the essential hero to become immortal and dwell with the gods on Olympus. He shows us another hero, a very different one, in the aged Oedipus, who comes at the end of his long life to the suburb of Colonus, outside Athens, and there, in a grove sacred to the Furies, disappears from human view, destined to become a demigod protecting the city in which his mortal remains are buried. As early as the late eighth century B.C. the Greeks began to venerate the tombs of heroes, even trying to restore their remains to their native city. Thus the bones of Orestes were brought from Tegea to Sparta, and those of Theseus from Skyros to Athens.

But rather than follow this line of inquiry, let us look at one play of Euripides that gives us unusual insight into the preparation for death and the situation of the dead in the tomb. The *Alcestis,* the earliest surviving play by Euripides, may be dated 438 B.C. (in the next decade after the two earliest plays of Sophocles, hence reflecting the same stage of Greek beliefs). The story is rooted in folktale: Admetus, king of Pherae in Thessaly, is privileged to escape death on the day fated for him to die, if he can persuade someone else to take his place. His wife, Alcestis, has consented, after his parents have refused, and as the play opens Death *(Thanatos)* comes, with drawn sword, to cut a lock of hair from her head, an action that will dedicate her to the gods below.[18] In the prologue Death talks with Apollo, the god who has won for Admetus his extraordinary privilege. Apollo prophesies that someone is on his way to save Alcestis from *Thanatos.* Then the Chorus of citizens is told by a maid, coming out of the house, how Alcestis has prepared herself for death.

When she understood the fatal day was come, she bathed her white body with water drawn from running streams, then opened the cedar chest and took her clothes out, and dressed in all her finery and stood before the Spirit of the Hearth [Hestia], and prayed: "Mistress, since I am going down beneath the ground, I kneel before you in this last of all my prayers." [She prays for her children, that they may marry and lead a happy life, without untimely death such as hers.] Afterward she approached the altars . . . made her prayers, and decked them all with fresh sprays torn from living myrtle.[19]

Next, Alcestis is carried out of the house, accompanied by her husband and children. It is necessary to bring her out because the structure of the Greek theater made interior scenes difficult, but Euripides typically converts this constraint to an advantage. He has Alcestis invoke the light of the sun, on which she is looking for the last time. She then describes a vision of Charon, the ferryman of the dead, at the oars of his boat, calling impatiently for her to hurry. She sees *Thanatos* also (invisible now to the audience) and describes him as a winged figure, frowning from under dark brows. Admetus begs her to wait for him in the grave and promises to be buried in the same coffin. When at last she dies, he proclaims public mourning throughout Thessaly. The citizens are to shave their heads and wear black robes; their horses shall have their manes cut, and there shall be no sound of music in the city for a full year.

If we compare the events and rituals of Alcestis's last day with those of other figures, such as Ajax, or Socrates in the *Phaedo,* we find certain common elements: a ritual bath, the committal of one's children to the care of others, a prayer, and a formal farewell to family and friends. These elements must have been familiar to everyone in the theater. But what happens next in the *Alcestis* is unique: Herakles, out of gratitude for the hospitality shown him by Admetus, goes to the tomb and wrestles with Death. As he later tells Admetus, "Beside the tomb itself, I sprang and caught him in my hands." Victorious over Death, he brings back Alcestis to her husband's house. She must remain silent for three days, until she has been, in effect, deconsecrated,[20] released from her obligations to the gods below. This is one of the few occasions in Greek mythology when a dead person is successfully retrieved from the power of Hades. Early in the play Admetus wishes for the melodious lips of Orpheus to charm Persephone into releasing his wife, but Orpheus himself did not succeed in bringing his own wife, Eurydice, all the way back from Hades. In dramatizing this myth Euripides has used a formula (loss, escape, reunion) that he takes up again in some of his later plays, such as *Iphigeneia in Tauris* and the *Helen,* achieving an effect that is not tragic, but tragicomic. In the *Alcestis* the fact that the initial loss is to death makes the escape and reunion the most surprising and joyful reversal imaginable.

We have here a vivid example of what the poetic imagination can do with the raw material of popular religion. It was believed that in dying, the soul struggled to get loose from the body. (There was a special word—*ψυχορραγεῖν*

—to describe this struggle.) Euripides has dramatized and externalized it by giving Alcestis the helper foretold by Apollo in the Prologue. Herakles takes over the soul-struggle from the dead woman and makes the impossible wish that we all know so well come true. Wish fulfillment is characteristic of folk-tale, not tragedy.

PLATO

Turning to the second part of our topic—death and the afterlife in Plato—it may be helpful to review some of the beliefs that the philosopher makes use of in his discussions of death and especially his eschatological myths (eschatology is the study of precisely what we are examining, the "last things," death and what comes after, the realm of the dead, and—something new to our discussion—the transmigration of souls, return to life, not, as in the case of Alcestis, the same life, in the same body, but another life, in a new body). First, a brief look at some of Plato's predecessors in philosophy, who, although familiar with the traditional popular beliefs we have already noticed, add to the sum of our knowledge about Greek speculation, particularly with regard to the nature of the soul and its destiny.

The pre-Socratic philosophers of the sixth and fifth centuries B.C. were essentially physicists, and so far as we can tell from the few fragments of their teachings that survive, they tended to regard the soul as material, consisting of whatever primeval element—such as air or fire—they thought to be the basis of all that exists. But certain philosophers, especially those in the western part of the Greek world, southern Italy and Sicily, are identified with an additional belief, that of reincarnation (metempsychosis, transmigration of souls), according to which an individual soul might live through a number of lives (sometimes retaining a memory of earlier ones) and only after a long period escape from repeated incarnation, returning at last to its original, presumably happy condition. Belief in reincarnation, as a philosophical and religious principle, is associated with the name of Pythagoras of Samos, who went to Croton in southern Italy around the middle of the sixth century B.C. and there established communities in which a philosophical society organized and ran the government. By the end of that century, belief in transmigration entered popular thought. Another Western philosopher, Empedocles of Akragas in Sicily, in the middle of the fifth century B.C., evidently adopted this belief and claimed to have led several lives. A famous Fragment says, "I have been a boy and a girl, a bush and a bird and a dumb sea-fish"—a sign that reincarnation need not be into a human body. Other Fragments of his poem, entitled *Purifications,* suggest that the soul (which he calls a *daimon*) falls from its original state of bliss to involvement in the body because of something like original sin, which seems to be identified with meat-eating. Purification of some kind is necessary before the soul can escape from incarnation.

Similar beliefs seem to have been accepted in the fifth century by people who called themselves Orphics, after Orpheus, the famous musician, noted for his sexual purity as well as for having descended to Hades and returned in safety while still alive. How early an actual cult of Orphism existed, before the Hellenistic period, it is hard to determine, but already in the fifth century (in the *Hippolytus* of Euripides, for example) there are allusions to Orphic abstention from meat. A papyrus discovered in 1960, in a fourth-century B.C. Macedonian tomb near modern Derveni, contains a philosophical commentary on a poem ascribed to Orpheus, and gold leaf plates found in tombs in southern Italy (of the Hellenistic period and later) seem to refer to Orphic teachings about the destiny of the soul.[21] The essential teachings of these mystery cults seem to have included the divine origin of the soul, its need to be released from the prison of the body (either by a diet free from meat or by rituals of purification), and its return to its original divine state after many lives that might last for thousands of years. Implicit and often explicit in accounts of such beliefs is the judgment of the soul after death and the imposition of retributive punishment or reward.

I mention this background because Plato makes such frequent reference to metempsychosis, purification, punishment and reward, usually in the context of myth. Several dialogues conclude with a mythical description of the soul's experience after death; we will shortly look at some features of these myths and try to determine their effect on the dialogue as a whole. Before doing so, I should like to emphasize two points:

1. Plato makes use of traditional material familiar to his readers; its presence in the dialogues does not guarantee that either Plato himself or his readers took it literally. What we see in the dialogues is a reflection of certain beliefs about death and the afterlife, coming to us through the mind of the most complex and elusive of the Greek philosophers. It is what Plato does with the beliefs of popular religion and esoteric mystery cults that is significant; the myths are as much a part of his philosophy as is his dialectic.
2. The Platonic Socrates effects a tremendous change in the developing concept of the psyche—the soul. What was the breath-soul that leaves the body at the moment of death, in Homer, what was the vehicle of passion, emotion, fear, anxiety, hope, or desire in tragedy (especially that of Sophocles and Euripides), now becomes the center of intellectual and moral activity. The "care of the soul" is, for Socrates, the most important activity human beings can engage in. This new understanding of the soul has a profound effect on the concept of death and the afterlife in Plato's dialogues.

It is appropriate to begin with a look at the *Apology,* Plato's version of Socrates's defense when he was tried in 399 B.C. for corrupting the youth of Athens, denying the existence of the traditional gods, and substituting new gods for old. (Let me remind you that this *Apology* is the work of Plato and need not bear any resemblance to what the historical Socrates may have said.

There is in fact a strong tradition that he said nothing.) In Plato's *Apology* Socrates affirms the priority of the care of the soul, urging his fellow Athenians to consider all other aims—wealth, reputation, honor, and the like—less important than the *epimeleia psyches,* the care of the soul, so as to make it as good as possible.[22] On this belief hinges the entire defense, indeed the entire life of the Platonic Socrates.

In the *Apology* we also find an expression of Socrates's complete agnosticism about the destiny of the soul after death. In his first speech to the jury, before he has been condemned, he says that no one knows whether death may not be even the greatest of blessings to man. To fear it, as if it were the greatest of evils, is a most disgraceful form of ignorance.[23] And in the last of the three speeches of which the *Apology* is composed, the address to the jury after sentence of death has been pronounced, he speculates at greater length about what lies immediately before him. Because his *daimonion,* the mysterious voice that prevents him from doing something that he should not do, has not prevented him from leaving home to come to court, or from saying anything he was about to say, he is convinced that the outcome for him will be good. He then goes on to say that death is one of two things, either nothingness or some kind of change of location for the soul from this place to another.

If it is like a sleep without a dream, death would be a wonderful gain. If it is a change of location and it is true that all the dead are there, what greater good could there be? Socrates imagines himself in the presence of real judges (Minos, Rhadamanthys, Aeacus, and Triptolemus) and such figures as Orpheus, Musaeus, Hesiod, and Homer. He would die many times over if this were true because he would find it wonderful to meet Palamedes or Ajax or any other men of old who had died because of an unjust judgment. The greatest pleasure would be to spend time examining and refuting some of the dead, to find out who is wise and who merely thinks he is. Agamemnon, Odysseus, and Sisyphus are mentioned. Here Socrates is following in the footsteps of Homer, who, in the *Odyssey,* Book XI, represented some of the dead heroes as doing in Hades what they had done on earth. He adds that to associate with the dead and examine them would be a source of incomparable happiness; moreover, there would be no danger of being put to death for doing so, since according to tradition, the dead are not only happier in other respects than the living, but also are immortal for the rest of time.[24]

We should note that in this dramatic situation, Plato makes no mention of reincarnation, nor does he let Socrates contemplate a third option where death is concerned. That is, he does not consider that there might be punishment after death, only the two alternatives of nothingness or transfer to a place of greater happiness where the dead could continue doing what they had chosen to do on earth. A study of fourth-century Attic epitaphs has shown that almost never do tombstones refer to an afterlife, and never to the fear of punishment. When Cephalus, the old man in Book I of the *Republic,* speaks of his concern, as death approaches, that there may be truth in the stories told of punishment in Hades for those who have done wrong in life, he raises a question that has left few other traces in the literature or inscriptions of the period.[25] Yet in each of the three dialogues that contain a mythical account of the afterlife—the *Gorgias, Phaedo,* and *Republic*—Plato includes the concept of punishment for wrongdoers, and in two of them he includes the concept of reincarnation, as he also does in the *Phaedrus,* in which the myth in the second speech of Socrates, although it focuses on the experiences of the soul before birth, takes for granted the prospect of repeated incarnations in which the soul is tested and either does or does not escape from the prison of the body.

The variation in detail in these four myths proves, if proof were needed, that Plato does not hold a dogmatic view of the afterlife, and the differing emphases in the four myths show why he uses the theme. In each case the description of death and the afterlife is integrated into the particular dialogue in which it occurs. Just as the tragic poets choose what will serve their poetic purposes, so Plato chooses what will serve his philosophic purpose. Each myth is as much a part of his philosophy as the dialectic that (usually) precedes it, and each, when analyzed, proves to be a rhetorical or even poetic method of reinforcing emotionally what is presented dialectically elsewhere in the dialogue. It is no accident that in three cases the myth comes at the end of the dialogue.

Without taking the time to report the details of each myth, let me summarize the eschatological myths in *Gorgias, Phaedo,* and *Republic,* to demonstrate Plato's selectivity and his focus on a different aspect of the afterlife appropriate to each dialogue.

In the *Gorgias,* at the close of a dialogue ostensibly about the nature and functions of rhetoric, but actually about the fundamental question of how one should live—whether in a constant search for power and the satisfaction of appetite, or in the effort to make one's soul as good as possible (a link with the *Apology*)—Socrates relates a myth, which he explicitly describes as true. In it the soul after death undergoes judgment and receives proper recompense for its deeds on earth. After three long conversations aiming to convince three interlocutors (and the reader) that a life of justice and moderation is to be chosen for its own sake, Socrates reinforces his argument with a powerful piece of persuasive rhetoric. He now defines death as the separation of soul from body; earlier in the dialogue he had suggested that the body is the prison of the soul. Now, freed from the body and its possibly deceptive appearance and adornment, the soul is judged in a meadow from which two roads lead off, one to the Isles of the Blessed, the other to Tartarus. Three sons of Zeus are the judges: Rhadamanthys for souls from Asia, Aeacus for those from Europe, and Minos for cases about which the others are in doubt. When the judges examine the souls, naked and indelibly marked by the actions performed in life, the wicked are sent to Tartarus, where, if they are curable, they endure therapeutic pains or, if incurable, they suffer exemplary punishment as a deterrent to others. The good are sent to the Isles of the Blessed. These are the philosophic souls—a significant reminder that the destiny of heroes in earlier myth is now reserved for philosophers.

The origins of most elements in this myth are easy to identify (Homer, Hesiod, tragedy, the mystery religions). Plato has used them as the framework within which he recalls arguments put forward in the dialectical portion of the work, most notably the comparison of virtue to health, wickedness to illness. As Jaeger said, "If the soul's purity from injustice is its health, and its infection with guilt is its deformity and sickness, then the judgment in the next world is a sort of medical examination of the soul. Naked, it appears before the judge (himself a naked soul); he examines every scar, every wound, every blemish left in it by the sickness of its own injustice during life."[26] Rather than taking literally the description of eternal punishment for the incurable sinners, we should see this as a way of expressing a profound truth, that a seriously deformed personality must live with the consequences of its wickedness as long as it continues to exist.[27]

Absent from the afterlife of the *Gorgias,* which in other respects recalls the beliefs of the mystery religions, as well as the more traditional ones of Homer and Hesiod, is any reference to reincarnation. This, however, is prominent in the *Phaedo* and the *Republic,* though with different emphases appropriate to two such different dialogues.

The *Phaedo,* whose dramatic setting is the prison in which Socrates will shortly drink the hemlock, is much concerned with the immortality of the soul. After a variety of proofs for immortality have been examined and criticized, Plato invites us to imagine the afterlife, where the souls of the dead gather at the Acherusian lake. There they are judged and sent to places of punishment or reward. The incurable sinners are sent to Tartarus, from which they will never emerge. Those who are curable will spend a year in Tartarus, but then, if they can win the pardon of those they have offended in life, they may emerge and be sent back to earth to enter on a new life. Souls that have led lives of holiness are freed from the underworld and sent back to earth, except for those that have been purified by philosophy: They alone are freed at once from the body, and they pass to dwellings so beautiful as to be impossible to describe.

Here the emphasis is on the immortality of the soul and the supreme value of philosophy. Details of the judgment are ignored, as are the punishments of the wicked. In the *Republic* the emphasis is on another element, the choice of the new life. Both the actual judgment and the circumstances and motives of the choice are set forth in great and original detail. This myth is the longest of Plato's eschatological ones; it serves as the conclusion to a long dialogue and shares the leisurely concentration on detail that we find in the first nine books.

You may remember the situation: A Pamphylian named Er, who was thought to have been killed in battle, recovered on the funeral pyre and told what he had seen "there"—*ekei,* a euphemism for the world beyond. Much that he saw is new to us, whether Plato's free invention, as seems most probable, or echoes of Orphic or Pythagorean doctrines otherwise unknown to us. I select a few details. The souls journey to a mysterious place where there are two openings into the earth and two into the sky. Judges sit between the openings and send the just upward, by the right-hand opening, and the unjust downward, to the left. By way of the other pair of openings other souls return, either full of dust and dirt from below or pure and clean from above. The returning souls camp in the meadow and tell one another of their experiences above or below, during the passage of a thousand years, each soul having suffered or been rewarded tenfold. The worst souls—for the most part those of tyrants—are not permitted to emerge like the rest, but are carried off, tortured, and hurled into Tartarus. The others, after seven days in the meadow, travel to a place where they behold a gigantic Spindle balanced on the knees of Necessity and supporting the planetary spheres. (I omit many vivid details, involving the presence of the Sirens, who provide the music of the spheres, and the Fates, who guarantee the choices to be made by the souls as they enter a new life.)

Plato directs our attention to the actual choice and the reasons for it in each case, reasons connected with the previous life and the experience just completed in the afterlife. Thus the souls that have recently come down from an interlude of bliss are less cautious than those who have emerged from a thousand years of suffering. Thus, too, Orpheus, who in his last existence was torn to pieces by women, chooses the life of a swan, rather than be born again of woman. Agamemnon chooses to become an eagle, Ajax a lion. Unwary souls choose to become tyrants—always the most evil destiny in Plato. Odysseus, tired of his labors in his previous life, renounces ambition and chooses the life of a private citizen. Each makes a completely free choice. There is no compulsion.

As with the *Gorgias* and *Phaedo,* it is manifest that Plato selects, invents, and weaves together with his incomparable power of imagination and equally incomparable rhetorical skill details that will support, complete, and reinforce the arguments set forth in the first nine books. No one can take any of it literally, but everyone can be moved and inspired by such myths. What remains constant is the insistence that the life of philosophy—the examined life that Socrates praised in the *Apology*—is the source of the greatest happiness. The Orphic or Pythagorean notion of release from the prison of the body through purification of some kind is reinterpreted so as to substitute intellectual activity for abstention from meat or initiation into the mysteries. It is the souls that have practiced philosophy that depart for the Isles of the Blessed in the *Gorgias,* the souls have been purified by philosophy that are freed from the need for reincarnation in the *Phaedo,* and the souls that philosophize that have the smoothest journey in the *Republic.*[28] Even before the myth of Er in the *Republic* Plato describes the death of the philosopher and his destiny thereafter with the phrase "to depart into the Isles of the Blessed and live there."[29] He makes the Isles of the Blessed a metaphor for the intellectual life, an image that survives in Aristotle's description of the supreme happiness of the life of contemplation,[30] and also in many other echoes down the years, including the Paradise of Dante.

Even in the myth of the *Phaedrus,* which, as I have said, is more concerned with what the soul experiences before birth, the best life on which the soul can enter when incarnated is that of the philosopher, and after death the souls that have the best chance of escaping from reincarnation (in the language of the *Phaedrus,* "regaining their wings") are those that have three times chosen the life of a philosopher.[31] I recommend to you the *Phaedrus* as a wonderful dialogue in which to study the integration of all the most important Platonic themes, including the nature of the soul and its destiny, but in every one of the dialogues equipped with an eschatological myth we find two things: the concept of the psyche that we first encounter in the *Apology,* as the center of intellectual and moral activity, whose care is the principal duty of every human being, and the conviction of personal responsibility for the actions chosen in life. It is to convince us of these fundamental truths that Plato makes inspired use of traditional Greek beliefs about death and the afterlife.

NOTES

This chapter was written in memory of Werner Jaeger on the centenary of his birth, 1888.

1. Consult David B. Claus, *Toward the Soul: An Inquiry into the Meaning of "Psyche" Before Plato* (New Haven, Conn.: Yale University Press, 1981).
2. Aeschylus, *The Suppliant Maiden,* 230–231.
3. "For the Lord of Death (Hades) is mighty in holding mortals to account beneath earth, and he surveyeth all things with his recording mind," Aeschylus, *Eumenides,* 269ff.
4. For a detailed discussion of the evidence, with attention to the stratification of beliefs, see Christiane Sourvinou-Inwood, "To Die and Enter the House of Hades: Homer, Before and After," in Joachim Whaley, *Mirrors of Mortality: Studies in the Social History of Death* (New York: St. Martin's, 1981).
5. See H. J. Rose, "Ghost Ritual in Aeschylus," *Harvard Theological Review* 42 (1950): 257–80.
6. For the relation of this antiphonal lament to actual practice, see Margaret Alexiou, *The Ritual Lament in Greek Tradition* (Cambridge: Cambridge University Press, 1974).
7. Aeschylus, *The Libation-Bearers,* 485ff.
8. Sophocles, *Antigone,* 431.
9. Ibid., 247.
10. Homer, *The Iliad.* Book 23:71f.
11. Sophocles, ibid., 76.
12. Ibid., 454.
13. Ibid., 459.
14. Ibid., 52.
15. Ibid., 519.
16. Ibid., 900.

17. Ibid., 905–12.

18. Euripides, *Alcestis,* 75f.

19. Ibid., 158–72, trans. Richmond Lattimore, *Euripides 1, The Complete Greek Tragedies* (Chicago: University of Chicago Press, 1955).

20. Ibid., 114ff.

21. See M. L. West, *The Orphic Poems* (Oxford: Oxford University Press, 1983).

22. Plato, *The Apology,* 36C.

23. Ibid., 29A–B.

24. Ibid., 41A–C.

25. This point is made by Jon D. Mikalson, *Athenian Popular Religion* (Chapel Hill: University of North Carolina Press, 1983), 80–81. For Attic epitaphs, see 74–79.

26. Werner Jaeger, *Paideia: The Ideals of Greek Culture,* 3 vols. (New York: Oxford University Press, 1944).

27. See R. E. Allen, *The Dialogues of Plato* (New Haven, Conn.: Yale University Press, 1984), 1:229.

28. Plato, *The Republic,* Book X, 619E.

29. Ibid., 540B.

30. *Nicomachean Ethics,* 10, 7; cf. Jaeger, *Paideia,* 2:418–19.

31. Plato, *Phaedrus,* 249A–B.

II

DEATH AND AFTERLIFE IN WESTERN RELIGIONS

5

From Witchcraft to Justice: Death and Afterlife in the Old Testament

George E. Mendenhall

INTRODUCTION

Though the title seems somewhat eccentric in dealing with such a serious topic, there is, nevertheless, a twofold purpose involved in its choice. It indicates, in the first place, that there was no simple uniformity in the concept of death and afterlife that was characteristic of the thousand years of history involved in the Old Testament traditions. More important is the fact that such concepts were and are inevitably involved with that social experience that we term "history," and thus are inseparably related to the nature of the society itself, the characteristics of its social relationships, and, above all, the nature of its operating system of values.

This chapter attempts to describe those changing features, though the sequel clearly lies almost outside the scope of the Old Testament itself. Only in the latest sources is there some indication of the kind of belief in life after death that became normative in both Judaism and Christianity. This development in turn was accompanied by the rise of apocalyptic literature that has its roots in the Old Testament as well. Though it is true that the specific content of those beliefs can hardly derive from direct experience, it is equally true that the changes in such beliefs attested in the historical record are inseparable from the historical experience of the community. It is part of the purpose of this chapter to trace the continuity of fundamental convictions through drastic changes in the system of communication by which they are given expression.

It generally is agreed that the Old Testament furnished the foundations for the constructions in later times of rabbinic Judaism and Christianity. It is not so clear in what ways the Old Testament constitutes the "interface," to use contemporary computerese, between the ancient Near Eastern polytheistic paganism, on the one hand, and postbiblical Judaism and Christianity, on the other. That interface is indicated in the title "the witchcraft associated with the cult of the dead derived from the ancient Near Eastern paganism," and is abundantly illustrated in Old Testament narrative, law, and prophets,[1] but the concern for justice was almost always a "voice crying in the wilderness."

As the title indicates, drastic changes in the concepts of death and afterlife took place in the course of the biblical history. As anthropologists have frequently pointed out, the customs and ideology associated with death and burial normally are remarkably resistant to change, and therefore, drastic changes in such beliefs and practices imply equally drastic causes. We are thus involved in the problem of the history of religion. In a topic such as this there are enormous difficulties in entering the minds of the ancients to discover what thinking lay behind the texts and the archaeological artifacts that constitute our evidence. They were not speculative philosophers to be sure, but on the other hand, they certainly were not a primitive culture (whatever that term may mean), and what happened in their experience and thought laid the foundations for the next couple millennia in world civilization outside the Far East.

To what extent can we know? Fortunately, human beings and human societies are finite, not infinite, and the range of possibilities is limited so that some reasonable understanding of ancient customs and ideologies is not impossible. In many cases we can say what was not true, but frequently enough all we can do is to argue for the relative probabilities of various interpretations of the literary and archaeological evidence. A significant part of the problem is the fact that even if it were possible to reach accurate conclusions concerning the ancient social consensus regarding death and afterlife, it is certain that those conclusions would be rejected by a considerable segment of both scholarly and unspecialized contemporary society. At any rate, the task is to do the best we can with the resources that are available.

THE CURRENT CONSENSUS

Most of the scholarly world agrees that there is no concept of immortality or life after death in the Old Testament.[2] The human body was shaped by God from the earth, and animated with the "breath of life" *nefeš hayyim* (Genesis 2:7–8). At death, the person becomes a *nefeš mēt,* literally, "a dead breath" (Numbers 6:6), and the body returns to the dust whence it came. In the very late source of Ecclesiastes 12:7, "the dust returns to the earth as it was, and the spirit [*rūh*] returns to God who gave it." At the same time, when people die, they descend to Sheol, which can only be defined as the place where the dead are dead. As the psalmist put it in a complaint to Yahweh, "In Sheol who will praise You?"[3] The presumption is that the deceased are inert, lifeless, and engaging in no activity.

Furthermore, the deceased is "gathered to his ancestors," a conventional phrase that doubtless derives from the fact that the body was placed in the family tomb, where the bones of the ancestors already lay. This complex of beliefs and customs is probably age-old, and has many similarities to the Mesopotamian picture of the underworld so well described by Jerrold Cooper earlier in this book. The biblical traditions preserved, however, contain almost nothing of the various descriptions of the state of the dead in that shadowy underworld so vividly portrayed in Mesopotamian sources. It is historically probable that in this case, as in so many others, it was the common Amorite heritage of both Babylonia and ancient Israel that accounts for these formal similarities between the two cultures, though the direct evidence is meager.

That such traditions about the state of the dead in the underworld did exist, at least in popular religion, is probable. This can reasonably be inferred from various passing references. For example, in Job 3:11, 13–15, 17–19 there is a vivid description of the democracy of death:

> Why did I not die at birth,
> come forth from the womb and expire? . . .
> For then I should have lain down and been quiet;
> I should have slept; then I should have been at rest,
> with kings and counselors of the earth
> who rebuilt ruins for themselves [a delightful irony],
> or with princes who had gold,
> who filled their houses with silver. . . .
> There the wicked cease from troubling,
> and there the weary are at rest.
> There the prisoners are at ease together;
> they hear not the voice of the taskmaster.
> The small and the great are there,
> and the slave is free from his master.

It clearly states what must have been the common doctrine that the dead are equal in the abode of the dead, including the stillborn, who also are the subject of specific attention in Mesopotamian sources. As many scholars have observed, we have only fragments of what was certainly a great variety of popular as well as official views of death and the afterlife that existed in the ancient Israelite culture. Yet the very language of the Bible indicates that there was not any concept of the human makeup that included an element that survived after death, nor was there personality or activity in the abode of the dead.

The current consensus that there was no belief in life after death in the Old Testament is actually a description of what was regarded in later times as the normative belief, and certainly did represent the mainstream of the early biblical tradition. What was handed down to later generations as sacred scripture was a selection from what was available, particularly in folk tradition, and therefore, it screened out almost everything that was incompatible with those beliefs and ideas that were characteristic of the period of transmission. Fortunately they did preserve the polemics against nonstandard beliefs and practices that we find especially in the prophetic literature, and also a number of narratives as well as laws that illustrate the attempt on the part of government at one time or another to prohibit what was regarded as incompatible with true Yahwism. It is certainly a complex picture that we now have, in contrast to the simplism of the standard works on biblical theology.

THE "INNER HISTORY"

Beliefs concerning the hereafter cannot be separated from the actual practices that were associated with those beliefs. The practices fall into two main categories: the customs associated with burial itself and those connected with the cult of the dead after interment. In a vast variety of forms and ideologies the cult of the dead has been much studied and recorded, and it is not necessary here to reiterate the details. Cooper has touched on this in his excellent description of the Mesopotamian evidence, and it is now probable that analogous customs and ideas did exist in ancient Israel. Studies have seemingly concentrated on the description of the formalities that were associated with the cult, but little attention that I have seen has been given to the question of the motivation and the social function of such rituals.

Anthropologists recently have emphasized that ritual is a powerful means in primitive societies for the perpetuation and reinforcement of the society and its value system, "whatever it may be," as one anthropologist put it. Most of our evidence has to do with ritual forms associated with the king and his court, or comes from literary works produced by ancient urban elites. Most of the people who wrote documents in ancient time were part of the political establishment, and there was no cultural reason for them to describe the quaint customs of nobodies. Central to the royal cult of the dead were the periodic feasts dedicated to the king's ancestors, so richly documented in the Mari archives. Probably such royal cults are, in all historical probability, mere elaborations on folk customs at a much humbler level, and had their origins in some remote prehistoric past.

If we take into account the fact that the early Israelites were village farmers and shepherds, much that otherwise seems incredible and inexplicable falls quite well into place. The biblical traditions themselves emphasize that the old Canaanite cities that were the political power structures in pre-Mosaic times remained polytheistic Baal-worshipers. With the possible exception of Hebron, of which we hear virtually nothing until the time of David, none of the old Canaanite cities had become Yahwist. What this means is that the biblical Yahwist community was composed of those population elements that had rejected and condemned the entire paraphernalia of ancient Near Eastern political regimes and for good reason: Their constant struggle for power had impoverished everyone and brought civilization to an end. This phenomenon was civilizationwide, though it did not take place at the same time everywhere. The power structures of the urban political establishments had become irrelevant, and everything associated with them, whether monumental art, palaces, temples, rituals, elitist scribal traditions and even language, and, above all, the worship of the ancestors, had become objects of scorn and vehement rejection.

The peculiar aspects of the normative Old Testament concepts of death and afterlife are inseparable from the circumstances that attended the sudden emergence of that religious confederation that was called Israel. The utter chaos that reigned over all the civilized world at the transition from the Late Bronze to the Early Iron ages certainly cannot be reduced to some simplistic explanation, though archaeologists seem, as a rule, to try to explain such phenomena as the result of natural catastrophes. There is not enough evidence or theoretical foundations to enable us to understand the vast cultural, religious, and linguistic changes that took place at that time. Yet it was precisely under these circumstances that the religious confederation of ancient Israel came into existence in the period between 1200 and 1150 B.C.

The cult of the royal ancestors had to be abolished, as were the royal regimes themselves. According to Joshua 12, thirty-one kings were done away with in the process of establishing the kingdom of Yahweh. Every one of those ephemeral royal regimes must have had, for a short time, the usual paraphernalia of cult symbols, ancestral cults (no doubt largely phony), and rituals. Though we do not have direct biblical or archaeological evidence for this conclusion, the compulsive conformity of ancient pagan political ideologies makes it virtually certain that they did exist.

It was against this complex of cult objects and political symbols that the second commandment was directed: "You shall make no graven image." What the cult of the ancestors really involved was the appeal to the past as an authoritative justification and legitimation of the present. In legal terms, it was an appeal to precedent as an authority for a current decision. In other words, it was what jurists have termed the *main mort,* "the dead hand" of the past. Though the king may have died, his power and influence live on by virtue of the fact that he became a god at his death. As a god with power to affect the welfare of the living, he had to be appeased and treated with proper respect. With the removal of the thirty-one kings and their associated paraphernalia of symbols (we call them flags) and rituals, the cult of the dead also had to die out, but such folk customs die hard.

Early Israel had to do away with the expensive ritual customs of the royalty, but what about the ritual customs of the important tribes, clans, families whose customs probably, at the grass roots, went farther back into antiquity than those of the upstart kinglets who sprouted up everywhere out of the woodwork in the twelfth century B.C.? This is the first commandment of the covenant that created the community called Israel. "You shall have no other gods in my presence."

This excluded the divine symbols of party, clan, village, and city. So far as we now know, there was no concept of god that was not associated with an existing social organization, though the correlation of gods with social organizations is a concept that has hardly entered into the agenda of modern academic studies in any systematic way.[4] There were two distinct functions of the death-cult and its associated symbols that were incompatible with the covenant-based ethic of early Israel: First was the fact that local cults of this sort could only serve to elevate local, parochial concerns to a status of prime importance, an effect that would endanger, as it always does, the larger unity that is always in jeopardy. The perennial tendency on the part of small social segments to sacrifice all larger concerns for the sake of a temporary local or private interest lies at the foundation of an incalculable amount of social and historical calamity and suffering.

The second function of the death-cult was its tendency to substitute ritual and superstition as a determinant of behavior in place of the historically based concept of cause-and-effect relationships within history itself. It is probably this phenomenon of early Israelite religion that constituted one of its most important features, and that led to the development of historiography as a major form of the system of communication. The moral and ethical concept of history lay at the very foundations of the religious community itself, and the substitution of ritual forms for ethical decision making could result, as it did, only in catastrophe.

Though there can be little doubt that early Israel did covenant to do away with the cult of the dead, there is equally little doubt that many of the customs associated with the age-old practice continued. The custom of burial with grave goods, for example, illustrates the persistence of burial customs, even though the rationale for the practice ceased to be legitimate. The idea that the grave goods furnished the necessities to the deceased in the underworld is dramatically illustrated by two episodes that happened in 1971 during our survey of archaeological sites in the Euphrates valley in Syria. They also illustrate the fact that folk customs can and do survive long after the dominant religious ideology ceases to furnish rational support for the customs.

We received an urgent call one morning to investigate a tomb that had been discovered by a bulldozer in the course of digging a ditch for a new road. It was a quite ordinary Early Bronze Age tomb, but when we cleared the debris filling it, we found the articulated skeleton lying on its back with the right hand resting on the shoulder of a water jug. Only a few days later we came to an obscure and remote village not far south of the Turkish border. The village cemetery was unusual for a Muslim one, in that each grave had single square block tombstone, and on the top of each stone was a carved cup hole. We asked a young man passing by what was the meaning of the cup hole. Without hesitation he replied, ''Every time it rained, the dead would have water.'' The concept of the ''thirsty dead'' is age-old, but it is only a fragment of the deeply engrained body of customary lore that the care of the dead is the responsibility of the living descendants.

If such continuities extending from the Early Bronze Age to the present day (one of the tombstones had an inscription dating it to just five years before our visit) exist in village life despite well over a thousand years of Islam, it is not surprising that in ancient Israelite life, such age-old customs and no doubt beliefs also continued despite the drastic changes brought in with monotheistic Yahwism. Consequently it should be no surprise that the archaeological evidence for burial customs of Israelite villages of the Early Iron Age indicates little difference from the burial customs of the pre-Israelite period or of the non-Israelite neighbors.

SAUL AND THE WITCH OF ENDOR

The bizarre and eerie narrative in 1 Samuel 28 illustrates very well the ideological contrasts that characterized early Israel, and also illustrates the difficulties and conflicts that attended the rise of the revolutionary new religious system of the Mosaic and Sinaitic covenant. There also are beautiful ironies in the narrative that probably arose out of the historical situation itself. During Saul's reign there were repeated episodes in which the felt needs of the kingship came into conflict with premonarchic Yahwist ethic. The result was a final estrangement between Saul and his mentor Samuel.

After the death of Samuel, Saul was bereft of counsel, guidance, and encouragement in trying to cope with the increase in the Philistine power. On the eve of the last battle of his life he was in desperation, evidently deserted by most of his own citizenry, no doubt deservedly so because of his irrational and manic behavior, while faced with hopeless odds in the coming battle with the Philistines. Under the circumstances it is not surprising that Saul believed that the inherited Yahwist faith and ethic had failed him, and therefore, he resolved to have recourse to the time-honored and well-nigh universal pagan practice of consultation with the dead through a witch or medium.[5]

The narrative itself emphasized most powerfully the fact that such procedure was illicit, and had been banned by Saul himself. There is no good reason to question the foundations of the contrast in historical fact, and the narrative furnishes most valuable information concerning the conflict in value systems that inevitably accompanied the transition from a religious community to a political monopoly of force. It is difficult to point to a more dramatic and sharply focused illustration of the difficulties faced by the cultural and religious revolution that was called Israel in the Early Iron Age than this episode from the end of King Saul's life. After only a few years of kingship the ruler was reverting to the ways of the pagan kings that he had removed in the first place. The narrative, as we have it, even emphasized the fact, when the witch of Endor (who unfortunately is not named) refuses to give in to Saul's request on the ground that the king had done away with such witchcraft in his kingdom. Only after he swore an oath to protect her would she proceed to ply her craft.

It is rare that we have such a historically based correlation between the early narratives and the earliest law code—that of Exodus 21–23. Though the narrative in its current form typically for the ancient Near East does not cite the law of Exodus 22:18—"You shall not permit a sorceress to live"—it does emphasize what was important in ancient law: Not what the text said, but what the legal authority *did,* namely, that Saul has "cut off the mediums and the wizards from the land" (1 Sam. 28:9). Therefore, she would be risking her life to do as he had asked. One has a strong impression that the narrator treated the witch of Endor in a sympathetic manner, emphasizing the fact that she was determined to see that King Saul had something to eat before facing his final trial of the next day. There may be a conscious irony in this aspect of the narrative also, since the usual concern was to furnish a banquet for the spirits of the dead (see note 5).

Probably the point of the entire narrative was to emphasize that what Samuel represented was the polar opposite to that which King Saul wanted and thought necessary, but at the same time it was what was really necessary for the success of Saul's regime. Saul's recourse to age-old and prestigious specialized techniques flew in the face of policies that he himself had established, and the ironic conclusion of the entire episode was merely the reinforcement of the fact that for him there was no hope: All he learned was the inevitability of the consequences of his own irrational and irresponsible behavior. It is characteristic of the ancient Near Eastern cultures that they do not preserve in writing systematic descriptions of ancient thought patterns, and thus the narrative, like ancient parables that serve a similar purpose, presupposes that the reader can understand the underlying principles implied in the narrative. Here at least it is clear that Saul's unprincipled behavior resulted only in the reinforcement of the principles he had rejected. To put it in modern terms, the specialized technology that enjoyed high prestige in powerful circles was no substitute for and could not avert the consequences of a whole series of actions that violated basic principles of the society that he was supposed to rule.

This fundamental opposition to the ancient Near Eastern pagan value system described in the covenant Decalog of Exodus 20 (Deuteronomy 5) and in the various law collections of the Pentateuch, and the ancient Near Eastern paganism is difficult to describe, and even more difficult to explain, but it goes to the very center of the biblical faith. It also constitutes a persistent, if not constant, contrast throughout the history of culture. The opposition to witchcraft, necromancy, and the various forms of omenology that were so highly developed in all ancient pagan systems is based on a most profound conviction of the rationality and predictability of human experience. This in turn was based on the blessings and curses that constituted an important part of the entire biblical covenant tradition. The obligations voluntarily accepted in the covenant were enforced, not by any arbitrary power structure, but by a profound conviction that obedience to those obligations must result in well-being of the sort that was sought by all in the ancient and modern world: long life, health, prosperity, and peace. Conversely, violation of those obligations must result in the opposite: war, famine, disease, and death.

These historically based connections between cause and consequence heightened individual as well as collective responsibility to a great degree, for all were really beyond the capability of ancient people to bring about; in other words, both the benefits and the ills were regarded as acts of God that ordinary mortals could not control. For this reason they were blessings and curses brought about by divine agency in all the ancient world, but nowhere else were those blessings and curses so firmly tied to the ethical behavior or misbehavior of human beings. For this reason any ideology, or any technology that claimed to guarantee well-being or avoid calamity by means other than ethical conformity to the covenant obligations that furnished the very foundations of the community was tantamount to treason, entailing the sentence of death. Technology and arcane arts could not be substituted for Yahweh's inexorable rule over human history in accordance with principle, not mere arbitrary caprice.

The blessings and curses as an integral part of the original constitution, so to speak, of the Yahwist community also was the foundation of its understanding of the dynamics of history. It was at the same time a powerful affirmation of the fundamental rationality of the course of history and the processes of the natural world that were so much involved in the divine application of the blessings and curses. Though this early Israelite ideology proved to be too simplistic, the basic affirmation of a discernible order and rationality in both nature and history furnished the foundations for further development in all of Western civilization. In contrast, the superstitions and irrationalities of ancient pagan necromancy and omenology have long been rejected by the modern scientific world view, though they still appeal to many people who suffer from the same irrational instincts and insecurities to which King Saul fell victim.

THE MONARCHY

By the end of Solomon's reign the monarchy in Jerusalem had all the paraphernalia and organizations characteristic of a typical Syro-Hittite state of that time. Though it is not until much later that we have definite references to the cult of the dead and the associated necromancy, especially in Isaiah (e.g., 8: 19), there is no reason to doubt that such practices were characteristic in both paganized kingdoms, Judah as well as Israel, for virtually all of the canonical prophetic writings preserved include condemnations of the royal and urban practices of witchcraft and sorcery. Unfortunately we do not have evidence, such as the written collections from Mesopotamia that constitute the training or reference manuals of those specialists in such practices.

In the ancient world all arcane and occult arts enjoyed high prestige, for they were patronized and consulted by kings and others in high places. Witches and sorcerers were, so to speak, the practitioners of social science research whose findings had to be followed by the powerful decision-makers, lest they risk catastrophe. It is not surprising that under such circumstances, mere ethical considerations fell by the wayside as unimportant, and as an inevitable accompaniment of this systematic excursion into modernity on the part of the monarchy and its bureaucracy, the old religious tradition was increasingly ignored and probably even unknown.[6] The prophetic tradition that represented the continuity of the pre-Monarchian covenant theology and faith constantly cited the capitol cities as the centers of apostasy and corruption, as they no doubt were.

This compulsive conformity to prestigious pagan superstitions of the time resulted in an increasing irrationality in political decision making and social policy. As prophets from Amos on complained, it was the powerless and the righteous who were victims of the pagan political establishment. At the same time, the policies of the government, innocent of any concern for or knowledge of the religious tradition, with its emphasis on a reasonably predictable order of cause-and-effect relationships, could not possibly be tolerable to its neighbors. Almost from its beginning the political state was characterized by wholesale murder of neighboring populations.

The result was predicted by all of the pre-exilic prophets: A political state that rejected all ethical controls over its behavior was not compatible with the divine order of Yahweh, which it systematically rejected, and therefore, it had to be destroyed by Yahweh himself. The destruction came on the northern kingdom first, and it is not hard to imagine the politicians and population of Judah saying, "They certainly got what was coming to them" (see 2 Kings 17: 1–18). Yet, as the historiographer of 2 Kings 17 goes on to point out, the situation in Judah was not that much different. It took another century before the same fate befell Judah, in 586 B.C. With that event the biblical tradition concerning life after death was placed into a new context, and it took centuries before a new consensus, so to speak, emerged to become normative religious doctrine.

THE SEARCH FOR JUSTICE

No doubt long before the destruction of Jerusalem it was evident to many people that the excessively simple formula of the curses and blessings of the old covenant tradition did not always conform to experience. The old concept of innocent blood crying out to Yahweh from the ground illustrates the fact that awareness of unrequited suffering and death existed from the earliest times, though there was exception of Yahweh's vindication in due time. In normal life, however, such anomalies did not call in question the fundamentals of the covenant faith, for after all, the belief structure primarily was a matter of religious faith and integrity, not an empirically demonstrable scientific account of history.

With the destruction of Jerusalem and the Judean state at the hands of the Babylonians in 586 B.C. the situation theologically as well as historically was drastically changed. In the first place it is a predictable constant in the history of culture that when a social system is destroyed, many of the characteristic features of that system lose their validity or legitimacy. In other words, ideas, customs, doctrines, and, especially, ethical and moral standards that seemed immutable and eternal in the old society no longer have their binding nature simply because the social system that upheld it no longer exists. By no means does this imply that there was a discontinuity from earlier social and cultural systems. Rather, under these circumstances there was a freedom—indeed a necessity—to reexamine the old ways and to search for new and more fruitful ways to cope with the new present and the future.

It cannot be denied that the destruction of the state of Judah was followed by the highest degree of intellectual and religious creativity that the society had known since the formative period of Moses. Indeed, since the nineteenth century many scholars have argued (against all reason and reality) that most of the Old Testament came into existence at this time, and next to nothing is known, if anything important developed, of the social and religious culture of the preexilic period.

The purpose here is to trace the development of one particular complex of ideas that were of crucial importance to both the earlier and the later religious communities, to discover and describe what happened to the original structure of the covenant tradition and, especially, the sanctions: the blessings and curses formulae.

Before the destruction of the political state there already were serious questions concerning the reliability, if not the validity, of the age-old doctrine of the divine order of retribution. The irrationalities of the political state faced with insoluble problems both domestic and foreign resulted in irrational acts that constituted a fundamental challenge to any concept of an orderly universe. The problem of the "righteous sufferer" was already raised, and no answer found except merely to wait, in Habakkuk (chapter 1) some time before the destruction. Jeremiah also (12:1–4) lamented the lack of divine justice evident in the prosperity of the wicked in his time, and was himself the victim of such unscrupulous people. The only answer seems to have been the reaffirmation of the inevitability of divine justice: The wicked eventually will be rewarded with their just deserts.

The destruction came as predicted, but with it came another terrible problem. Granted, the destruction was thoroughly deserved and was caused by the policies of the insane government, but the experience turned out to be no consolation: The catastrophe of suffering, famine, disease, exile, and death afflicted the faithful as well as the evil. Calamity was no respecter of people, and therefore, the old formula that the wicked are punished and the righteous rewarded did not hold true. In the misery of exile and the loss of everything held dear there was no place for hope in the old formula. In calamity, as in death, the good and evil, the great and small are equals, and therefore, Job's dialogue with his "comforters" begins with his long soliloquy (chapter 3) asking why he should have existed at all if there was to be no differentiation between the good and the evil.

Though there is no evidence that the book of Job had any influence in the later course of biblical thought, it does excellently illustrate the climate of thought after the destruction. The gross inadequacy of the old curses and blessings formula was powerfully emphasized in the speeches of Job, while his comforters endlessly reiterated the old Deuteronomic orthodoxy that the divine order of the universe was still in place: Job had sinned, as Zophar, with the incredible callousness of the self-righteous, confidently asserts: "Know then that God exacts of you less than your guilt deserves" (Job 11:6). Thus does orthodox doctrine triumph over all objective reality. Or, on the other hand, if Job merely confesses, then all the blessings of the covenant will come to him, as Eliphaz, in a much more kindly manner, promises (Job 5:17–27).

The difficulties involved in the interpretation of the book of Job are well known and need not be further elaborated on here. The argument of the current discussion is the fact that the old concept of blessings and curses, rewards and punishments was drastically challenged as *the foundation for religious faith and integrity,* or as the basis for the understanding of human experience. What it meant was that the divine order of justice was not predictable or reliable within the framework of human historical existence, and that faith in God and obedience to divine command could not be founded on this laudable, but unreliable doctrine.

Under the old Sinai covenant structure the faith and the obedience were *not* founded on the blessings and curses formula. The faithfulness and the relation to God were based on the prior experience of grace—of benefits received before the establishment of the covenant relationship. The blessings and curses formula served as further sanction for obedience, but it was subsidiary, not primary, in the relationship.

The problem was not and could not be solved with this discovery. For this reason there is no evidence that the book of Job had any influence on subsequent thought for centuries. The problem came back to that of the very nature of God himself. If God could not be relied on to render blessings and curses within the framework of mortal existence, how, then, could God be regarded as being the source of justice and righteousness (cf. Jeremiah 9:24)? Was God merely to become another arbitrary powerful despot ruling, like the old Mesopotamian pagan gods, by caprice rather than by predictable principle? It is here that the faith faced a terrible dilemma. The book of Job ended, as many have observed, with no solution, but merely a reaffirmation, which was itself a step far beyond the tired old Deuteronomic orthodoxy, that the vision of God was a good in itself, not exchangeable with the material blessings of life (Job 42:1–6). This was too rarefied a position to serve as the foundation of a popular religion, especially under the circumstances of grinding poverty and general low morale that characterized the early postexilic society.

The paradox ultimately was resolved by projecting the realization of the divine rewards and punishments to a dimension other than that of normal earthly experience and history. It is not probable that the process of ideological change can be traced in detail, and within the increasingly diverse cultural backgrounds represented in the far-flung society of Jewish ideology in the Hellenistic period, there was by no means a unanimity of thought. As is well known, the important and powerful group of Sadducees in New Testament times still had not accepted the concept of life after death (Acts 23:6–10). As so often is the case in the history of religion, innovations or reforms gained acceptance in popular religion and practice long before they were accepted into the corpus of belief and practice of official religion, that is, of powerholders in the religious organization.

Some 400 years after the destruction of Jerusalem we have in Daniel 11:2 a clear statement affirming the resurrection of the dead, and it is combined with the affirmation of reward and punishment meted out after the resurrection. What both the good and the evil had not received, though much deserved, during their lifetime was meted out to them after their resurrection. Though such transitions in thought are rarely clearly describable or explainable in ancient (or modern) history, it may tentatively be suggested that the transition took place in two main stages that are well represented in our preserved literature.

In the first stage, usually termed apocalyptic, which is illustrated already in some oracles of the preexilic prophets, there is affirmation of a future that radically contrasts with the normal course of human and natural events. This motif ranges from the hopeful vision of a peaceful future of Micah 4:1–4 to the equally hopeful expectation of peaceful relations in the natural world of Isaiah 11:6–9. Whatever else may be implied in such passages that appear in one context after another in the preexilic prophets, it is clear that their vision was a powerful affirmation that their contemporary state of affairs characterized by violence and hopelessness was neither intended by God nor was it necessary. Because most of the prophets came from nonestablishment social circles, their visions state emphatically that "things don't have to be like this." Against all deterministic myths of ancient or modern times the visions affirm the possibility of more fruitful and happier alternatives.

This affirmation of a radical discontinuity from the unsatisfactory present is combined in Job and elsewhere with the affirmation of divine justice. Though it is true that the present is not compatible with the faith in a just and loving God, the apocalyptic future will set all things right. Ezekiel's vision of the "valley of dry bones" (37:1–14) is a classic and hyperbolic illustration of the theme. The result was the frequent emphasis on "waiting for God," the emphasis on patience in suffering and, above all, on maintaining religious and moral integrity in the face of powerful temptations to give up. Contrast the question of Job's wife (2:9): "Do you still hold fast your integrity? Curse God, and die." Such visions also are, then, inseparable from the conviction that it is neither necessary nor desirable to adapt to the irrationalities of societies that are bent on self-destruction. Though the modern scientific world view would agree that Isaiah went too far in predicting that the lion would become a herbivore, we should not lose sight of the fact that fanatic determination to maintain the present status quo usually excludes the possibility of something much better, and often enough determines the destruction of the system.

The second stage in the development of doctrine that proclaimed life after death is the eschatological. In the first, apocalyptic stage it seems at least that the scenario is played out on the level of historical time and space. In the second, eschatological stage the scene shifts to one that is entirely transhistorical: It takes place in the unseen world of eternity—of heaven and hell, as it eventually became in postbiblical thought. The blessings and curses become completely systematized in their eternal realization in the world to come. But this belongs to and is described in the essays that deal with postbiblical Judaism and Christianity.

CONCLUSION

There are traces in the Egyptian "Negative Confession" of a concept that the quality of life after death depends on the quality of life led while on earth. It seems, however, that the systematic development of this doctrine took place only in the postbiblical tradition, and as is true of the apocalyptic and eschatological literature in general, the socioreligious function of the doctrine was not to convey information about the unseen and unknowable, but to furnish foundations for a religious and ethical integrity that had its own independent source and dynamic, not forever a "reed shaken in the wind" of whatever ideology or propaganda happens to be fashionable.

There seems to be no doubt that any religious, political, or philosophical doctrine or concept can be put to evil and vicious use by the unscrupulous, and this doctrine of reward and punishment in the eschatological future has, on occasion, degenerated to the idea of "pie in the sky, bye and bye." There is a delicious irony in the fact that those who concocted this parody of ancient doctrine did so in the hope of recruiting support from the disaffected by promising them "a lot and all at once" right here and now. The result of such promises usually has been another chapter in the sad history of human inhumanity.

NOTES

1. For example, the prohibition of witchcraft in Exodus 22:18, referred to in 1 Samuel 28:9.

2. For a lengthy description and critique of this consensus consult H. C. Brichto, "Kin, Cult, Land and Afterlife—A Biblical Complex," *Hebrew Union College Annual* 44 (1973): 1–54, and Mitchell Dahood, *Psalms III 101–150*. The Anchor Bible (Garden City, N.Y.: Doubleday, 1970), XLI-LII. Brichto hopelessly confuses the condemned pagan practices that did exist with the normative Yahwism of the Mosaic and prophetic faith, evidently unaware that there was a difference.

3. Psalm 6:6. Compare the similar complaint in Psalm 30:9, "Will the dust praise thee?"

4. It is most probable that any ancient pagan social organization had a god that was its cosmic counterpart, its tutelary deity. It was the ancient and universal means by

which to give expression to the sense of value that was associated with the organization. See Ramsay MacMullen, *Roman Social Relations* (New Haven, Conn.: Yale University Press, 1981), 82: "for the assembled Butchers, Youths, or whatever opened their meetings with a prayer to the deity they had inevitably chosen at the moment of their incorporation." See also p. 86: "We have the record of a patron deity chosen, its image set up, and prayers offered to it by the tenants of the Bolan Building in Rome." The Bolan Building was an ancient apartment building.

5. For an excellent description of the cross-cultural practices and ideology associated with necromancy, see Harry A. Hoffner, Jr., "Second Millennium Antecedents to the Hebrew *'OB'*," *Journal of Biblical Literature* 86 (1967): 385–401.

6. Note the complaint of Hosea (4:6) that the priests themselves did not know the religious tradition.

6

Death and Afterlife in the New Testament

Leander E. Keck

The New Testament assumes that to understand life, we also must understand death and the afterlife. Yet the New Testament contains not a single chapter that summarizes the Christian view. What it says about the subject is found in a wide variety of contexts because, characteristically, the New Testament deals with death and the life after death when it talks about something else. Moreover, because the New Testament was written by many people, most of whom are unknown, and over a period of a hundred years, it says different things. Faced with such a situation, we do well to begin with a general orientation.

INTRODUCTION

Two sets of considerations will get us ready to understand what the New Testament says about death and the afterlife. The first set of considerations is that of the vocabulary and its logic. The word "death" itself is used in two senses, the literal and the metaphorical. Literally, "death" refers to the cessation of life; metaphorically, it also refers to a spiritual and moral condition. In other words, the New Testament knows as well as we do that some people are dead morally before they are dead physically. The New Testament has a different attitude, however, toward physical death. Whereas we often regard death as a neutral physiologic fact, as in the antiseptic expression "She expired," the New Testament often reflects the ancient Near East view of physical death as an enemy. Never does it speak of death as a friend who releases one from pain. Consequently death and mortality are religious and theological problems: If God is the author of life, why must everything that lives die? Above all, suicide is not even considered a viable option. In the New Testament, death is never in human hands; rather, it is we who are in the hands of death.

The second word we need to clarify is immortality. Is there something in the self that is naturally immortal? The idea that the soul is naturally immortal, deathless by definition, is at home in much of Greek thought but not in the New Testament. Not all the ancient Greeks thought that the soul was immortal, but those who did were dualists, emphasizing the fundamental difference between what is physical, material, and mortal and what is immaterial and immortal. For them the soul is a splinter of the divine, and so is naturally immortal. The New Testament has a unique idea of immortality: The whole person will become immortal by resurrection.

So the third word we need to understand at the outset is resurrection. In the New Testament, resurrection is not simply coming to life again. That would be resuscitation or reanimation. A resuscitated corpse will die later, but a resurrected person will never die because resurrection entails being transformed into an immortal being. According to the New Testament, we are born mortal, but our destiny is to become immortal by resurrection.

Finally, there are certain words for the place of the dead. In the Hebrew Bible, which Christians call the Old Testament, the dead go to the underworld, to Sheol, a place the Greeks called Hades. Neither Sheol nor Hades is a place of punishment. The Hebrew word for that place is Gehenna, a fiery place of torment. The English word for that is Hell. The New Testament never confuses Hades and Hell. In traditional Roman Catholic vocabulary we find the word "purgatory," the place where the dead are purified of their sins before going to heaven. The New Testament does not mention purgatory because that idea came into the Christian vocabulary much later.

These words, each with its own logic, did not simply appear; each is part of larger complexes of ideas that have important histories. This brings us to the second set of considerations that will prepare us to look at the New Testament, that is, some historical matters.

We begin with the Greek tradition of radical dualism of the eternal, immortal soul and the mortal body made of matter. No one knows how old this dualism is in Greek thought, for it is much older than Plato, who, in the fourth century before our Era, developed it philosophically. By the beginning of our Era the dualistic view had undergone many developments, one of which combined it with ancient Near Eastern mythology and astrology to form a widespread movement that offered salvation, a movement we call Gnosticism, from the Greek word *gnosis,* or knowledge.[1] According to Gnostic thinking, the immortal soul is a prisoner of the mortal body. Some Gnostics coined the slogan *soma sema:* The *soma* (the body) is a *sema* (a tomb) for the soul. What makes this doubly tragic is that the body causes the soul to forget that it is a splinter of the divine. So the soul is doomed to amnesia and to one body tomb after another until it receives the true *gnosis,* the saving knowledge, of what it really is and where it came from. Armed with this knowledge from a heavenly revealer, the soul can escape at death and return to its eternal heavenly home outside the cosmos.

The New Testament had to contend with this dualism because Christianity began with a different view of the self, one at home in the Hebrew Bible. Here the self is a besouled body, a body animated by the breath of life. The ancient Hebrews never regarded the body as the prison of the life-breath; for them the self was what we call a psychosomatic entity, God being the creator of both body and life-breath. At death a shadowy self went to Sheol, the place of the dead. This view prevailed until the second century before our Common Era, when for the first time a new idea emerged—that the righteous would be resurrected. This idea solved a major theological problem created by martyrdom. It previously was believed that those who obeyed God's will would prosper, and that calamity was God's punishment for disobedience. But when it became illegal to be a practicing Jew,[2] obedient to the Law of Moses, the old theology was in a crisis because now the disobedient prospered and the obedient suffered and were killed. And so there arose the view, first clearly expressed in the Book of Daniel,[3] that at the end of history, God would intervene and vindicate the righteous who had paid with their lives for being obedient, and that God would do this by resurrecting them. Not all Jews believed this, but those who did bought into a view of history known as apocalyptic.[4]

In the apocalyptic view, all history is rushing downhill toward the End, when the world as we know it, dominated by evil and death, will be replaced by the Age to Come, when everything will be made right by God. There was no single apocalyptic scenario for the End, but belief in resurrection became so important that it was retained even by those Jews who later gave up much of apocalyptic thought, the rabbis.

The point is that the Gnostic and the apocalyptist had quite different views of the self. What would have made a Gnostic shudder—the news that the soul would be reunited with the body—was exactly the basis of hope for the apocalyptist; conversely, what would have been final defeat for the apocalyptist—the unending separation of the soul from the body—was redemption for the Gnostic. To a large extent, the history of the Christian understanding of death and afterlife is the story of how Christianity came to terms with both of these views. That story begins in the New Testament.

This brings us to the second historical consideration: the fundamental shift of early Christianity's center of gravity. Early Christianity began as a sect within apocalyptic Judaism, but soon became a largely gentile religion in the Greco-Roman world. The initial Christians were Jews who brought with them their apocalyptic views of death and afterlife; later, the gentile Christians—Greeks, Romans, Celts—brought their dualistic ideas into the church, some of which were combined with the Jewish legacy and some of which were rejected. In the New Testament we see the beginning of this interaction.

The third historical consideration concerns the nature of the New Testament. Historically, Christianity did not come from the New Testament; rather, the

New Testament came from early Christianity. The New Testament did not produce Christianity the way the Book of Mormon produced Mormonism. Rather, the New Testament is an anthology of twenty-seven booklets written by Christians between the years 50 and 150 C.E. Each booklet was written for a particular purpose, and so takes a good deal for granted. As a result, the New Testament is not a comprehensive summary of everything early Christians believed, but a collection of writings occasioned by various needs in the churches. We should not be surprised, therefore, to find that it contains a variety of ideas about death and life after death.

JESUS

These orienting remarks have prepared us to look at what the New Testament says about our theme. Even though Jesus wrote not a single word in the New Testament, we will begin with him. Then we will examine what Paul the apostle says. After that we will look briefly at the Book of Revelation, and then turn to the Gospel of John.[5]

Jesus did not speak often about death and life after death, but what he did say shows that he was influenced by apocalyptic thought. For example, he expected that the righteous would be resurrected at the End of history.[6]

The Gospel of Mark reports that once the Sadducees, who rejected the idea of resurrection, tried to trap Jesus with a trick question (12:18–27). According to the Law of Moses, when a man died, his brother was to marry the widow. Now, the Sadducees asked, suppose this happens repeatedly in the same family, so that finally the woman had married all seven brothers. In the resurrection, whose wife will she be? Jesus rejected the question: "When they rise from the dead, they neither marry nor are given in marriage, but are like angels in heaven" (12:25). In other words, resurrection is real transformation, not simply resuscitation. This is virtually the only thing Jesus taught about life after death. Elsewhere he simply refers to things like the coming Judgment to underscore the importance of living rightly now.

In the Gospel of Matthew, Jesus uses the phrase, "kingdom of heaven." In such cases he is not talking about the place where the blessed will go after death. Rather, "kingdom of heaven" is simply a paraphrase for "kingdom of God," since the word "heaven" is a circumlocution for God, as in our phrase, "for heaven's sake." So when Jesus speaks about having treasure in heaven (Matthew 6:19, 21), he means one will have a good relation to God (see also Luke 12:13–21).

Jesus could simply allude to various parts of the apocalyptic scenario because it was not his aim to provide information about death and afterlife, but to call people to a new way of life on earth. He frequently calls attention to the coming judgment, as in some of his stories, the parables. Some of them end with a warning about people being thrown out into "outer darkness" where they will "weep and gnash their teeth" (e.g., Matthew 8:12; 22:13). So, too, he urges people to deal decisively with whatever causes them to sin. "If your hand causes you to sin, cut it off; it is better for you to enter life maimed than with two hands to go to hell, to the unquenchable fire" (Mark 9:43). In all such sayings, Jesus is not providing instruction about life after death, but is referring to the future to say that the consequences of not acting rightly now are serious.

PAUL

Death and life after death are much more important in the teaching of the apostle Paul. We will first see why this is the case and then see what Paul had to say about our theme.

Paul was a Jew, from Tarsus, a city in the southeast corner of modern Turkey, who went to Palestine when he joined the Pharisees,[7] for whom resurrection was a basic belief. This means that Paul believed in resurrection long before he became a Christian. Why, then, were death and the afterlife more important in his teachings than in the teachings of Jesus? Because he became a Christian when he believed the news that a resurrection had already occurred, but in one case only—that of Jesus. Resurrection was supposed to happen for the righteous, but Jesus had been executed on a cross as a criminal. But if God resurrected him, then he was not a criminal, but a righteous man whom God had made Lord, the heavenly regent, so to speak. The resurrection of Jesus meant even more. If resurrection marked the transition from This Age to the Age to Come, when all things would be made right, then the resurrection of Jesus implied that the time of salvation has begun. But everything seemed to be just as it was before. So how could the time of salvation have begun? Because Paul could not give up the conviction that God had raised Jesus from the dead, he, like his Christian contemporaries, reinterpreted salvation as a new right relation to God for those who believed the news of Jesus' resurrection. The complete transformation would occur when the Lord returned, at the so-called Second Coming of Christ, which would happen soon. In the meantime, believers could begin living the life of the New Age ahead of time. In other words, the death and resurrection of Jesus were the pivot on which his thinking turned. This was true of other Christians as well, but what distinguished Paul was the way he thought through the deeper and wider consequences of his conviction that God had resurrected Jesus.

One thing Paul saw clearly was that the New Age that had begun with Jesus' resurrection was decisive for the whole world. Therefore, Paul took the news of Jesus, climaxed by his death and resurrection, to the Greco-Roman world. Gentiles need not wait until the return of the Lord Jesus before they could benefit from the salvation of the New Age. They could get in on this now by believing the gospel and by being baptized and becoming members of the church, a new international, interracial community. So Paul became the first great

Christian missionary, founding congregations of believers in Asia Minor and Greece.

The Letters of Paul in the New Testament were written for these groups.[8] Paul did not write essays on topics or a book of theology. So if we want to grasp his thought, we must combine the various things he did say, risky as this may be. We cannot summarize everything he said, but we will reach for what is essential and characteristic.

Paul, being deeply influenced by the Bible, interpreted the story of Adam and Eve to mean that death entered the world as a result of Adam's disobedience or sin, and so death became the fate of humanity (Romans 5:12–21). In other words, it was sin that brought death, not the other way around. To paraphrase it, according to Paul, we do not sin because we are mortal; rather, we are mortal because of sin, not only because of what Adam did, but because ever since then everyone sins and so ratifies Adam and his consequences. This idea is so strange at first that it is useful to reflect on it a bit more.

Suppose Paul had said that we sin because we are mortal. We are more familiar with this way of thinking because it often has been said that we resist our mortality, deny our death. To assure our immortality, we devise all sorts of strategies that enhance our power over others. We exploit, suppress, and kill. In a way, we are a death-driven humanity. Paul might agree that this is a true description of what we do, but he also would insist that it is wrong as an explanation because it implies that the root problem is that we are mortal. If our mortality is the root problem, then we are innocent victims of the way we were created. But this implies that the real responsibility for our sin is with the Creator who made us mortal to start with. According to Genesis, God created us good, and we sinned and brought about our mortality. Human sin cannot be traced back to the Creator, but must somehow be our responsibility.

Paul does not spend much ink explaining the origin of sin and death. His real agenda is showing how the human dilemma is overcome by God's act in Jesus Christ. How can we escape the tyranny of sin and death? By participating in Jesus' own resurrection. How can we do that? According to Paul, by being baptized because baptism makes us shareholders, so to speak, in the one event that broke the power of sin, the resurrection of Jesus (Romans 6:1–11). Paul evidently relies on the ancient view of sacraments, according to which a religious rite actually does something—imparts the life of a divine being to humans. Does this mean that baptism makes us immortal? Not at all. Paul assumed that baptized Christians would still die like everyone else. But the new Christians in Greece had problems with Paul's teaching, perhaps because he had not fully explained things before moving on.

In Thessalonika, which we call Salonika, the new Christians were distressed because some of them had died. They concluded that those who died before the coming of the Lord have forfeited their salvation. They thought that only those alive then would share in the coming salvation. Paul's First Letter to the Thessalonians corrects their thinking. When the Lord comes "the dead in Christ will rise first; then we who are alive, who are left, shall be caught up together with them in the clouds to meet the Lord in the air; and so we shall always be with the Lord'' (1 Thess. 4:16–17). Paul does not say where they will be with the Lord, or anything about what will happen next. He simply assures the readers that the dead Christians will not lose out.

The new Christians in Corinth seem to have had a more serious problem, one influenced by the Greek dualism we noted earlier. Some of the Corinthian Christians were saying flatly, ''There is no resurrection of the dead'' (1 Cor. 15:12). Apparently they did not deny life after death. Rather, they rejected the resurrection because they saw the material, mortal body as the problem—a problem solved by releasing the soul from it, like liberating a bird from a cage. Paul cannot let this go unchallenged because it undercuts the gospel based on the resurrection of Jesus. In 1 Corinthians 15 we have his response.

First, he exposes the self-contradiction that the denial of resurrection implied. On the one hand, if there is no resurrection for Christians, then there was no resurrection of Christ either because his resurrection is unique only in that it is the first. So if the Corinthians deny that Christ was resurrected, then they deny the very salvation that they prize. In fact, Paul declares, ''as in Adam all die, so also in Christ shall all be made alive'' (1 Cor. 15:22). On the other hand, he exposes the contradiction in what the Corinthians are doing—baptizing on behalf of the dead (v. 29). This is the only reference to such a practice, and no one knows exactly why it was done. In any case, Paul sees that if the body is not resurrected to be reunited with the soul, why bother with baptizing on behalf of the dead? Their souls are already free.

Then Paul explains what he means by the resurrection—the only passage in the New Testament that does this. He uses an analogy: We plant a seed in one form, but it comes up in another form, in another body. A grain of wheat has a brown body, but when it is planted it becomes a green one when it sprouts. So, he infers, we are buried in one kind of body but raised in another kind, what he calls a ''spiritual body''—the only time he uses the phrase.

He also says why this is important: ''flesh and blood [that is, our ordinary phenomenal existence] cannot inherit the kingdom of God'' (v. 50). The Corinthians agreed completely. But they had a quite different solution: Get the soul out of the body, out of flesh and blood, altogether. Paul's solution is that flesh and blood will be transformed into the spiritual body, like the grain of wheat is transformed into a green plant.

This will happen at the end, when the Lord comes: ''The dead will be raised imperishable, and we shall be changed. For this perishable nature must put on the imperishable, and this mortal nature must put on immortality'' (vv. 52–53). In other words, the Corinthians solved the problem of our mortality by relying on the old Greek dualistic solution of releasing the immortal soul from the body, but Paul solved it by appealing to the Jewish apocalyptic resurrection that transforms the entire psychosomatic self into an immortal being. Immortality is in store for the whole self.[9]

Finally, Paul points out what is at stake in this view—the defeat of death. Death is the ultimate enemy, the ultimate antithesis of God, the author of life. If there is no resurrection, if we must shed our bodies, if our bodies are so much unusable slag because they are material and mortal, then death has the last word after all, and God will have created something that God cannot redeem. For Paul, this is completely unacceptable. So he writes that at the end, when resurrection occurs, "the last enemy to be destroyed is death" (v. 26). In other words, by resurrecting the mortal body and transforming it into an immortal spiritual one, God triumphs over death. Anything less ends in a standoff: death being sovereign over what is mortal because of Adam's sin, God being sovereign only over souls. From Paul's angle, if that is the bottom line, then the whole event of Jesus Christ was a waste of time because as far as death is concerned, we would be exactly where we were before.

In the Letter to the Romans he goes even farther. In chapter 8 he returns to Genesis, which says that because of Adam's disobedience, the earth was cursed. Paul takes this to mean that all nature is subject to death, to what he calls "bondage to decay" (see Romans 8:20–21). He sees that everything that lives must die, and that nothing is permanent. So Paul says that creation itself will be liberated from this bondage to death. In other words, the defeat of death and decay will be total; the whole creation will be redeemed from death.

Before leaving Paul, some concluding observations are useful. First, although Paul writes in Greek to Greeks, he does not approach the problem of death and afterlife in Greek terms; he does not begin by analyzing the nature of the self as an unfortunate compound of body and soul. He clearly recognizes that our physical bodies are mortal, and he knows that there is an immaterial element, our spirit. But for Paul, the mortality of the body is not a fixed starting point, not a given, but the consequence of Adam and of our own ratification of Adam by our own sinning. In other words, in the last analysis, the mortality to which we are subject is not natural, but unnatural—the result of Adam. To have accepted it as natural would have implied that the human dilemma can be traced back to a jerry-built creation and an incompetent Creator.[10]

Second, what is really at stake, therefore, is the understanding of God as the creator of an originally good world, who at the End is capable of reclaiming it from its tragic history and its bondage to the consequence of sin, to death.

Third, Paul shows no interest whatever in Hades or in Hell. In fact, these words never appear in his letters. Nor does Paul have any interest in exploring where the souls will be before the resurrection, just as he says not a word about life in heaven. For him, it is enough to know that the whole person will be redeemed from death, and be with the Lord.

Fourth, Paul's thinking is both mythic in character and cosmic in scope. It does not describe phenomena like death or the resurrection body, but interprets these realities in language that is actually inappropriate to the subject matter because all our language is time-bound and earth-bound. Yet this is the only language that he has to talk about that which transcends time and space. Paul does not describe the undescribable, but is content to walk the boundary where he believes the decisive transformation will occur, and there to affirm what the logic of the situation requires in light of the resurrection of Jesus.

THE REVELATION OF JOHN

Whereas Jesus and Paul rely on certain apocalyptic ideas, there is one book in the New Testament that is permeated by apocalyptic themes—the Revelation of John. This book was written thirty years after Paul's death and more than sixty years after that of Jesus. No other book in the New Testament has captured the imagination of Western art or influenced the imagery of Christian hymns more than the Apocalypse of John. It apparently was written when Christians in Asia Minor were being persecuted by the state for not worshiping the divine genius of the emperor, a stance that cost them their lives. Because it was Jewish martyrdom that led to the emergence of apocalyptic theology in the first place, it is not surprising that Christian martyrdom led John the Elder to use apocalyptic to interpret the situation that now faced Christians. From this fascinating book only the elements most important for our topic will be noted, and but briefly.

The book is a series of visions that interpret John's own time and what is expected to happen shortly. Right at the outset, the resurrected Christ announces, "I died, and behold I am alive for evermore, and I have the keys of Death and Hades" (1:18). Thus those who may be killed because of their faith in Jesus are assured that death does not have the last word because Jesus has the final authority over it. As the visions of almost indescribable disaster pass before our eyes, again and again we are shown the blessed state of the martyrs. It is these visions that have provided much of the Christian imagery of life after death.

In chapter 7 John sees "a great multitude which no man could number, from every nation, from all tribes and peoples and tongues" (v. 9), standing before God's throne and before the Lamb (the resurrected Christ, who had been killed like a sacrificial lamb); these people wear white robes, the symbol of purity, and wave palm branches, the symbol of victory. Who are they?

> These are they who have come out of the great tribulation; they have washed their robes and made them white in the blood of the Lamb.
>
> Therefore are they before the throne of God,
> and serve him day and night within his temple;
> and he who sits upon the throne will shelter them with his presence.
> They shall hunger no more, neither thirst any more;
> the sun shall not strike them, nor any scorching heat.
> For the Lamb in the midst of the throne will be their shepherd,
> and he will guide them to springs of living water;
> and God will wipe away every tear from their eyes. (vv. 14–17)

For our topic, three closely related things are distinctive in the Apocalypse of John. The first is the idea of the millennium, the 1,000 years when Christ will rule the earth as the Messiah. During this time Satan will be bound. At the beginning of the millennium the righteous will be resurrected, the Christian martyrs. After the thousand years are over Satan will be released and a final battle will take place between good and evil. Satan will be defeated and "thrown into the lake of fire and brimstone" (20:10, King James version) to be tormented forever. Now comes the second resurrection, when all the dead will be raised and the Last Judgment will take place. The third thing is a new heaven and a new earth, to which a new Jerusalem descends (Revelation 20—21).

The reason for this scenario is clear: The first resurrection represents the vindication of the righteous martyrs. Their millennial reign is God's reward for being faithful unto death. The second resurrection is necessary to bring all the dead to the Judgment. The new heaven and earth, with its new Jerusalem, is the decisive and ultimate answer to history, with its agony and rebellion against God. No other New Testament book has this scenario.

More than any other book in the New Testament, the Apocalypse of John has given us the images of eternal bliss, and eternal damnation in a fiery hell. In a book not in the New Testament, the Apocalypse of Peter,[11] we get even more detailed pictures of the torment in store for sinners in Hell. Many readers find the Revelation of John to be a horrifying book; actually, its horrors have the function of providing the dark background for a profound hope.

THE GOSPEL OF JOHN

The Gospel of John was written at about the same time as the Apocalypse of John, but by someone else in quite different circumstances. It reflects a quite different outlook as well because whereas apocalyptic theology insisted that salvation and eternal life will be given only in the future, at the End, when the Lord comes again, the Gospel of John insists that salvation and eternal life are available here and now.

Why does John insist that Jesus brings eternal life now? Because it presents Jesus as the Logos in the flesh. The term "Logos" has many meanings: word, reason, argument, rationale. In John it refers to the Word of God, not a book or a saying, but an eternal reality through which God created the world. This is clear in the opening lines: "In the beginning was the Word, and the Word was with God, and the Word was God. He was in the beginning with God; all things were made through him, and without him was not anything made that was made. In him was life, and the life was the light of men" (John 1:1–4). This Word "became flesh and dwelt among us," John declares (v. 14). In other words, for John, the story of Jesus is the story of what happens when the Creator becomes a man and offers real life, eternal life, to people who, it turns out, mostly refuse it. This new life means beginning all over again one's relation to the Creator by acknowledging that Jesus is the Son of God who gives life that is eternal: "For God so loved the world that he gave his only Son, that whoever believes in him should not perish but have eternal life" (3:16). But whoever does not believe "is condemned already, because he has not believed in the name of the only Son of God" (3:18). In other words, the Last Judgment is not in the future either, as in apocalyptic thought, but occurs whenever one says no to Jesus. Because, for John, Jesus is the Creator Logos in the flesh, saying no to Jesus has ultimate consequences that no future judgment could surpass. On the other hand, "he who believes in the Son has eternal life" (3:36). John's Jesus, therefore, declares, "Truly, truly, I say to you, he who hears my word and believes him who sent me, has eternal life; he does not come into judgment, but has passed from death to life" (5:24).

But the very next paragraph promises the traditional future resurrection.

> The hour is coming, and now is, when the dead will hear the voice of the Son of God, and those who hear will live. . . . The hour is coming when all who are in the tombs will hear his voice and come forth, those who have done good, to the resurrection of life, and those who have done evil, to the resurrection of judgment. (5:25, 28–29)

John evidently works with a double meaning of death. The first meaning of death refers to what we call spiritual deadness. Everyone is spiritually dead until one responds positively to the Son of God, and so finds real life. The second meaning of death is literal, and so refers to all the dead who will be raised as in apocalyptic thought. John affirms the second meaning as part of the Christian tradition, but is really interested in emphasizing the metaphorical meaning: Eternal life can begin now in the midst of ordinary life. Eternal life is not simply endless ordinary life, but a qualitatively different life. This life eternal is not described any more than is Paul's spiritual body. It is affirmed as a gift that one receives whenever one responds positively to Jesus, the incarnate Word. This true life transcends physical death. The person who receives it remains mortal but will be resurrected. As Jesus says later, "For this is the will of my Father, that every one who sees the Son and believes in him should have eternal life, and I will raise him up at the last day" (6:40). It is not explained why resurrection is necessary, but we may assume that the same consideration is at work here as in Paul: What God created, the body, God will redeem.

Another idea is found only in John. During Jesus' last night with the disciples he says, "In my Father's house are many rooms; if it were not so, would I have told you that I go to prepare a place for you? And . . . I will come again and will take you to myself, that where I am you may be also" (14:2–3). In other words, Jesus promises to come to the believers in the hour of death and to take them to where he is—with God in heaven. Here, too, it is not clear why a person who has gone to the heavenly room will still need to be resurrected. In any case, this passage has become one of the most influential in Christian thought, and is read regularly at funerals.

CONCLUSION

By no means have we looked at everything in the New Testament that concerns our topic, but enough has been seen to invite some concluding observations.

To begin with, not only does the New Testament contain a variety of ideas, but even a single author like Paul or a single book like John can say things that do not seem to fit logically. For example, Paul insists on a future resurrection, as we saw, but he also can say that if he should die, he will be with the Lord (Philippians 1:23). We have seen two important reasons for this variety. On the one hand, the New Testament reflects two cultures, the Hebraic and the Hellenistic, both of which had multiple views of death and afterlife. On the other hand, because all Christians believed that Jesus was resurrected, they had to think through the consequences of this event for a whole range of questions, including beliefs about their own death and afterlife. The New Testament shows the various ways they did this in widely differing situations. More comprehensive treatments, based largely but not exclusively on the New Testament, will appear much later, when Christian theologians begin to systematize Christian beliefs.

Second, what the New Testament says about death and afterlife is always part of a much larger complex of ideas. This is inevitable because what one thinks about death and afterlife always affects what one thinks about the current life, and what makes it what it is or ought to be. Death and life are coordinate concepts. This is why, in learning what the New Testament says about death and afterlife, we found it necessary also to consider the nature of the self and the human dilemma and its resolution.

Third, many questions that people have about death and afterlife are simply ignored in the New Testament. One thinks of questions like, Will we know one another in heaven? What will the next life be like? What will happen to those who died before Christ or before they heard of Christ? One passage gives a hint of an answer to this question. According to 1 Peter 3:19–20, Christ "preached to the spirits in prison, who formerly did not obey." This often is taken to mean that Christ, before his resurrection, preached to the dead in Hades. This idea became part of the Apostles' Creed, in the line "He descended to hell" (i.e., to Hades). The theme became popular in medieval art.

Fourth, the New Testament writers consistently assume that each person is unique and of infinite value, even though no writer explains why this is the case. They all believe that the soul is not naturally immortal; none of them thinks that an eternal, immortal soul goes from body to body. There are two reasons for this. On the one hand, the New Testament, like the Old, believes that only God is eternal and that nothing created is coeternal. On the other hand, the idea of the transmigration of eternal souls undermines both the uniqueness of the self and the ultimate consequences of this life. What one does with this life has ultimate significance for the whole person, forever. The New Testament would accept the modern slogan "You only go around once."

Finally, it is clear that the New Testament ideas of death and afterlife are at home in a quite different world from ours. We think differently about the world, time, history, the nature of the self; and we no longer think that Hades is "below" and heaven is "above." As a result, many people no longer take literally what the New Testament says about these matters, but interpret them poetically, regarding them as powerful, and perhaps necessary, religious images that express a deep truth about the self in relation to ultimate reality, to God. In the last analysis, images are more powerful, and more important, than descriptions because images interpret and energize.

The New Testament images of death, resurrection, and eternal life have energized Western culture as well as the Christian community because they are permeated by hope in the face of pain and futility, and because they point to the Creator who does not rest until life is redeemed from death.

NOTES

1. Until the late nineteenth century, Gnosticism was regarded as a Christian heresy that developed in the second century C.E. This view reflected the fact that until then, our knowledge of it depended on the Christian theologians' polemics against its influences in the churches. Since then texts from Egypt, Iraq, and central Asia have been published; this evidence makes it quite probable that "Gnosticism" refers to a widespread religiophilosophical movement that absorbed a great variety of ideas, myths, and practices to explain a sense of alienation from the world and to offer salvation from it. Most scholars regard Gnosticism as a movement that developed alongside early Christianity; some early forms of Gnosticism appear to have influenced Christianity already in the first century. The discovery of a Gnostic library in Egypt (the Nag Hammadi Collection) in 1947 has generated wide-ranging debates over the definition, nature, origin, and influence of Gnosticism. For a useful, succinct discussion, see Elaine H. Pagels, "Gnosticism," *Interpreters Dictionary of the Bible.* Supplementary Volume (Nashville: Abingdon Press, 1976), 364–68. The Nag Hammadi texts are available in *The Nag Hammadi Library in English,* ed. James M. Robinson (New York: Harper & Row, 1977), and Bentley Layton, *The Gnostic Scriptures* (Garden City, N.Y.: Doubleday, 1987). The most important descriptions of and quotations from early Christian opponents of gnosticism are available in Werner Foerster, *Gnosis. A Selection of Gnostic Texts,* trans. and ed. R. McL. Wilson (Oxford: Clarendon Press, 1972), vol. 1, *Patristic Evidence.*

2. The allusion is to the effort of one of the successors of Alexander the Great, Antiochus Epiphanes IV, to prohibit the practice of Judaism in Palestine in 168 B.C.E. This resulted in the Maccabean revolt, whose success three years later is celebrated in the Jewish community with the festival of Hanukkah. The story is told in 1 Maccabees, which is found in what Protestants call "The Apocrypha" and which Roman Catholics regard as deuterocanonical.

3. The Book of Daniel, most scholars agree, was written during the Maccabean revolt.

4. As in the case of Gnosticism (see note 1), scholars continue to debate questions of the nature, origin, and influence of apocalyptic. The word itself comes from the Greek term *apokalypsis,* revelation. It has become clear that one must distinguish texts

that claim to be apocalypses—revelations of the future—from apocalyptic ideas that are found in a wide range of literature. For a convenient survey, see Paul D. Hanson, "Apocalypticism," in *Interpreters Dictionary of the Bible*. Supplementary Volume (Nashville: Abingdon Press, 1976), 28–34. For an introduction to the major Jewish apocalypses, see John J. Collins, *The Apocalyptic Imagination* (New York: Crossroad, 1984). For a discussion of the themes of apocalyptic thought, see Christopher Rowland, *The Open Heaven. A Study in Apocalyptic in Judaism and Early Christianity* (New York: Crossroad, 1982), espec. 73–189.

5. The Gospel of John is treated separately from the Gospels of Matthew, Mark, and Luke because scholars agree that it presents a different portrait of Jesus, for it relies on traditions about his teaching that diverge significantly from those used in the other three (the Synoptic Gospels). Most scholars are convinced that the earliest Gospel is Mark, written about 70 C.E., forty years after the death of Jesus. The others were written later, before 95 C.E. The Letters of Paul, on the other hand, were written in the 50's C.E. In other words, in the New Testament the Gospels come first even though they were written later than the Letters of Paul.

6. "When you give a feast, invite the poor, the maimed, the lame, the blind, and you will be blessed, because they cannot repay you. You will be repaid [i.e., by God] at the resurrection of the just" (Luke 14:13–14).

7. The Pharisees were not priests, but laymen committed to scrupulous observance of the Torah, the Law of Moses. After the Jewish revolt against Rome in 66 to 70 C.E., other groups, like the Sadducees, disappeared, but the Pharisees survived to lay the foundations of rabbinic Judaism.

8. The New Testament contains thirteen letters that claim Paul as their author. Because of the differences in vocabulary, style, and content, critical scholarship has concluded that some of them were probably written in his name by his followers. Although scholars have varying judgments about the genuineness of some of the letters, all agree that seven are beyond dispute: Romans, 1 and 2 Corinthians, Galatians, Philippians, 1 Thessalonians, and Philemon.

9. In 2 Corinthians 5:1–5 Paul appears to have in view a somewhat different scenario, or at least a different detail, for here he does not write of the resurrection that transforms the buried body, but of receiving a heavenly body that apparently already exists, which he calls "a house not made with hands, eternal in the heavens" (v. 1). But even here he is careful to point out that the goal is *not* for the self to be "naked" (stripped of body categorically), but to be "further clothed, so that what is mortal may be swallowed up by life" (v. 5). The passage is difficult, and interpretations vary considerably.

10. One theme found in many forms of Gnosticism is a repudiation of the Creator (often called the Demiurge) as a being greatly inferior to the true God, who is not responsible for the world. It is precisely this cleavage between the true God and the Creator that is rejected by the Apostles' Creed: "I believe in God . . . maker of heaven and earth."

11. The Apocalypse of Peter is available in *The Apocryphal New Testament,* ed. M. R. James (Oxford: Clarendon Press, 1953), and in *New Testament Apocrypha,* ed. E. Hennecke and W. Schneemelcher (Philadelphia: Westminster Press, 1969), vol. 2.

7

Bound Up in the Bond of Life: Death and Afterlife in the Jewish Tradition

Robert Goldenberg

INTRODUCTION

This volume quite properly distinguishes between the scriptures of ancient Israel (the so-called Old Testament) and the literature of postbiblical Judaism: The religion we call Judaism rests on a biblical foundation, but only in the sense that the upper floors of a building rest on its foundation. A building cannot stand without the support of its base, but no good can come of forgetting the difference between them, and those who look in either location for things or people whose place is in the other will end up finding nothing. The reader should keep in mind that except for some references to the very late Book of Daniel, this chapter deals with postbiblical Judaism and not the Bible. The biblical antecedents to Jewish conceptions of death and the hereafter are a subject in their own right, treated elsewhere in this book.

JEWISH ATTITUDES TOWARD THE AFTERLIFE

It will be useful to begin with some general observations. First, it should be remembered that most ideas of the afterlife are ungrounded in experience; to be more exact, the only experience that underlies such conceptions is our experience of learning about them as we grow up. Such conceptions may carry the authority of tradition, but they have no empirical basis, and cannot be confirmed or refuted in the ways that other sorts of ideas usually can be tested. Nevertheless, such conceptions have arisen in many parts of the world and have been preserved because they fill a need: Individuals (or whole cultures) project into the next world the fulfillment of those needs and the satisfaction of those desires that have remained frustrated in this one. The Jews, like all other people, reveal something of their deepest hopes and frustrations in the postmortem dramas they have permitted themselves to imagine.

Second, it must be kept in mind that the Jewish tradition never reduced its conceptions of death, resurrection, and the afterlife to an authoritative dogmatic scheme. Around the year 200 C.E. the Mishnah ruled[1] that anyone who denies the resurrection will be excluded from the World to Come; beyond that single requirement the tradition provided no more than striking images and phrases. These are so powerful that they have given strength to innumerable Jews over many centuries, but there are certain questions the tradition simply does not enable us to answer, questions of the following sort: Will all the dead be resurrected to stand at the Last Judgment, or will the Judgment take place first, to determine which of the dead are worthy of renewed life? Will the Messiah be the judge at this final tribunal, or appear only later to rule over those deemed worthy to witness his glory? Will the Messiah's kingdom last forever, or be followed by something else? Is the so-called World to Come identical with the Messianic kingdom, or something that will come after? The Jewish tradition never supplied a definitive answer to questions such as these; it created the raw materials for a gripping drama but never put them together.

Third, this chapter speaks of Judaism and of Jewish ideas and practices, but not all Jews accept these ideas any more, and not all Jews still observe these practices. Ordinary devoted Jews, people who belong to their local temple and attend it regularly, who frequently read books of Jewish interest and maintain a high level of committed Jewish activity, will react with astonishment to any suggestions that contemporary conceptions of Heaven and Hell have their origin in ancient Judaism. They will insist that Christianity believes in Heaven and Hell, whereas Judaism does not, and will justify their insistence by reporting that their own rabbi has told them so. In fact, classic Jewish sources are full of references to the fate that awaits us after we die. It is true that such references have played a smaller part in Jewish piety than fear of hellfire often has played in Christian piety, and many rabbis of the nineteenth and twentieth centuries have indeed tried to cover them over altogether. Nevertheless, there can be no question that classic Judaism had a strong expectation—disorganized, but strong just the same—that certain events will await us all after we die.

Why would anyone seek to deny these things? Why would anyone want to reject the tremendous religious comfort these ideas have provided? Two important implications arise from these questions. The first arises from the fact already mentioned that all traditional conceptions of the afterlife are nonscientific in the usual senses of that term: They are not based on evidence, and there is no empirical way to test them. As Jews began around 200 years ago to pour out of the European ghettos that had confined them for centuries, they became fervent admirers of the scientific rationalism that inspired those who had let them out; this admiration carried them so far that they began to reject those aspects of their own tradition that rational thought could not support. Belief in an afterlife and divine judgments are examples of this process; they illustrate a far-reaching general change in Jewish religious attitudes over the past two centuries.

The second implication is this: The fate of the individual has never been quite so central in Jewish religious thinking as it necessarily became in Christianity. To drop the concepts of Heaven and Hell from Christianity is to drop the need for salvation, and that is to remove the heart from the Christian religion. To remove these concepts from Judaism leaves certain questions unanswered, but allows the basic outline of the religion to stand. Therefore, when these ideas became embarrassing many rabbis simply removed them from their teaching and filled in the resulting gaps with other things. The resulting transformation succeeded so well that intelligent, well-read people like the ones just mentioned sometimes have no idea that anything of the kind had ever existed.

"The basic outline" of Judaism just mentioned means the following: Later generations of Jews inherited from the Bible a basically collective understanding of their religion. They felt that they belonged to a covenant inaugurated by Moses linking the Creator of the World to the entire people of Israel—the people as a whole, not its members one by one. They understood that the system of reward and punishment laid out all over the Bible, but most clearly in the Book of Deuteronomy, offers its promise and warnings to the nation as a single entity, and they accepted the law brought down by Moses at Sinai as the law of an entire society. This view has extremely important implications for the question of death and afterlife, since after the death of any person a covenant relationship of the kind just described can go on without interruption. As a result of these considerations, classic Jewish thinking saw national catastrophe, not individual extinction, as the worst imaginable disaster; the meaning of history, not the meaning of life, has been the ultimate concern of Judaic thinking. Even for those who shared this point of view death remained a matter of deep concern; men and women will mourn their loved ones whatever the dominant theology, and a vision of projects unfinished or joys unshared will cause anxiety in anyone who contemplates it. Nevertheless, the effort of the covenant people to abide by the law of its God will continue even after any individual is gone.

RABBINICAL CONCEPTIONS OF HUMAN BEING

Despite the similarities just discussed, almost all later Jewish conceptions of human nature differed from biblical forerunners in an important regard. In the Bible[2] the human organism is essentially unitary, an indivisible amalgam of body and animating principle. Death represents not so much the breakdown of this amalgam as its transfer to a new locale, a shadowy other world known as Sheol. Almost all biblical treatments of this matter consider the trip to Sheol a one-way journey; it occasionally was possible to establish contact with the departed shades now exiled there, and some knowledge about what went on there could be acquired, but in the dominant biblical conception all people eventually move from here to there and then stay there forever, some sort of body and some sort of spirit combined.

Later Jewish thinking, possibly under the influence of Greeks or Persians during the period that these two nations ruled Judaea, developed an entirely different conception of human nature, a conception that implied an entirely new understanding of death and its consequences. The human being was now viewed as an artificial and unstable combination of body and something else, and death now appeared as the inevitable rupture of this bond. This conception left room for important differences—some might see the two components of personhood as equally valuable, and therefore see death as a great misfortune, whereas others could see the body as a corrupt prison from which the pure spirit or soul longed to be free, and therefore see death as a kind of liberation—but in either case it now became possible—indeed necessary—to consider the ultimate fates of body, on the one hand, and mind or spirit or soul, on the other, as two separate questions.

The idea that the body, which seems to decompose and disappear after death, might in fact someday be revived finds its first clear expression in the biblical Book of Daniel, dated by most modern scholars to the time of the Maccabees, around 165 B.C.E. It is plausible to see a connection between the circumstances then prevailing and the acceptance of this apparently new idea. Traditional Judaism was then suffering the first major persecution in its history. Those loyal to the Torah as traditionally interpreted were being rounded up for torture and death, whereas those eager to violate its rules and worship after the manner of the Greeks were being lavishly rewarded for this act of betrayal. For the first time in history the biblical link between prosperity and virtue, on the one hand, and wickedness and suffering, on the other, had been turned inside out. Suddenly those who remained faithful to God's Torah were suffering horribly for just this reason, whereas those who eagerly violated that same Torah in public were receiving great honor and reward. This development offered a violent challenge to traditional conceptions of divine justice, and seemed as well to deny the age-old idea that national fidelity to the holy covenant was the only true basis for national well-being; in time it gave rise to the idea that those who constituted the true nation, which meant those who kept the Torah, would indeed inherit God's blessing, even if they had to be roused from the sleep of death to do this.

RESURRECTION AND ITS IMPLICATIONS FOR THE JEWISH FUNERAL PRACTICES

It thus turns out that the idea of resurrection, although the most individualistic of all religious conceptions, has its origin in the collective character of Judaism already described: Those people who would rise from the dead were those who had remained faithful to the nation's ancestral covenant. It turns out as well that an idea apparently separate from the this-worldly dynamic of penalty and reward laid out so sharply in Deuteronomy and other biblical writings may in fact have arisen precisely to defend that dynamic from collapse. In addition, the concept of resurrection maintains the fundamentally positive evaluation of bodily existence presupposed in the Hebrew Bible itself. In all these ways the developing Judaic tradition continued to reflect its scriptural origins even as it began to incorporate breathtaking innovations.

The new ideas of resurrection and afterlife were not welcomed in all Jewish circles. In particular, a group called Sadducees were notorious for their unwillingness to accept these new beliefs. They defended this rejection on the ground that such ideas are not found in scripture, and except for the admittedly very late Book of Daniel, they were more or less correct in this claim. It also is important to note that the Sadducees were the aristocrats of ancient Jewish life, people who enjoyed this world so well that they had no need to look forward to another in which they might enjoy benefits they had missed here. Their thoughts on this subject are recorded in ancient rabbinic literature. "We mock you," they are said to have taunted their rivals, "because you deprive yourselves in this world but then will have no pleasure in any other."[3] In every generation it has been easier for the well-off to be religious scoffers than for those who suffer, but such indifference to the situation of others did not endear the Sadducees to their fellow Jews, and by the end of the second century they had disappeared.

By the time of the Mishnah affirmation of the hope for resurrection had become one of the few dogmatic requirements of the Jewish religion; the Mishnah appropriately warns that those who deny the resurrection will indeed be excluded from the joys of the World to Come. The great philosopher Moses Maimonides (1138–1204) identified this affirmation as one of the thirteen basic principles of Jewish belief, and in the standard basic prayer of the rabbinic liturgy, the so-called Standing Prayer or *ʿAmidah,* the second benediction concludes by acclaiming the Creator for his faithfulness to "those who sleep in the dust" (see Appendix A). This prayer was for centuries recited daily by every Jew in the world.

The belief in resurrection had its effect on Jewish funeral practices as well. Rabbis and others had long been used to compare resurrection to apparently similar processes in nature: The seed disintegrates and gives birth to the new plant, and so, too, the old body decomposes, but the new one springs forth from its dust. This conception led to the idea that even as the body returns to dust, a small bone in the base of the spine, a bone called *luz,* never entirely disappears; this bone eventually becomes the kernel around which the rest of the resurrected body can take form. The need to protect the *luz* from accidental destruction thus assumed enormous importance in Jewish folk conceptions. Those who disappeared at sea were believed to have suffered an unspeakable fate because their bodies could not be laid to rest in the dry ground and there was no telling what might happen to them. Every Jew was considered bound to drop anything else he might be doing and see to the burial of an exposed corpse found by the roadside. This obligation was thought to rest even on those preparing sacrifices for the Holy Temple, despite the fact that contact with the dead would bar them from completing their offering; even a high priest on his way to perform his duties could not go on if he encountered such an anonymous, untended corpse along the road. Such a discovered corpse was called in rabbinic terminology a *met mitzvah,* in literal but clumsy translation an obligatory corpse; Judaism could think of no more sacred act than to bring the remains of such an unfortunate to burial. The need to preserve the dead body from utter destruction also is one of the roots of the well-known and ancient Jewish abhorrence of cremation. Even during those centuries that the nations among whom Jews lived practiced cremation rather widely, the Jews themselves avoided this means of laying their dead to rest.

No single one of these attitudes is unique to Judaism. Anthropologists tell of many cultures in which an unburied corpse provokes dread and must, therefore, be removed from view; the ancient Greek tale of Antigone is perhaps a familiar example of the anxiety that could be provoked when the obligation to bury the dead could not properly be carried out. Psychologists, too, have studied the importance of offering a last farewell to beloved figures who have died, so it is not surprising to learn how difficult it must have been when the death of loved ones could not be confirmed and their bodies laid to rest. In the particular case of Judaism, it also is important to remember the tradition that Adam and Eve were created in the image of God, along with the paradoxically contrasting notion that the punishment of Adam and Eve when they were expelled from the Garden of Eden included the detail that their bodies would someday have to return to the dust from which they had been made.

Jewish funeral practices thus reflect many basic considerations. There is a tradition, for example,[4] that Rabban Gamaliel in the first century C.E. decreed that all people, whether rich or poor, should be buried in simple white shrouds; Gamaliel had in mind here the important idea that all Jews stand equal in the sight of their creator, and was concerned that no one be put to shame in his last appearance on earth.[5] The strong Jewish aversion to any burial practice, such as cremation or embalming, that prevents the natural decomposition of the body reflects the ancient tradition that all people, although created in the image of God, are destined to return to dust; Jewish tradition did not want to see the image of God consigned to the flames, or our return to the dust held back by artificial means. Finally, it is important in this connection to mention the traditional Jewish conception of the stages of mourning. In contrast with the widespread Christian custom of a public wake before the funeral, Jewish bereaved are left alone with their grief until after the departed have been buried and the last responsibilities of the living carried out. Then, for a week after the funeral, they stay at home but remain surrounded by their friends and relatives while their grief subsides. After this brief, but intensive mourning they gradually return to normal activities, in part after a month and in full after a year. (For Jewish prayers of mourning, see Appendix B.)

PHILO AND MAIMONIDES: THE IMMORTALITY OF THE DISEMBODIED SOUL

Since ancient times there has been alongside the belief in resurrection a well-known alternative conception of personal survival after death: the immortality of the soul. By the time of the Greeks and the Romans there was a widespread tendency to conceive of every human being as an unhappy partnership, so to speak, between a bodily and a nonbodily element. Either of these could become the focus of the hope or expectation that death is not the complete end of our existence. More favorable conceptions of bodily or material existence led people to conceive such survival in terms of resurrection or restoration of the body, whereas hostility to material existence led others to hope for something else. The rabbinic traditions preserved in the Talmud and related writings are of the first sort, and represent the predominant attitude among Jews, an attitude inherited from the Bible itself: Our bodies, too, are part of divine creation, and our existence as human beings is inconceivable without them. On the other hand, the Jewish philosopher Philo, who lived in Egypt during the first century C.E., represents the most successful ancient blending of Jewish tradition with Greek philosophy; he clearly followed the second course. Here is Philo's description of the fate he expects for his body and soul, respectively, after he dies: ''But then we who are here joined to the body, creatures of composition. . . , shall be no more, but shall go forward to our rebirth, to be with the unbodied, without composition'' (*de Cherubim,* 114). Philo speaks of rebirth, but not of his body; he evidently expects that his body, a product, as he puts it, of composition, eventually will decompose and simply disappear. Indeed, the highest bliss he can imagine is to join the unbodied, as he calls them, to be free of his body forever.

Now Philo lived in the most deeply Hellenized Jewish community known; he lived surrounded by Greek culture, before the rabbis' rise to prominence in Jewish life, and outside the area in which rabbinic teachings first appeared. In the mainstream rabbinic tradition as well a similar idea eventually gained wide circulation under the name of the World to Come. In its origin this conception reflected the hope that the current world, with its sorrows and oppression, would soon be replaced by a better one. This coming world would not necessarily differ from the current one in a dramatic way; it would simply be better, chiefly in the sense that the righteous would overcome their subjection to the wicked and inherit the power that properly belonged to them.

Certain visionaries, to be sure, had from the beginning imagined this future world in a much more dramatic way; the Bible contains Isaiah's famous prophecy[6] of lions resting peacefully with lambs, and also led the way toward linking such dramatic imagery to the basic themes of the Jewish religion, as in Ezekiel's vision of the dry bones,[7] in which the image of decomposed bodies being reassembled and brought back to life represents the exiled Judaeans' hope for restoration to their homeland. At the time of the Book of Daniel the idea that the martyred righteous of Israel would be restored to life apparently implied that the scene of their renewed lives would be a world rather like this one, except that they could enjoy the honor and strength so cruelly denied them so far. In this early stage the concept of a World to Come still presumed an earthly world to come, one that would be enjoyed by the righteous in their resurrected bodies.

As time went on the imagined future world came to differ more and more radically from the world in which we all now live. Most strikingly, the rewards of the World to Come came to be detached from bodily pleasure. Not all Jewish teachers approved of such detachment, and some continued to talk of a banquet reserved for the righteous at which they would feast on the flesh of legendary creatures such as Leviathan and Behemoth[8]; by the period of the Talmud (300–500 C.E.) others conceived of the World to Come as one in which there would be no eating or drinking or urge to reproduce the species.[9] This conception is far from the ideal that death represents a separation of body and spirit that must be overcome; this is really another version of Philo's notion (though the early rabbis did not get it from him) that death represents an opportunity for our souls to escape their fleshly jailhouses.

Those trying to integrate this idea into the rabbinic tradition faced a rather difficult task; the hope for resurrection of the body and the hope for disembodied bliss in the World to Come represent ideas in tension, and it is not obvious how or why any single person should accept them both. Philo most emphatically did not; his great successor Maimonides about a thousand years later agreed with him philosophically but faced a different situation. In the meantime the rabbinic tradition had assumed a dominant role in Jewish religious thought all over the world, and the rabbinic tradition taught that anyone who denies the resurrection is a heretic with no personal hope of redemption.

Maimonides' solution to this dilemma was to affirm the doctrine of resurrection, indeed to list it among the indispensable dogmas of the Jewish religion, but then to define the ultimate bliss of the World to Come in such a way that there was no need for resurrection. For Maimonides, the experience of the World to Come was one of disembodied union with the Active Intellect, which, in rather crude shorthand, can be identified with the mind of God. For Maimonides, such union was quite impossible for those still tied to bodily existence; in fact, emancipation from the body was one of the aspects of such union that made it so attractive for him. It was difficult for others to believe that he was genuinely looking forward to the restoration of his bodily existence after he had been freed of it, and he was accused of having dropped the resurrection under cover of theological double-talk; finally, in the year 1191, he wrote an impassioned essay denying these accusations. It is not for a modern reader to give a ruling on Maimonides' sincerity; he has had his passionate defenders and equally passionate detractors for almost 800 years. He does represent, however, a striking example of one of the features of Judaism mentioned early in this chapter: Jewish tradition presents a varied picture of the ultimate fate of humanity, and sometimes even the greatest Jewish thinkers have had trouble ironing out the variations and creating a single clear version that all Jews everywhere could be expected to affirm.

THE FINAL JUDGMENT

One link between the two great images of future bliss under discussion was provided by the third great Jewish contribution to eschatology, the idea of a final judgment. The idea of the Last Judgment links the concepts of resurrection and the World to Come, though in a way that allows for no definite relation among them; recall the earlier question whether all the dead will be raised to stand for judgment, or first be judged according to their records and only the worthy among them then allowed to enter the bliss of renewed life. Because no evidence is available according to which such matters can be decided, those who consider these questions must acknowledge that we cannot ever answer them with certainty; the Jewish tradition implies just such an acknowledgment in its inability over history to work out a final, universally accepted dogmatic teaching in regard to matters of this kind.

Despite such uncertainties, rabbinic teachers eagerly looked forward to the time when divine judgment would separate those who had lived as one should—that is, according to the Torah—from those who had not.[10] The same chapter of the Mishnah that begins by excluding those who deny the resurrection from the World to Come goes on to list various categories of biblical villains: Certain wicked kings have no place in the World to Come; the generation of the Flood neither has a place in the World to Come nor any hope even of facing judgment; the people of Sodom and Gomorrah, two cities miraculously destroyed on account of their wickedness, have no place in the World to Come but will be allowed to stand at judgment; and so on.[11] It may seem that being allowed to stand at judgment is no great advantage when you know in advance that you will be found wanting, but such distinctions teach the modern reader how important these hopes were to many, many people over a long period of time.

The notion that all human beings will finally have to give an accounting of their lives became part and parcel of the Jewish folk consciousness. The sacred text most often studied by the common folk over the long centuries of Jewish history is a tractate of the Mishnah commonly known in English translation as the *Ethics of the Fathers;* this long collection of aphorisms contains repeated exhortations that reflect the beliefs described in this chapter. Each good deed, said R. Eliezer ben Jacob (4:11), becomes a defense advocate on our behalf, whereas each bad deed becomes a prosecutor; the court before which these attorneys will plead is left unnamed, but the reference would have been clear enough to anyone who heard this saying.[12] Elsewhere (2:1) Rabbi Judah the Patriarch, editor of the Mishnah, identifies the court in question more clearly: "Keep your eye on three things and you will never come to transgression. Know what is above you: a seeing eye, a hearing ear, and all the deeds written into a book." The most eloquent of these references (4:22, by R. Eleazar haKappar) amounts to a complete existential statement:

> Those who are born are destined to die, those who die are destined to return to life, and those who return to life are destined for judgment. . . . Know that all is according to the accounting of deeds, and do not let your [wicked] impulse assure you that the grave can be your refuge, for against your will you are formed, and against your will you are born, and against your will you live, and against your will you die, and against your will you are destined to give an accounting to the Blessed Holy One, the King of all kings.

More than 1,500 years later the famed Yiddish author Y. L. Peretz (1852–1915) could use these same themes in his most powerful and best-known stories; in a tale called "Three Gifts" Peretz wrote of a man who had committed exactly the same number of good and bad deeds in his life and so was permitted to return to earth just long enough to bring back three gifts for the heavenly tribunal that would tip the scales in his favor, while in a famous and rather subtly satirical tale called "Buntshe the Silent" *(Buntshe Shveig)* Peretz wrote of a man who had been so saintly that even the heavenly prosecutor could find nothing to say against him when he stood before the heavenly court. These stories were written in the twentieth century, a time when sophisticated intellectuals might have been expected to mock such simple conceptions, yet these ideas remained part of the nation's cultural heritage and found their way into literary classics treasured even by those who no longer accept the old beliefs.

CONCLUSION

In the centuries after the completion of the Bible, Jews developed two conceptions of human nature, one that preserved the Bible's own positive evaluation of the body and one that did not. Each of these conceptions suggested a different way of imagining the bliss that awaits the righteous at some later time: Positive evaluation of the body required that the body be restored to life before such bliss could have any meaning, whereas negative evaluation of the body required, on the contrary, that the truly precious part of our being—our spirit, or soul, or mind—be liberated from its material prison to enjoy its own proper reward. Some rabbinic teachers eventually combined these two conceptions into a single, rather unclear scheme, affirming both the resurrection of the dead and the disembodied bliss of the World to Come, whereas for others, the World to Come simply meant a world like this one in which the righteous would live when they were restored to life. A drama of judgment came to play an important role in people's expectations. It was important to know that only those judged worthy would ever enjoy these blessings and that a time was coming when all people, or at least all members of the covenant people of Israel, would be brought for review before a divine judge, perhaps the Creator himself, perhaps one charged by the Creator with this task.

Even before the ancient world had given way to the Middle Ages, almost all Jews everywhere had embraced one form or another of these basic beliefs. These particular conceptions have by now lost much of their following among Jews, but the general attitudes they reflect have survived even among so-called modernized or emancipated Jews; they represent deeply ingrained and remarkably persistent features of modern Jewish life. The story of their survival and transformation in the modern world is a fascinating chapter in its own right, but goes too far beyond the subject matter of this book for inclusion here.

NOTES

1. Sanhedrin 10.1.
2. See chapter 5 in this volume.
3. Cf. Avot de-Rabbi Nathan, ch. 5.
4. Mo'ed Qatan 27a–b.
5. This tradition offers a good example of the observation above that many contemporary Jews have abandoned large parts of their heritage; we now live in a day of $6,000 funerals, not uniform white shrouds.
6. Isaiah 11:1–9.
7. Ezekiel 37.
8. See Bava Batra 74b, Leviticus Rabba 13:3.
9. Berakhot 17a.
10. Goodness and following the Torah were considered more or less interchangeable concepts, at least for Jews.
11. See Genesis 19.
12. The abbreviation "R." stands for "Rabbi."

APPENDIX A: THE JEWISH AFFIRMATION OF THE RESURRECTION

The following is the second paragraph of the so-called Prayer of Eighteen Benedictions *('Amidah)* recited every day by observant Jews. It portrays resurrection of the dead as a sign of both the power and the loving faithfulness of the Creator.

> You, O Lord, are mighty forever; you give life to the dead, you have great power to save. You sustain the living with loving kindness and revive the dead with great mercy; you support those who fall, heal those who are sick, release those who are captive, and keep your faith with those who sleep in the dust. Who is like you, powerful Master, and who resembles you, O King who kills, gives life, and brings forth salvation? You are faithful to bring the dead to life; blessed are You, O Lord, who revives the dead.

APPENDIX B: JEWISH PRAYERS OF MOURNING

The following prayer is recited at all occasions of memorial in Jewish life: at the funeral or on the anniversary of the death of a loved one, or at the public memorial service *(Yizkor)* held at each of the major festival seasons of the Jewish year. The reference to the "bond of life" that has given its name to this chapter is taken from the Bible—1 Samuel 25:29.

O God full of mercy who dwells in heaven, prepare perfect rest under the wings of Your presence, in the ranks of the pure and holy, shining like the splendor of the firmament, to the spirit of . . . who has gone to his eternal [home]. May his rest be in Paradise; may the Merciful One shelter him forever in the protection of His wings, and bind his spirit into the bond of life—the Lord is his inheritance; may he rest in peaceful repose, and let us say Amen.

The "Mourner's Kaddish" is the Jewish prayer most commonly associated with death and mourning, yet its text barely makes reference to these themes. It received its name because mourners were thought to earn merit for their departed relatives by reciting this prayer at the end of every public service of worship; this gave the entire congregation one last chance to join together in reverent praise. All words printed in italics are recited by the entire congregation, the rest by the mourners alone.

May His great name be magnified and sanctified *(Amen)* in the world He created according to His will. May He establish His kingdom in your lives, during your days, and during the lives of all Israel, quickly and soon, and say, Amen.

May His great name be blessed forever and for all eternity.

Blessed, praised, glorified, exalted, elevated and beautiful, high and honored be the name of the Holy One *(may He be blessed),* above all blessings and hymns, praises and consolations that have ever been spoken, and say, *Amen.*

May abundant peace from heaven, and life, come upon us and upon all Israel, and say, *Amen.*

May the One who makes peace in His heavens also make peace upon us and upon all Israel, and say, *Amen.*

8

Death and Eternal Life in Christianity

Hiroshi Obayashi

DEATH, RESURRECTION, AND THE KINGDOM OF GOD

Eschatology is a religious thought about the end times toward which the whole of history is viewed as a process. Evaluating the current situation in the light of the end (politically, socially, morally, as well as religiously) and choosing a future course of action accordingly were practices already known in Old Testament prophecy. But given the historical experience of oppression, exile, and humiliation that the Jews experienced during the last several centuries before the Common Era, the old prophetic outlook was no longer sufficiently comforting and motivating to the suffering people in Judea. They needed a stronger, more urgent sense of hope that conventional prophecy could not offer. A new resource was needed to be tapped for renewed inspiration. This was apocalypticism. The apocalyptists envisioned their future not as the smooth outcome of the process from the past and present, but rather its abrupt termination and the introduction by God of the utterly new. The apocalyptic envisioning of the future often has inspired a revolutionary fervor through the announcement of the end of the old age and the impending arrival of the new as its negation.

In the midst of this apocalyptic situation Christianity arose. The disciples of Jesus were so thoroughly steeped in the apocalyptic eschatology; they lived with a sense of imminence about the approaching end of the world, which they believed would be brought swiftly by Jesus himself with his triumphant second coming. This Final Judgment that will end the current history, replacing it with a new reign of the Messiah, they believed, would happen within their own lifetimes, vindicating at last God's justice and goodness for the faithful. And it was for this purpose that the raising of the just and then of all the dead would take place.

The apocalyptically conceived Christianity was not supposed to last for a long time. It was a movement announcing the quick end of history, thus necessarily a quick end of itself. So when the Christian movement lasted for more than a century it was forced to reinterpret its own message. In the apocalyptic framework the relationship between the postmortem fate of the individual, whether in heaven or in hell, that is to ensue the departure from the current life, on the one hand, and the final universal judgment of all humankind, on the other, did not present much problem. Whether the dead are believed to be "asleep" or not, the cosmic end was so near at hand that all would be brought to stand in judgment one way or the other. When the final end began to be conceived as far away, Christians were forced to rethink about death and afterlife as independent issues from, though still in close dialectical relationship with, the end times. And in this rethinking the biblical dualism about human beings—as sharply divided into the fleshly existence that is corrupt and the spiritual being that is holy—played an important part. Though the influence of oriental and Greek dualism of body and soul is evident, the early Christian dualism, particularly that of Paul, was not that of two constituent elements in one human being. It was a dualism between one form of life governed by the principle of flesh and another guided by the principle of spirit. No human being who remains in the former can enjoy the vision of God and eternal life. One has to be reborn, recreated by divine power into a spiritual being—die to the old self and be raised into a new self. The death and resurrection of Jesus Christ, the Son of God, made it possible for all humankind to undergo such a transformation. This became the fundamental pattern in understanding death and afterlife for the Christianity of the early centuries as well as the Middle Ages and further, both in doctrine and in popular piety.

To start with "death," Christianity is convinced from the early period of its history that human beings are mortal. Any attempt to see them as immortal and infinite is rebuffed by the power of God, the creator. Human beings as creatures possess no "natural" immortality of their own. Natural immortality would be an endless life apart from any relationship with God. A demon's immortality as conceived by the popular belief is a case in point. Though fallen and rejected by God, the demon does not have to die the way human beings do. Such an immortality without God's blessing means no more than a curse. Tatian (c. 160), an early Christian father, unequivocally denied that human beings possessed any immortality of that kind. "Living endlessly" in itself contains no delight, or any good. It is living in communion with God that makes immortality delightful and desirable. For this reason Christianity prefers to use the expression "the eternal life" instead of "immortality" to avoid its vicious implication of a meaningless prolongation of life. There is "nothing desirable about living forever. Those who ask for an endless life should realize what they are getting into. Not immortality, but the life eternal, is a good to be pursued and cherished. For Christianity 'the life eternal' means . . . being alive in God, both now and always."[1] Grasping for (natural) immortality on one's own is not only a futile attempt, but also, even if possible, will never lead to a desirable state. Human beings are mortal, and only by faith in God's power of resurrection, conquering death, can they hope to be raised into a new life. Thus Christian faith does not preach the circumvention of death; it teaches the acceptance and overcoming of death as exemplified by the cross of Jesus himself.

Deeply historical in orientation, the early Christianity refused to speculate beyond the confine of the historical existence of human beings. Tatian and other early fathers are firmly rooted in the New Testament attitude in this respect. It was Clement of Alexandria (c.150–c.250) who, influenced by Greek thought, was tempted to let his imagination fly into the realm of immortality.[2] His preoccupation with what lies beyond the mortal existence of human life only led to the depreciation of the significance of earthly, historical life a la Greek philosophy. Origen (c.185–c.254), also influenced by a version of Platonism, crossed the creaturely boundary over to speculate about the eternality of the human soul by espousing the idea of its preexistence, which had to be condemned by a church council in the sixth century.[3]

So the immortality that the Christians could embrace was not "natural" immortality, but that which is the gift of God realized by Christ. Early Christian fathers, particularly those of the Greek-speaking world, such as Irenaeus, understood the work accomplished by Christ to be not only the destruction of sin, but, more important, the achievement of immortality for the rest of humankind.[4] Human beings, as those Greek fathers considered did initially, have a created capacity for immortality, but losing that capacity because of the fall, they found themselves in inescapable mortality. It is exactly the restoration of this possibility of immortality that the saving work of Christ accomplished for all humankind. Salvation means to them the gift of immortality from God made possible by the work of his begotten Son.

To acknowledge mortality still leaves open possibilities of two attitudes on the part of the Christians toward death: one that views it as an opportunity for a renewal or a step in the process toward a higher plane of life, and the other that abhors death as the wage of sin, unavoidable only because sin is unavoidable because of the fall. Augustine is the most eloquent exponent of the latter, which later formed the mainstream idea. It was by Augustine that Paul's position in the New Testament about death's having entered into the destiny of humankind because of the fall was made decisive for the official teaching of the church. Augustine (354–430), the North African theologian who represents the pinnacle of the ancient Christian thinking, consummating the development of the early theology and vastly influential over the ensuing history of medieval Christianity, carries the torch of the paradox of death. Death is an inexorability of nature, on the one hand. But on the other hand, Augustine refused to yield to the naturalistic acceptance of it. We all die naturally but without acquiescing to its naturality.[5] Death has that dimension that defies simple naturalistic explanation. For how else does it hold such a terror to all human beings?

If, then, death is evil and the wage of sin, does that mean, since we all inevitably die, that we are all defeated by this common enemy? To deal with this question Augustine differentiates two kinds of death. One is the separation of the soul from the body, which he calls "the first death." What he calls "second death" occurs only with the Final Judgment, when the damned are forsaken by God. So, "of the first and bodily death," Augustine maintains, "then, we may say that to the good it is good, and evil to the evil. But doubtless, the second, as it happens to none of the good, so it can be good for none."[6]

So for "the first death" there is a possibility of bearing a positive significance, especially when it is the death that vindicates the unswerving faith of the martyrs. The good, that is, those redeemed by grace, have but to suffer the first death. They "do not pass to that second endless and penal death." With this theological tactic Augustine manages to preserve a special and positive significance for the deaths of the good and righteous that occur within the framework of the universality of the first death. And it is the mercy and power of God demonstrated through Christ's conquest of death that overpowers the evil of death to make it serve the ultimate goodness. "Not that death, which was before an evil, has become something good, but only that God has granted to faith this grace, that death, which is the admitted opposite to life, should become the instrument by which life is reached."[7]

One reason for this persistence on the part of Augustine in connecting death to sin is that the Christians perceive death to be a phenomenon that runs counter to God's creation, the divine act of calling things, including life, into being. Death is seen as a counterforce that pushes them out of being. If being is good, then death that is seen to occasion nonbeing must be its opposite, evil. Another reason is that Christians believe that Christ's redemptive act effected, among other things, the conquest of death. Death is opposition to God's redemptive as well as creative act. Christ accomplished the redemptive task by conquering the power of death for humankind, not in the sense of removing "the first death" from all humankind, but in the sense of not allowing the final word to death, even when it occurs to all humankind without exception. For those who believe in Christ, death, even with its full power of negation, is made to serve the goodness of God.

The realization by the Christians after the first century of the apparent postponement of the final end resulted in toning down the overtly futuristic language. Christians understandably shifted the emphasis from the remote eschatological future to the present and the immediate future that awaits a person after death. What was the futuristic kingdom of God in the New Testament became in the popular imagination a heavenly region of reward prepared for the individual souls to enter on departure from the earthly life through God's judgment and admission. Heaven is now timelessly available at any point in time, not only at the end of history. On the other hand, on the theological level, it came increasingly to imply a sphere of influence already present and spreading that manifests itself in the reality of the visible institution of the earthly church, though not identical with it. This is the manner in which Augustine conceived his "City of God." The City of God is the domain of influence in which love of God *(amor Dei)* prevails as its guiding principle, whereas the earthly city *(civitas terrena)* is the domain of the power of self-love *(amor sui)*. The Roman empire is the embodiment of the latter but not identical with it. Augustine sees the history of humankind as the stage on which the drama is unfolded by the struggle of these two forces for ultimate victory of the City of God over the other. In this sense the kingdom of God is very much behind the spreading influence of the earthly church.

Augustine interpreted the early Christian teaching according to the requirements of the changing historical situations into which Christianity survived. He has little to say about "heaven." And when he does refer to it, it is only because references are made to it in the Bible itself. He always uses a thoroughly symbolic and, at times, allegorical interpretation to the biblical heaven and hell.[8] It was the City of God in the transcendent but at the same time historical sense of the term, that in which he invested his entire theological energy, leaving heaven and hell mostly to the popular imagination.

Augustine's theological thinking becomes even more pointed if we focus on the topic of resurrection. Just as he differentiated between the first and second deaths, he now distinguishes two concepts of resurrection. By the first resurrection Augustine refers to the regeneration that is effected by means of baptism in the current life. It is the resurrection according to faith. The second is the bodily resurrection that is to take place on the Judgment Day at the end of time.[9]

Thus Augustine, by assigning the second, bodily resurrection to the Judgment Day, highlights the importance that he attaches to the first resurrection, which is to happen to us in our current life, the resurrection from death (the life lived in sin) to life (the life lived in God's grace). He even chides those who confuse the two to believe as if the second one were going to happen to the current life, branding them "spiritual chiliasts" or "millennarians" in the derisive sense of these terms.[10] Augustine's emphasis falls on the first resurrection because that is what ensures that the soul, when brought to the second (bodily) resurrection at the Final Judgment, "shall not come into damnation . . . ; into which death, after the second and bodily resurrection they shall be hurled who do not rise in the first or spiritual resurrection."[11] So the weight of the biblical concept of resurrection was in substance concentrated in what he considers the most crucial, that is, the first resurrection in the sense of "redemption" (from the divine point of view) or "conversion" (from the human point of view). The resurrection in the bodily sense is preserved in his discourse only because it is, in the tradition, implying almost that it is no longer crucial to the Christian faith. For he accepts healthy skepticism about such a bodily resurrection when he says, "[B]ut if we are unable perfectly to comprehend the manner in which it shall take place, our faith is not on this account vain."[12]

Furthermore, even this "bodily resurrection" of the Final Judgment is no longer understood by Augustine in a literal sense. Using the distinction between the flesh and the body, the former representing the physical and organic aspects of the human life and the latter, the totality of one's existence, Augustine removes the veil of absurdity from the "resurrection of the body." It is the raising of the person who is understood mainly in terms of his soul after physical death, not the turning of the flesh into spirit. The flesh cannot be turned into the spirit. It can only be made spiritual by being brought under the control of the spirit. "For as," Augustine says, "when the spirit serves the flesh, it is fitly called carnal, so, when the flesh serves the spirit, it will justly be called spiritual. Not that it is converted into spirit, . . . but because it is subject to the spirit with a perfect and marvellous readiness of obedience, has entered on immortality."[13]

HEAVEN, HELL, AND PURGATORY

As was made clear by Leander Keck in chapter 6, the message of the New Testament was addressed to the issues of death, resurrection, and the kingdom of God, not so much heaven, hell, and purgatory. Though the references are by no means scarce in the Bible to this latter set of concepts, and in fact Christ is indeed described to have ascended to heaven or even references to hell are ascribed to Jesus himself (Matthew 25:30, 41), they did not constitute the central thrust of the biblical message. So the major theological developments through the history of Christianity also maintained the same focus, as did the Bible, of death, resurrection, and the kingdom of God. It was mostly the popular piety, which is no less important to the life of the Christians, that fostered and kept alive beliefs about heaven, hell, and purgatory. The popular beliefs about heaven and hell developed, particularly through the Middle Ages, with their increasingly vivid imagery. With the final universal judgment pushed back into a remote future, people's concern became sharply focused on the individual fate immediately after their death. The dualism of soul and body now firmly set by the Middle Ages, forming the Roman Catholic pattern of understanding the constitution of the human being, death was considered the separation of the soul from the body. The postmortem journey of the soul to heaven or hell became the most widely accepted pattern of understanding the destiny of the departed. This type of understanding relying heavily on the pictorial imagery, we find that the soul in turn often was depicted in corporeal terms as traveling to or residing in heaven or hell, and enjoying the bliss or suffering the pain of torment therein. Heaven and hell are conceptually integrated, and sometimes even physically located, within the three-tiered Ptolemaic universe of the Middle Ages. Heaven always up above and hell down below, the departed souls are to be consigned to their respective deserts. The Old Testament word for "heaven" denoted the physical sky where God's abode was, and only special people, such as Enoch and Elijah, were thought to be raised there. Though the New Testament continued to locate heaven high above the earth to which Christ raised his eyes in prayer (Mark 6:41), Christians began to consider it to be opened to all the faithful. For Christians, the distinctive accomplishment of Christ was the conquest of death, thereby liberating all the faithful from the yoke of death and preparing them for the entry into heaven. All the biblical themes about heaven were revived and kept vivid in the medieval art and literature. Heaven is where there is no more privation, pain, or sorrow. It is where joy and pleasure prevail in God's presence with all the problems of this world eliminated. In heaven, souls were to be reunited with those of all the loved ones who preceded them, even though apparently the earthly relationships, such as between husband and wife, were not supposed to be carried over into it. There the inestimable spiritual rewards and compensations await those who suffer unjustly in this world, or toil for justice's sake; the final truth is to be revealed to those who seek it. In short, the ultimate blissfulness characterizes this community of all souls now redeemed and perfected to the level at which they can see God face to face.

Heaven is the realm of perfection. Humans are in the state in which God meant them to be in "creation in His own image," God-oriented and totally free of moral imperfections. But "perfection" connotes "no further growth," which in turn implies staticity or inactivity. Though logical consistency is not an important part of ancient religious imagination, particularly about heaven and hell, "perfection" does have such undesirable implication of inactivity. If activity and growth are the hallmarks of life, then their absence could imply lifelessness or death. Perfection ascribed to heaven, therefore, had to be carefully qualified so as not to lead to such an opposite effect. Thus heaven was meticulously conceived as a community in which fellowship takes place among the blessed human souls and between them and God. This heavenly fellowship is the prototype and support for the fellowship among Christians *(sanctorum communio)* in this world.

Heaven, thus, is not a realm of such a deadening boredom, but of an ongoing activity of those saved who enjoy the beatific vision of God. No longer corporeal, the citizens of heaven require no optical medium to see God "face to face." It is more an intellectual "seeing," unmediated perception, or even "knowing" of God immediately. In this beatific vision of God, the knowing of God transcends the earthly epistemological framework of the subject knowing the object, that is, the ordinary gulf between the knower and the known. The blessed will know God in contemplative interpenetration with God's knowing of himself. Thomas Aquinas (1225–74), the monumental theologian of medieval Scholasticism, was the most eloquent proponent of the theology that made this beatific vision the ultimate goal of human beings, whose created purpose as intellectual beings was to know God. Faced with the infinite fullness of God, the created intellect of human beings will never cease to wonder and enjoy in amazement the inexhaustible source of knowledge, God himself.

Quite in contrast, hell evolved from the archaic concept of the underworld. As we learned in the chapters on ancient Mesopotamia and the Old Testament, the underworld, called Sheol in the Hebrew scripture, was initially the place of all the dead, regardless of their moral worth. It was only later in Jewish history and then in Christianity that this underworld of all the dead was bifurcated into the realm of reward (heaven) and punishment (hell, Gehenna). Hell came to denote the underworld to which unrepentant sinners were to be consigned. Sinners were to be cast into "outer darkness" with weeping and gnashing of teeth (see Matthew 25:30), or they are to be thrown into "eternal" (Matt. 25:41) or "unquenchable fire" (Mark 9:43), or even into a "lake that burns with fire and sulphur" (Rev. 21:8).

These and other graphic depictions of hell notwithstanding, the biblical references to hell still leave room for the understanding of hell simply as the opposite of God's blessing. That is to say, instead of being the physical place of torment, hell was still a metaphorical reference to the state of being excluded from God's fellowship. Being left in the state of sin, hence excluded from God's grace, in itself already constitutes a punitive measure, without an additional punishment, say, of "going to hell," awaiting. In other words, in the New Testament "hell fire" still maintained nuances that permitted it to be a metaphorical reference to "falling out of" and "being excluded from" God's grace (e.g., Hebrews 10:27), just as much as "heaven" was a metaphorical expression of being "in grace."

It was not so much the Old Testament itself as the later rabbinical teachings in Judaism, not so much the New Testament itself as the teaching of the later church in Christianity, that solidified the concept of hell as a place of punitive torment with all the gory details of gruesome torture under which the sinners are to suffer the unending pain. Dante's *Divine Comedy* and Milton's *Paradise Lost* are the definitive literary representations of the widespread beliefs about hell, established enough to find their way into the teachings of the church.

It is understandable that the beliefs in hell's torment in the literal sense were needed, and actually functioned for many centuries as the "carrot and stick" for the moral fabric of Christendom as well as the encouragement for faith and repentance. But Christians have always been aware of the absurdities and the logical gap between the infinitely forgiving God of love and the sadistic cruelty of the unending punishment. The major thrust of the gospel of Jesus was in God's love and forgiveness. To exact infinite agonies of punishment for finite human acts of sin is too sadistic to befit God, who even fulfills justice through love, the love that could only be expressed through self-sacrifice. So there has always been an undercurrent in Christian sentiment that even hell is not final. Those damned, though they may have to remain in hell for a long time for punishment, ultimately will be restored from there into heaven. This undercurrent of "universal salvation," surfacing often since the ancient times, is an important impulse of the Christian faith.

As heaven and hell were conceptually separated and firmly established in the medieval Christian minds into two ultimate realms of reward and punishment with such graphic details of celestial blissfulness and ghastly underworld pain, some unresolved practical problems arose in popular piety. The idea of purgatory addresses these problems.

The great majority of us are aware of our own inadequacies, whether we openly admit it or not. If heaven represents the beatific condition in fellowship with God and all angelic beings, then most of us ordinary human beings who die in a state of moral and religious imperfection realize that we are not ready for it. For this reason a thought has come to prevail in popular piety since ancient times that there should be an intermediate realm between this world and heaven. This intermediate state or place, called "purgatory," finds references in the Old and New Testaments as well as among the church fathers throughout the early centuries. But it was not until the councils of Lyons (1274) and Florence (1439) that the Roman Catholic Church gave it an official definition, though it did not go beyond the points that such a region exists and that prayer and merit-making are valid means to prepare for it. In purgatory a process of cleansing and purifying takes place by way of the pain of fire. Though the capital (mortal) sins lead one directly to the damnation of hell, venial (minor) sins are dealt with differently. They are to be expurgated in purgatory so that one may be purified enough to be ready for admission into heaven. Concurrent with purgatory is the idea of indulgence developing through the history of the Roman Catholic church, which is the remission of the temporal punishment of the venial sins. It is this temporal punishment that takes place in purgatory, from which the sinner is expected to emerge cleansed and ready for the final beatitude. The indulgence, then, is the remission of this limited punishment in purgatory, or a shortening of the stay therein.

As developed by the church, the practice of indulgence involved praying, doing penance, and merit-making in preparation for the eventual departure from this world and the journey through purgatory. For hundreds of years during the Middle Ages this practice remained important for vast numbers of Christians in Europe, playing an integral part in the process of salvation in Catholic theology. As the validity of the belief of indulgence and purgatory became fully established, the practice was extended from the living, preparing for their own postmortem itinerary, to the souls of the deceased, who are believed to be in purgatory already. By the end of the Middle Ages praying and merit-making by the living on behalf of their deceased relatives had developed into a major religious practice. Offering masses for the souls of the dead became widespread and deeply rooted in popular piety, enough for the church to consider it an adequate basis for the institution of the sale of indulgence. That the financial abuse of the religious beliefs of purgatory and indulgence ignited the fuse for the world-historical event of the Protestant Reformation is too well known to be recounted here. The practice of the sale of indulgence provoked Martin Luther (1483–1546) into uttering unsavory diatribes such as, "No doubt the majority [of the papal hierarchy] would starve to death if purgatory did not exist," and

> How can you bear on your conscience the blasphemous fraud of purgatory, by which treacherous deception they have made fools of all the world and have falsely frightened it and stolen practically all their possessions and splendor. For by this teaching they have completely destroyed the sole comfort and confidence in Christ and have taught Christians to gape at, to wait for, and to rely on the endowments they would make. For he who in death gapes at, and trusts in, the endowments he intends to make must meanwhile take his eyes from Christ and forgets Him.[14]

Following Luther's lead, the Protestant Christians thus rejected all the teachings concerning purgatory and indulgence. But leaving aside the excessive tone of Luther's denunciation of these beliefs, one can still make the following observation.

Purgatory and the attendant practice of indulgence presuppose several beliefs as premises. First, sin calls for retributive justice even after reconciliation (redemption and forgiveness) was accomplished by Christ. Sin's needing to be punished further after redemption is considered by Luther as undermining the meaning of the redemptive death of the Son of God. Second, the practice of indulgence, especially the sale of it, is based on the belief about the "Treasury of Merit" accumulated over time from the surplus of merit bequeathed by all the saintly individuals as well as Christ himself. The belief was that Christ's infinite merit and finite but immense quantity of good works accumulated by all the saints of the ages were bequeathed to the church. Finally, they believed that the church had the authority to administer the Treasury of Merits and to dispense it as the church deemed fit, with the pope holding, as it were, the key to that treasury. This claim Luther fervently disputes. Some of the items in his initial protest formulated in the Ninety-Five Theses of 1517 make specific reference to this point.

Important in all of these premises is the frame of reference in which the Roman Catholic beliefs of indulgence and purgatory were formulated. These premises and beliefs make sense within an ancient and medieval soteriology (doctrine of salvation) shaped by a specific world view. One of the features of medieval thought is that things are to be viewed in terms of "substance" with "quantity" or "measure" as their predicate. This was largely due to the strong influence of Greek philosophy, particularly Aristotelianism, during the Scholastic period. Sin and grace were considered in quantitative terms. The distinction between mortal and venial sins is as much a quantitative distinction as it is a qualitative one. Thus, within the category of venial sins, the degrees of offenses are differentiated quantitatively and expurgated accordingly.

For Protestants, sin is rebellion against or conscious ignoration or distrust of God. There is no difference in the degree of offenses once one turns his back against God. Likewise, grace, for Protestants, is God's loving acceptance of sinners, through his gratuitous sacrifice and forgiveness. There are no gradations of graces. When Luther declared salvation to be by grace alone *(sola gratia)*, he meant that grace is the universal act of God reconciling humankind to himself, whether sinners acknowledge it or not. The Roman Catholic conception of grace, on the other hand, is thoroughly substantial, permitting the linguistic habit of referring to it as an entity capable of being, as it were, injected into the sinners. Thomas Aquinas made frequent reference to this "infusion of grace." Thus substantialized grace could further be quantified into something measurable, just as sin was measured and expiated accordingly.

Though Luther and other reformers were still living in the late medieval world, sharing many of the common beliefs and perspectives with most of their Catholic contemporaries, their theology was being developed with a view toward a new era with sufficiently different presuppositions within the framework of an emerging new world view. Their thinking was more "qualitative" than "quantitative," and more "attitudinal" than "substantial." Both sin and grace are more the "attitude" for the Protestant than the "conditions" or "entities" or "substance."

Even though at the close of the sixteenth century the Council of Trent rectified, by officially condemning, the past abuses of the sale of indulgence, the Roman Catholic church did not alter its basic posture toward the beliefs of purgatory and indulgence. The fundamental structure of the Roman Catholic soteriology was reaffirmed by the Council with a renewed vigor, along with the world view that sustains it. The quantitative and substantial ways of viewing sin and grace are still maintained as valid, hence indulgence and purgatory continue to be the accepted beliefs within the Roman Catholic piety and theology.

Prominent Catholic thinkers, such as Karl Rahner, have attempted a theological explanation that is to render purgatory intelligible to twentieth-century minds. According to Rahner, it is through the purgatorial stage after death that the human soul undergoes the readjustment in body-soul relationship from the wrong one we now have, with our individual physical bodies, to the right pancosmic one, with the entire universe where all share and contribute to the same total universe in communion.[15]

SALVATION AND THE ETERNAL LIFE

Martin Luther, who represents the Protestant Reformation and is largely responsible for the pattern of subsequent Protestant attitudes toward salvation and eternal life, considered the Pauline interpretation of salvation as "justification by faith" to be the single most important teaching of the Bible. No one devoted more energy to bringing this Pauline teaching to the center of Christian religion than Luther, who believed that salvation lies not so much in the context of the Final Judgment, the bodily resurrection and the messianic rule, as in the Christian life, lived in faith now in the present consequent to "justification."

Just as Augustine had harsh words about millennarians, Luther also rebukes them by saying, "This false notion is lodged not only in the apostles (Acts 1:6), but also in the chiliasts, Valentinians, the Tertullians, who played the fool with the idea that before Judgment Day the Christians alone will possess the earth and that there will be no ungodly."[16] Luther brushes aside any ideas about the imminent approach of the end, particularly the way the advent is anticipated by some of the millennarians, that is, the physical establishment of the messianic rule on earth. Though Luther does not dismiss the Last Judgment, his references are meager, and mostly homiletical rather than theological. The final resurrection, judgment, and the messianic rule are all mostly kept unsaid by Luther. Resurrection, for example, is alluded to only as the logical consequence of his pastoral and homiletic metaphor for death as a "sleep." Luther does not lend the full weight of his theological articulation to the eschatological concept of the general resurrection. It is the justified life now that counts. God's own righteousness, vindicated and maintained through the redemptive death of Christ on the cross, is imputed to sinful humankind out of his gratuitous love, which results in the declaration that the sin of humankind is forgiven (objective justification). Therefore, those who believe in Christ and God's grace are declared justified (subjective justification). The objective reality of God's forgiveness has to be received in faith by individual human beings to become the subjective reality of justification. Luther considers justification to "mean that we are redeemed from sin, death, and the devil and are made partakers of life eternal not by ourselves . . . but by help from without, by the only-begotten Son of God."[17] Justification carries the force of the entire soteriological and eschatological significance when Luther says that "the article of justification, which is our only protection, not only against all the powers and plottings of men but also against the gates of hell, is this: by faith alone (*sola fide*) in Christ, without works, are we declared just (*pronuntiari justos*) and saved."[18]

It is thus quite clear that the dimension of "the eternal life" hereafter is to be experienced in the reality of the justified life here and now. In Luther the ideas of immortality and heavenly blissfulness, which played such an important part in the popular Christian piety, particularly during the Middle Ages, are absorbed into the significance of eternity invested in the justified life of a Christian.

So the predominant pattern of the Protestant theological understanding of the eternal life has been to see it as the dimension of eternity in the present. Karl Barth (1886–1968), the representative Protestant theologian of the first half of this century, spoke of eternity entering into concrete time, thereby giving depth content to the otherwise empty finitude of temporal history. "The eternity in which He Himself is true time and the Creator of all time is revealed in the fact that although our time is that of sin and death, He can enter it and Himself be temporal in it, yet without ceasing to be eternal, able rather to be the Eternal in time.''[19] Barth obviously is referring to the divine incarnation in historical life of Jesus Christ. The eternal life, then, that we are to enjoy is not the immortality that awaits us in the hereafter, or the continuation or prolongation of our current life beyond the grave. Barth reacted against a ''naturalistic'' doctrine of immortality just as vehemently as early Christian fathers such as Tatian.[20] The eternal life that we are promised is rather the possibility of our current participation in the eternal that is realized by God in the temporality of history. And this participation is possible only in the form of faith, faith in the proclamation about the event of salvation, the incarnation of the Eternal in time. Thus the eternal life is the eternalization of life lived in faith in the present.

Rudolf Bultmann (1884–1976), concurring on this point with Barth, defines ''faith'' not only as faith in salvation that is to take place in the hereafter, but as in itself ''part of salvation-occurrence.'' That is to say, to have faith in salvation offered by God in itself constitutes part of salvation. For it is not possible for a sinful human being naturally to have faith. To be sinful, by definition, means not having faith or not being able to have faith in God. Faith, though on the part of an individual a voluntary act of decision, is still a gift of God. Without prevenient grace, even a human being's faith in God is not possible. Faith, then, is already ''the salvation-occurrence, the eschatological occurrence.''[21] To put it plainly, to be enabled by divine grace to have faith in salvation and the eternal life in itself constitutes, in the present moment of our mortal life, the state of being in salvation and the eternal life. Salvation and the eternal life, which are the eschatological events that lie beyond the end of time, are understood by Bultmann to be realized in the reality of faith that takes place in the present, hence ''faith as eschatological occurrence.''

This is further echoed in Paul Tillich's concept of ''eternal now.'' The eschatological end of history is born by all moments of the temporal process as their ''inner aim.'' The biblical concept of the ''eternal life,'' which is signaled by salvation, is possible at all points in history, not just at the final end, because it is always there as the inner aim (end, telos) of the whole of the historical process and each moment therein. Tillich (1886–1966) states:

> Past and future meet in the present, and both are included in the eternal ''now.'' But they are not swallowed by the present; they have their independent functions. Theology's task is to analyse and describe these functions in unity with the total symbolism to which they belong. In this way the *eschaton* becomes a matter of present experience without losing its futuristic dimension: we stand *now* in face of the eternal, but we do so looking ahead toward the end of history and the end of all which is temporal in the eternal.[22]

This Protestant emphasis placed on the discovery of the eternal in the present is true even of those theologians who recently emerged decrying and criticizing the loss of the futuristic vistas of eschatology in Protestant theology. The 1960s and 1970s were the decades of disenchantment with the status quo of Western civilization and the intransigent structure of the conventional society. With the rising tide of antiestablishment movements, theologians such as Jürgen Moltmann and Wolfhart Pannenberg rose with a call to rekindle the eschatological fervor and to reopen the futuristic vision.[23] But even they did not indulge in speculative imaginations about the end of time that lies far beyond the scope of human understanding. Their true aim was to recognize the power of the future felt in the present. Speculating about the future as future, particularly the absolute end of history that belongs only to God, is a futile and barren intellectual exercise. It is the power that the future exerts on the present, the pull of the future felt in the human aspirations that motivates us in the present struggle, that is the truly significant object of theological investigation. There is little wonder, then, that the Theology of Hope that Moltmann proposed to the Christian world in the sixties was inspired by the revolutionary ferment in the Third World and in turn became a catalyst for a wide-ranging theological movement, both Protestant and Catholic, characterized by the common goal of liberating humankind from the various yokes of the stifling past. Liberation Theology, Feminist Theology, Black Theology, and Political Theology all seem to have been inspired by the eschatological end vision, and yet all in unison meant to create changes in the concrete situations in the present. The eternal, thus, must be felt in the present as the inner aim and propelling force of human history. This is how "the eternal life" has been alive as a vital element in the Christian life.

NOTES

1. Jaroslav Pelikan, *The Shape of Death* (Nashville: Abingdon Press, 1961), 23.
2. Ibid., 48f.
3. Ibid., 80ff.
4. Ibid., 109ff.
5. Augustine, *The City of God* (New York: Modern Library, 1950), 419.
6. Ibid., 413.
7. Ibid., 415.
8. Ibid., 749ff.
9. Ibid., 718.
10. Ibid., 719.
11. Ibid., 718.
12. Ibid., 742.
13. Ibid., 430.
14. Martin Luther, *What Luther Says: An Anthology* (St. Louis: Concordia Publishing House, 1959), 1:388.
15. Karl Rahner, "On the Theology of Death," in *Modern Catholic Thinkers,* ed. A. Robert Caponigri (New York: Harper & Brothers, 1960), 138–176.
16. Luther, *What Luther Says,* 1:284.

17. Ibid., 2:701.

18. Ibid.

19. Karl Barth, *Church Dogmatics* (Edinburgh: T. & T. Clark, 1956), 4-1:188.

20. G. C. Berkouwer, *The Triumph of Grace in the Theology of Karl Barth* (London: Paternoster Press, 1959), 330f.

21. Rudolf Bultmann, *The Theology of the New Testament* (New York: Charles Scribner's Sons, 1951), 1:329.

22. Paul Tillich, *Systematic Theology* (Chicago: University of Chicago Press, 1963), 3:395f.

23. Jürgen Moltmann, *Theology of Hope* (New York: Harper & Row, 1967); Wolfhart Pannenberg, *Theology and the Kingdom of God* (Philadelphia: Westminster Press, 1969).

9

"Your Sight Today Is Piercing": The Muslim Understanding of Death and Afterlife

William C. Chittick

INTRODUCTION

From the beginning of Islam all Muslims have accepted the resurrection of the body and the existence of heaven and hell as fundamental articles of faith. Both the Koran and the Hadith (the sayings of the Prophet Muhammad) provide many details about the events that will occur after death. In brief, we are told that on the first night in the grave, people will be questioned by the two angels about their beliefs and will be put into a pleasant or an unpleasant situation according to their answers. They will remain in the grave until the Day of Resurrection, when everyone will be mustered before God. The Scales will be brought out, and each person will be judged. At this point, "whoso has done an atom's weight of good shall see it, and whoso has done an atom's weight of evil shall see it" (Koran 99:7–9). Finally, people will be given everlasting abodes in paradise or hell.[1]

Belief in the afterlife is so basic to Islam that Islamic thought has been divided into three basic "principles" from early times: the Unity of God (*tawhîd*), prophecy (*nubuuwa*), and eschatology (*maᶜâd*) or questions pertaining to the next world. To understand the third of these questions, we need some knowledge of the first two.

Islam defines the Unity of God with the statement, "There is no god but God," a formula that makes up half of the Islamic testimony of faith (the second half being "Muhammad is the Messenger of God"). This declaration of God's Unity does not mean simply that God is one. It means that everything in the universe has been brought into existence by a single Reality and is inextricably connected to it. Nothing can be correctly understood unless it is tied back to God. The Koran tells us repeatedly that whatever is found in the heavens and the earth is a "sign" (*âya*) of God. God created all things through his power and wisdom, so each and every creature gives news of his nature.

The second principle declares that God has sent prophets to every nation on earth, reminding people why he created them and what he expects from them. Prophecy is a fact of human existence, which helps to explain why Islam considers Adam the first of the prophets. He was granted this high station when God placed him on the earth to be his representative (*khalîfa*) among all creatures. After Adam, God sent 124,000 more prophets, but like all good things in this world, prophecy had to come to an end, and the last prophet was Muhammad.

The Koran maintains that all of the prophets have brought a single basic message: "There is no god but God." In other words, Islam holds that the declaration of God's Unity underlies every prophetic teaching. The prophets were sent to remind mankind of God's Unity and to point out the signs of his wisdom and mercy, which fill the cosmos. Their revealed teachings explain that human beings are inseparable from their Creator and Origin, and that he created them not because he had any need for them, but because he wanted others to share in the bounties of existence. Because human beings are God's creatures, they must follow the guidelines he set down for them to benefit from their situation. If they simply follow their own whims and desires, or the demands that a society forgetful of God makes on them, they will fail to take advantage of their existence in this world.

This brings us to the third principle of Islamic thought, eschatology. The literal meaning of the Arabic word is "return." The Koran tells us in many verses that all things have come from God and return to him. More particularly, human beings have been created by God for a specific purpose. The degree to which they succeed in fulfilling this purpose shapes their own selves, and their own self-nature then determines the mode in which they return to God after death. The modes of return to God are diverse in keeping with the diversity of human aptitudes and destinies. God is Merciful, Compassionate, Loving, and Gentle to many of his servants, but he also is Wrathful, Avenging, and Severe. He does not show the same face to each person. The face he does show depends on the creature's own self. If one person loves God and sincerely strives to live up to his own human nature, he will return to God and find him Loving and Compassionate. But if someone forgets God and ignores his human responsibilities, he will return to God and find him Severe and Wrathful.

What, then, is a human being? What are the potentialities of human becoming? Why does God tell people to do certain things and avoid other things? If God created human beings to enjoy the benefits of existence, why does he not let them enjoy life in the way they want to enjoy it? Why does he have to tell people that there are right ways and wrong ways of doing things? Why are they expected to do things they don't like to do? To answer such questions from the

Islamic point of view, we need to look closely at some of Islam's basic teachings concerning human nature.

DIVINE AND HUMAN QUALITIES

Human beings find themselves situated within the universe, which is defined as "everything other than God." The term includes as many galaxies and worlds and dimensions that may happen to exist, for all eternity. Because every phenomenon in existence is a sign of God, the universe is the sum total of God's signs.[2] The cosmos is created by God, to be sure, but more specifically, it is created on the basis of what God is in himself. If a generous man gives a gift, it will be a generous gift, and if a stingy person gives at all, he does so in keeping with his basic stinginess. Because God is fundamentally compassionate, merciful, and loving, he creates the universe as befits his compassion, mercy, and love. The universe manifests these qualities in a fundamental way.

Though everything that exists provides news of God's reality, God in himself is unknowable. How can the shadow know the sun? How can the artwork know the artist? Hence nothing provides a full picture of God. Human knowledge is only partial, though there is a sound basis for a certain understanding of God in the message brought by the prophets, since they were sent by God. When Muslims want to explain God's nature, they begin by quoting the Koran. There we read, for example, that God has many names. He is Alive, Knowing, Desiring, Powerful, Speaking, Generous, Just, Forgiving, Avenging, Merciful, Wrathful, Loving, Mighty, Bestower, Inaccessible, Life-giver, Slayer, Exalter, Abaser, and so on. Traditionally, there are said to be ninety-nine of these names.

To understand the universe in the context of the Divine Unity, we need to connect it back to the One God. A basic way of tracing things back to their roots in God is to show that everything found in the cosmos reveals God's names, since all the qualities of creation are his signs, reflecting his reality. The life of all living things derives from God's life, while all knowledge is a pale reflection of his knowledge. Every mother in the universe who shows love and compassion for her children participates in God's love and compassion for his creatures. The grandeur of mountains and sky is a dim reverberation of God's glory.

Each thing in the universe manifests an aspect of God, or, let us say, one or some of God's names. But nothing in the universe reflects God himself, God in his full glory as possessing the ninety-nine "Most Beautiful Names"—nothing, that is, except the human being. This does not mean every human being, but only those human beings who are fully human and who have actualized all the potentialities latent in human nature. It is the fact of manifesting every name of God—not only some of the divine names—that sets humans apart from all other created things, even the greatest of the angels. Man, in effect, is a little god, and for this reason God chose him as God's representative on the earth. This, in the Islamic view, is one of the meanings of the famous verse in Genesis, repeated by the Prophet Muhammad, "God created the human being in His own image."

As stated earlier, God created human beings because he desired that others should share in the benefits of existence. What are these benefits? A benefit, according to Webster, is something that promotes a person's well-being. Human well-being is promoted by everything that promotes a person's humanness, or everything that allows him to be truly himself. As soon as the true human self is defined as an image of God possessing all the divine attributes, it becomes clear that a person is truly himself only when he is Godlike. Only by becoming Godlike can he share in the benefits of existence, for only then does he possess those qualities that promote his well-being, that is, life, knowledge, desire, power, speech, generosity, justice, and so on.

It is clear that few human beings manifest all the attributes of God. During the course of an average person's life only a few human potentialities come to be actualized, and these are not found in their full strength. No doubt people gain many of God's qualities through the mere process of growth and maturation. An infant enters this world with several divine attributes already manifest, such as life, knowledge, desire, and power. But the divine qualities found in a child are in embryonic form. Only gradually do they expand and develop. Take the divine attribute of speech, for example. At the beginning, it is a mere potentiality, and a newborn infant is not much different from any other animal in this respect. But the attribute develops quickly, and there is no limit to the perfection it can reach.

If people want to actualize any quality in its fullness, somewhere along the line they will have to take the matter into their own hands. The natural growth of an attribute like speech is limited by a person's environment and personal gifts. If a person wants to transcend his environment and take full advantage of his gifts, he will have to discipline and train himself. No one becomes a great poet, writer, or speaker without effort. In any field of human endeavor and activity the full actualization of potential demands dedication. But any field of endeavor you can name involves the utilization of *some* of the divine qualities deposited within the human being, not *all* of them.

If people strive to become great athletes, they may develop desire and power to a degree unimagined by others. If they devote themselves to helping the underprivileged, they may develop and manifest a compassion unique among their family and friends. Human possibilities are unlimited, and the actualization of each human quality brings out one or more of the divine qualities present within us because we have been created in God's image. But each of these possible activities, in the eyes of Islam, is of secondary concern at best. To be truly human a person's activities and efforts have to conform to God's purpose in creating him. That purpose was to allow his chosen creatures to share in the full benefits of existence. The fullness of existence has to be defined in terms of *all* God's qualities, not only some of them. Hence the human task is not to concentrate on bringing out a single attribute, such as speech, or power, or desire, or compassion, but all divine attributes without exception.

How can this be done? Islam maintains that human beings are perfectly capable of developing some of their potentialities on their own. Their cultural, social, and personal situations define certain goals for them, and by working toward these goals they will manifest some of the qualities latent within themselves. But if individuals and societies set their own goals, there is one goal that is beyond their grasp. That goal is the full, total, and complete actualization of human possibility and perfection. No one can know, without guidance from outside himself, what potentialities are latent within his own soul. The reason for this is that human possibilities are defined by the divine attributes, and no one can know God unless God gives news of himself. A human being can set out to become Godlike, but he cannot possibly understand what it means to become Godlike or *how* he can become Godlike unless God tells him. This is the function of prophecy.

According to Islam, the prophets come with a twofold message. On the one hand, they provide knowledge of the Divine Unity. In other words, they explain the nature of Ultimate Reality and the interrelationship of all things. They set down how God is to be understood and point out the difference between those human beings who live in harmony with God and those who have turned away from God, occupying themselves with various secondary affairs on the basis of individual judgments of good and evil, right and wrong. The first part of a prophetic message is to provide a knowledge that places things in a proper perspective, situates man in the cosmos, and connects everything back to God. The second part sets down a path that people can follow to rectify the disharmony and disequilibrium so apparent in the human relationship with God. Islam often refers to this second part of prophecy as the "Revealed Law," or *Sharīʿa*.

The first part of prophecy defines the human situation. The second part describes a path of action whereby human beings can actualize to the fullest extent possible all the divine qualities latent within themselves. Many Muslim authorities speak of the Law as a "scale" *(mîzân)* within which all things can be weighed. By weighing knowledge and activity in the scale human beings can be guided to the actualization of the full range of God's attributes in perfect balance, without the fear that one attribute will outweigh the others and produce a distorted image of God, something less than human.

If human beings weigh everything in the scale of their own understanding, they will upset the proper measure of things. Like children, they will see reality as centered on themselves instead of on God. But this is a reversal of the correct order, since the Reality of God defines the standards of existence. By perceiving and acting wrongly, people upset the balance inherent in existence and in their own primordial human nature.

The Law sets up equilibrium within the soul in a complex manner that has formed the subject of innumerable studies by the learned masters of the tradition.[3] Here I can only offer a single example of what is involved: One of the principles of the divine scale is enunciated by the prophetic saying "God's mercy precedes His wrath." This means that God's mercy is more real than his wrath, and that wrath is itself a function of mercy. Within the original and primordial human nature, made in God's image, mercy and wrath are both present, but mercy predominates. Hence mercy and wrath cannot be used simply as a person sees fit. Just as God is essentially merciful and only secondarily wrathful, so also human beings must be essentially merciful and only secondarily wrathful. All the rulings and statutes of the Revealed Law are designed to put mercy before wrath.

Human beings cannot possibly discern the real and ultimate nature of mercy and wrath on their own, since this pertains to the divine nature, which is unknowable in itself. By the same token, the human sense of right and wrong cannot tell them how to establish the proper balance between mercy and wrath. They may understand that mercy is a desirable human quality and that it must outweigh wrath, which, in its proper measure, also is a desirable human quality. They also may perceive that it is possible to overemphasize mercy or to place too much stress on wrath. But the whole secret of human perfection is to find the proper measure and balance, and this is inaccessible to human understanding without help from God, the source of all ontological attributes.

Mercy and closely related attributes such as compassion, love, and forgiveness are comparatively rare in human beings. The reason for this is that such qualities demand that people concern themselves with the good of others, just as God has concerned himself with the good of creation by bringing the universe into existence. But most human beings are too self-centered to put the welfare of others before or even on the same level as their own welfare. As a result, they choose to interact mercifully and lovingly with other people only to the extent that this lies in their own interests, as defined by their own shortsighted understanding. Hence they are quick to judge their neighbors and to defend their own castles from real or imagined encroachments. All this means that mercy, compassion, love, and forgiveness get pushed into the background. But this is a reversal of the proper order of existence, in which mercy precedes wrath. If a person lives the whole of his life out of kilter with existence itself, he will suffer terribly when God makes the real nature of things manifest to him in the next world. This is the basic message of Islamic eschatology.

DEATH AND DREAMING

Let us now look more closely at the Islamic conception of the cosmos or universe, which, as said above, is defined as "everything other than God." This will allow us to answer the questions: Where are heaven and hell located? Why are they there and not some place else? How can the descriptions of heaven and hell found in the Koran and the prophetic sayings be understood as anything more than allegories or symbols?

The Koran and the Islamic tradition divide the created universe into two basic worlds. These are named by several sets of contrasting terms, such as invisible and visible, manifest and nonmanifest, high and low, subtle and dense, luminous and dark, spiritual and corporeal. Thus, for example, the visible world is defined as everything accessible to our sense perception, whereas the invisible world is that which can only be known through God's revelations. Among the most important creatures who inhabit the invisible world are angels, who are God's messengers to the visible creatures. According to the Prophet, the angels were created out of light. In contrast, the body of Adam was molded out of what the Koran calls "clay," which is the basic substance of the visible world. We should not be surprised to hear that the light of the angels is invisible, since even physical light can only be perceived because it is thoroughly mixed with darkness. If it were free of darkness, it would be so intense that we could not look at it without being blinded.

The Koran, along with a good deal of Islamic thought, bases its dialectic on juxtaposing opposite qualities and asking us to meditate on the differences. Hence it is important to grasp the nature of invisible angelic light to understand the nature of clay. Angelic light has many intrinsic qualities, such as life, knowledge, desire, power, speech, and generosity. In other words, the angelic light manifests all the names of God in a direct and intense manner.[4] In contrast, the basic attribute of the clay from which the visible world is constructed is darkness, which is the lack of light. This is not pure darkness, or else the physical world could not be perceived and would not even exist. But compared with the light of the angels, the light of clay is so dim that it has to be called darkness. Hence the concomitant attributes of light, such as life, knowledge, will, and speech, cannot be found in clay itself.

The created universe has two poles: the luminosity of the angels and the darkness of clay. One pole is pure light, life, knowledge, desire, and power, whereas the other pole does not manifest any of these qualities. Hence it is darkness, death, ignorance, listlessness, and weakness. But light and darkness make up only the two poles or two extremes of the cosmos. Between the two are found many degrees of mixed light and darkness. Islamic philosophy often refers to these degrees of mixed light and darkness as different degrees of spirit or soul, for example, the mineral, vegetal, animal, human, and angelic spirits. Each ascending degree of spirit manifests a greater intensity of the light of God.

A good way to grasp the structure of this universe is to picture an empty globe of practically infinite dimensions. The outward shell of the globe is the visible universe, made out of clay. At the center of the globe is the first creation of God, made out of pure light. Between the center and the shell is found a vast hierarchy of creatures who are neither pure light nor pure clay. They represent various degrees of light, or various mixtures of light and darkness. The closer we stand to the center, the more intense and purer is the light. The closer we stand to the shell, the weaker is the light and the greater the darkness.

In this cosmic globe whose center is light and whose shell is clay, human beings fill a special niche. As said earlier, human beings are made in God's image, while the cosmos, as a whole, is the sum total of all the signs of God, displaying his names and attributes in an infinite spatial and temporal expanse. In other words, the cosmos, as a whole, also is made in God's image, so the human individual is a mirror image of the cosmos. As a result, a human being is called a "small universe," or microcosm, and the cosmos is called the "great universe," or macrocosm. Everything found in the macrocosm also is found, in some manner, in the microcosm.

The Koran tells us that God shaped Adam's body out of clay and then breathed into Adam of his own Spirit. Though Adam's outer shell or body is made out of clay, his center is the Spirit of God, made of pure light. Hence human beings are compounded of spirit and body. If we want to know the characteristics of the pure human spirit, we list the names of God: alive, knowing, desiring, powerful, speaking, generous, just, and so on. As for the body, at best it is a pale shadow of these attributes. Loosely speaking, it is their absence.

But this is still not a complete picture of the human being, since here we have only a shell and a center. Just as the macrocosm contains many degrees of mixed light and darkness, so does the microcosm. The inward human dimension that fills the "space" between the Divine Spirit and the clay of the body is called the "soul" *(nafs)*. In itself, the spirit is pure light, whereas the body is almost pure darkness. The soul is an intermediary realm of mixed light and darkness.

When we think of a "person," whether ourselves or others, we have in mind the whole microcosm that makes up a human being, including spirit, soul, and body. It is important to grasp that all human beings are essentially the same in their spirits, since the spirit is the Divine Spirit, and in their bodies, since they are all made of clay. Where people differ is in their souls. Each soul represents a unique conjunction of light and clay, or spirit and body. Just below the surface each person displays a unique intensity of light. Some people manifest the light of the spirit more directly, and some less directly. But no two persons are the same.

What are the soul's attributes that combine to make up the unique personality of each human being? We can say that the soul is "neither light nor darkness," since it is the meeting between spirit and body. The attributes of light are the divine attributes, whereas clay represents the weakest reverberation of these same attributes. Hence the soul is neither pure life nor total death, neither pure knowledge nor complete ignorance, neither unlimited power nor total weakness, neither perfect speech nor plain inarticulateness. In every case, the soul is somewhere in between. Every soul manifests a unique configuration of all the divine attributes in differing intensities. No two souls possess exactly the same degree of knowledge, desire, power, speech, generosity, justice, or forgiveness.

The world of light is inhabited by angels, whereas the world of clay is filled with bodies. What or who inhabits the intermediate worlds between the angels and clay? As already mentioned, the philosophical tradition refers to some of these intermediary creatures as different degrees of "spirit" or "soul." The Koran speaks about some of this realm's inhabitants, using terminology that is especially interesting because of its symbolism: It says that a group of God's creatures are made out of "fire." They are called "jinn," which means literally "hidden," since, like the angels, they are invisible. But their invisibility is not the same sort as that of the angels, since their light is mixed with darkness. Mythically speaking, "fire" is halfway between light and clay. Hence the creatures made out of fire are both visible and invisible, corporeal and spiritual, high and low, luminous and dark.

In the Islamic intellectual tradition the Arabic words used to name the substance of these intermediate, fiery creatures can best be translated as "image" *(mithâl)* or "imagination" *(khayâl)*. This does not mean that the jinn are "imaginary"—far from it. In fact, they are more real than creatures made only from clay, since they possess more of the attributes of light, which are the attributes of true existence. Scholars commonly use the adjective "imaginal" to distinguish these intermediary beings from "imaginary" things and from fantasy.[5]

Because imaginal creatures are situated between spirit and body, their qualities stand between those of light and clay. The best way to find examples of such creatures is to look at our own imagination, especially in dreams. Though dream images are rather flimsy excuses for imaginal realities, they have certain characteristics in common with the imaginal creatures who inhabit the intermediary realms of the macrocosm.

Whenever we see anything in a dream, we see something that stands between light and clay. In other words, we see a body that is not a body. On the one hand, the dream image is bodily, so it has the characteristics of clay, which are those qualities that can be perceived by the senses. The dream image can be heard, seen, touched, tasted, and smelled. On the other hand, the image is a spiritual thing, since it is invisible to other people and is woven out of the light of our own awareness. If you see your friend in a dream, you have really seen your friend, since you saw that friend and not another. At the same time, you are in fact seeing only yourself—not your body, but your awareness and consciousness. You perceive, in other words, your own soul, which is woven of light and darkness, awareness and ignorance, power and weakness. You perceive imagination.

Whether imaginal things are found between the shell and the center of the macrocosm or in the dream images of our own souls, they share certain characteristics. One of the most important of these is that they appear in forms that can best be called "appropriate" *(munâsib)*. This point can be understood by looking at the science of dream interpretation *(ʿilm al-taʿbîr)*.

It is an axiom of Islamic thought that every form *(ṣûra)* in the universe manifests a meaning *(maʿnâ)*, just as every phenomenon is a sign of God. This is especially obvious in the case of the forms that we see in dreams. The Koran mentions dream interpretation as a science possessed by prophets such as Joseph. Muhammad himself used to interpret the dreams of his companions, and gradually dream interpretation was developed as one of the practical sciences of Islamic civilization, as important for everyday life as medicine. In dream interpretation it is assumed that a dream is an intermediate reality, since it hides and reveals at the same time. Dream images manifest invisible realities in visible form. The dream interpreter has to grasp the connection between the form of the dream and the meaning that lies behind the form. The outward form displayed through imagination has a necessary and appropriate connection with the spirit, meaning, concept, or mood that it manifests. The interpreter must understand this connection and express the invisible content of the image in an abstract and rational form, or in an imaginative form closer to our immediate understanding than the dream image itself.

Islamic cosmology adds that the imaginal realities of the macrocosm display a connection between form and meaning just like dreams. Anything that exists within the imaginal world combines corporeality with spirituality, or form with meaning, but not in a haphazard manner. Moreover, imaginal things appear in appropriate forms instantaneously, since, like fire, their shapes are not fixed. Their forms constantly change in keeping with the meaning they manifest at any given moment. Like dream images, they undergo continual transformation. This change of form in accordance with an inward meaning can be seen to a certain degree even in the world of clay, since the soul is able to shine through the shell of the body. When people are happy or angry their faces are likely to show it.

In the world of clay it is relatively easy for us to hide our feelings and true thoughts from others, since our souls are hidden behind the veils of our bodies. But suppose for a moment that our bodies were made not of clay, but of fire. Then we would appear instant by instant in a form appropriate to our own thoughts, feelings, and moods, just as we appear to ourselves while dreaming. This is one of the keys to Islamic eschatological teachings: When the veil of the body is removed, the soul—which is an imaginal creature—manifests itself in its true form. The meaning and content of the soul is no longer hidden by the shell made out of clay. The soul reveals its true nature for all to see. Hence the Koran says about the experience of death, addressing the human soul, "We have now removed from thee thy covering, so thy sight today is piercing" (50:22). Hence, also, the Koran refers to the resurrection as the day when "secrets will be divulged" (86:9) and when "that which is in the breasts will be brought out" (100:10). "On that day you shall be exposed, not one secret of yours concealed" (69:18).

THE MAKING OF THE SOUL

It was said earlier that God's purpose in sending the prophets was to lay down a path through which human beings can fully actualize all the divine qualities, which are latent within them because they are made in the divine image. The divine qualities will manifest themselves in any case, but unless they are shaped and molded by God's guidance they will appear without harmony and equilibrium. "Guidance," in sum, is itself a divine attribute that the soul must actualize. Its effect on the soul is to bring out the latent divine image in a balanced manner that will yield happiness and wholeness in the next stage of existence.

Because human beings are full and integral reflections of God, they possess an indefinite expanse of possibilities. God is infinite, and he manifests himself in an infinite variety of modes. Every creature other than a human being represents one of the modes in which God manifests his qualities and characteristics. An angel manifests light and transcendence, a lion manifests power and majesty, a bird manifests freedom and joy. Every nonhuman creature has a narrowly limited definition, certain tight bounds it cannot transgress. Creatures come into existence, follow more or less determined courses, and depart. A walnut tree never yields pumpkins, nor does a python turn into a rabbit. But a human being comes into existence as an almost unlimited potentiality. Everyone enters the world basically the same, but one person leaves as a bodhisattva, another as a Shakespeare, and another as a subhuman monster.

By putting human beings in touch with the divine attribute of guidance, prophecy leads them in a direction that will allow them to achieve a harmonious and healthy flowering of their potentialities. The process whereby people actualize their latent divine perfections can be described through the analogy of the animal kingdom. Each species and variety of animal represents a specific combination of divine attributes, or a particular kind of created perfection. An elephant has skills not possessed by a tiger, and a bee can do what an antelope can never hope to accomplish. There are literally millions of these perfections in nature, and they are nothing but the "signs" of God. Human beings are set apart from all other creatures because they can accomplish the tasks of all things, whereas other creatures can only accomplish their own specific tasks. Moreover, there are certain qualities that humans possess to the exclusion of other things, foremost among them an intelligence that can understand the other creatures and their tasks. Because of intelligence, human beings can control the other creatures. This expresses, in concrete terms, the fact that God appointed man as his representative in creation.

To be perfectly human, a person must actualize the perfections of all things—all the signs of God—within himself, for he is a microcosm containing everything in the macrocosm. In other words, people must come to manifest all the names of God, but in the perfect harmony and equilibrium that is set down by the scale of the Revealed Law. If a person fails to realize these qualities, he will, in effect, become less than human. When the body dies the soul will be set free to appear in an imaginal form that manifests its own less-than-human nature, just as the soul appears to itself in bodily form during dreams.

The Muslim authorities frequently use this animal symbolism to describe the form taken by the soul in the next world. In myth and fable each animal had traditionally been understood as representing one specific character trait. Thus the animals provided perfect symbols for incomplete souls that are dominated by negative qualities. For example, the famous theologian al-Ghazâlî (d. 1111) writes as follows:

On the Day of Resurrection, meanings are bared. Then form takes on the color of meaning. If a person had been dominated by passion and greed [in the world], he will be seen on that day in the form a pig. If he was dominated by anger and aggression, he will be seen in the form of a wolf.[6]

The great Persian poet Jalâl al-Dîn Rûmî (d. 1273) expresses the same idea when he writes,

Our existence contains thousands of wolves and pigs—
 good and evil, fair and foul.
The dominant trait determines man's properties:
 If gold is more than copper, then he is gold.
At the Resurrection you will appear in the form
 of the trait that governs your existence.[7]

In short, the next stage of human life, which Islam refers to as the "grave" *(gabr)* or the "interworld" *(barzakh),* is an imaginal realm in which the actual attributes of the soul display themselves in appropriate forms, exactly as in the dream state. But the interworld differs from dreaming in a number of ways. Thus, for example, we wake up from our dreams and quickly forget them, but we do not wake up from the interworld until the distant event known as the Day of Resurrection. Moreover, the interworld itself is a kind of waking up in relation to this world. As the Prophet said, "people are asleep, and when they die, they wake up." Hence the experiences of the interworld are more real and more intense than those of the present life, since the interworld stands closer to the luminous center of the cosmos. That is why the Koran says that a person's sight at death is "piercing." The soul will see clearly what it had only seen dimly when immersed in the world of clay.

STAGES OF THE AFTERLIFE

Islam distinguishes three major stages of becoming after death. The first, the just mentioned interworld, is the period from death until the Day of Resurrection, which occurs at the "end of the world," when the possibilities of human existence in this world have been exhausted. For each person the interworld represents an awakening in relationship to the life in the world, so the soul is more aware of itself and its surroundings than it was when it lived in clay. Because its existence is now totally imaginal, it perceives itself and its surroundings in appropriate bodily form. At this stage the soul does not enter into heaven or hell, since those two abodes will not be populated until after the Day of Resurrection. It receives, however, a foretaste of its ultimate and permanent state. As the Prophet said, death is the "lesser resurrection" and the grave is "either one of the pits of hell or one of the gardens of paradise."

Some of the later authorities have compared the period spent in the grave to the time spent in the womb. The soul undergoes constant growth and transformation on the basis of the deeds it performed in this world. Then, as the Koran reports, the Day of Resurrection draws near and the angel Seraphiel sounds a blast on the trumpet. On hearing this everyone in heaven and earth loses consciousness. When Seraphiel sounds the trumpet for the second time people wake up to face the events of the resurrection.

The Prophet provided many descriptions of what happens in the grave that only make sense as imaginal events. As soon as we stop thinking of these accounts as metaphors we see that there is no reason that they should not represent a description of the actual experiences of the soul in the imaginal state of existence. Certainly one should be able to see a close resemblance between these descriptions and dream experience. In the interworld human acts, which had concrete form in the world of clay, are brought back and made present in a form appropriate to the intention and content of the act. All the Koranic and prophetic accounts of what happens in the grave can be understood on this basis. For example, the Prophet reported that after the believer has been questioned by the angels in the grave,

> a crier calls from heaven, "My servant has spoken the truth, so spread out carpets from paradise for him, clothe him from paradise, and open a gate for him into paradise." Then some of the joy and fragrance of paradise comes to him, his grave is made spacious for him as far as the eye can see, and a man with a beautiful face, beautiful garments, and a sweet scent comes to him and says, "Rejoice in what pleases you, for this is your day which you have been promised." The person asks, "Who are you? For your face is perfectly beautiful and brings good." The man answers, "I am your own good deeds."[8]

The Day of Resurrection is itself a major stage of becoming. Some sayings of the Prophet speak of its length in terms of thousands of years. Many events take place, all of which are perceived in accordance with the state of the soul and the laws of imaginal existence. The happy souls destined for paradise experience these events as easy and pleasant, but the wretched souls undergo terrible trial and tribulation.

After the events of the Day of Resurrection people are divided into two groups. One group is taken into the Garden, and the other into the Fire, and there they remain forever. Both Garden and Fire are imaginal modes of existence in which the soul appears to itself and to others in keeping with its own real nature. The basic difference between the two is that the Garden is situated close to the source of light, whereas the Fire dwells in relative darkness. Hence a prophetic saying tells us that after the resurrection, light will be separated from fire and taken to heaven, whereas the heat of fire will remain in hell.

The Garden is said to have eight basic levels; the Fire has seven, though there are innumerable subsections to each level. Some authorities maintain that the degrees of heaven and hell are as numerous as human souls. No two souls leave this world in exactly the same form, and none develops and grows in the interworld in the same manner. The soul's perception is thoroughly shaped by its own characteristics, so no two persons perceive the same object in exactly the same way. In paradise once a week the faithful are taken for the Day of Visitation, in which they are given the highest blessing of the Garden, the vision of God. But, as the authorities remind us, "the water always appears in the color of the cup." In other words, no one sees God in exactly the same form. Everyone sees God in keeping with his own capacity and understanding. No believer has the same capacity as the prophets, and the prophets themselves are ranked in degrees. As God says in the Koran, "those prophets—we have preferred some of them over others" (2:253)—so some prophets have a more perfect vision of God.

If the highest bliss is to be given vision of God, the worst chastisement is to be veiled from God. That is why one of the Muslim authorities can sum up this whole discussion by saying, "The next world possesses two abodes: vision and veil."[9] To be veiled from God is the worst punishment, since it is to suffer the disintegration of oneself. Human beings, it must always be remembered, were created in God's image. By failing to live up to the divine qualities deposited in themselves they cut themselves off from God, who is the source of everything that they are. They had had the potentiality of becoming semidivine, but they have transgressed their own nature and become less than human. It is the grandeur of the divine attributes in man that allows him to suffer in hell.

In the Fire, people lose the integrating factor that made them human. They are torn this way and that by conflicting forces within themselves. But all the while they maintain an awareness of what they should have become. The Fire is their own regret assuming concrete, imaginal form, appropriate to the perceivers. By the way, most Muslim authorities maintain that the fires of hell eventually will abate. After many aeons those who dwell in the Fire will become so accustomed to the veil that they would not be able to bear entering into paradise. God's all-embracing and precedent mercy gives solace even to the damned.

NOTES

1. The best account of basic Muslim beliefs concerning death and the afterlife is provided by J. I. Smith and Y. Y. Haddad, *The Islamic Understanding of Death and Resurrection* (Albany: State University of New York Press, 1981). Despite its title, the work deals only with descriptions of the afterlife, not with the traditional "understanding" of these descriptions. For a survey of basic beliefs and the manner in which they have been understood, see W. C. Chittick, "Eschatology," in *Islamic Spirituality: Foundations*, ed. S. H. Nasr (New York: Crossroad, 1987), 378–409. Both of these

works provide bibliographies of the literature. Other works that deal with how the tradition has understood the descriptions of the afterlife include J. W. Morris, *The Wisdom of the Throne: An Introduction to the Philosophy of Mulla Sadra* (Princeton, N.J.: Princeton University Press, 1981); Chittick, "Rûmî's View of Death," *Alserat* 13, no. 2 (1987): 30–51; idem, "Death and the World of Imagination: Ibn al-ʿArabî's Eschatology," *Muslim World* 78 (1988):51–82.

2. The word "universe" in Arabic, *ʿâlam,* often is explained in terms of other words from the same root, such as *ʿalam* and *ʿalâma,* which mean "signpost," "mark," and "designation."

3. For a detailed discussion of this function of the Law, cf. W. C. Chittick, *The Sufi Path of Knowledge: Ibn al-ʿArabî's Metaphysics of Imagination* (Albany: State University of New York Press, 1989), ch. 11.

4. The angels, however, are divided into many kinds, and most of them manifest only some of the attributes of God. Although the light displayed by each kind of angel is pure and intense, in some cases the light of knowledge will dominate, in others the light of power, in others the light of love, and so on.

5. When the philosophical tradition speaks of some of the intermediary beings as "spirits," this does not imply that they are purely spiritual in nature. It simply means that there is an invisible, animating reality beyond the visible body. In relation to a plant's body, the "vegetal soul," which allows it to grow and reproduce, is invisible and, therefore, spiritual. In relation to the human rational soul, the vegetal soul can be called bodily, although this body is "subtle" *(latîf),* not "dense" *(kathîf).* At the same time, all levels of soul and spirit—except the Divine Spirit itself—can be referred to as "imaginal" creatures, since they dwell in an intermediary realm between pure light and pure darkness.

6. Ghazâlî continues by making the connection with dream interpretation: "That is why, if a person sees a wolf in a dream, it is interpreted as a wrongdoer, and if he sees a pig, it is interpreted as an impure and filthy man. The reason for this is that sleep symbolizes death: To the extent that a person moves away from this world through sleep, form follows the inward meaning." *Kîmiyâ-yi saʿâdat,* ed. A. Ârâm (Tehran: Markazî, 1319/1940), 18.

7. *Mathnawî,* ed. R. A. Nicholson (London: Luzac, 1925–40), Book 2, vs. 1416–19. Cf. W. C. Chittick, *The Sufi Path of Love: The Spiritual Teachings of Rumi* (Albany: State University of New York Press, 1983), 101–107.

8. Tabrîzî, *Mishkât al-masâbîh* (Delhi, 1325/1907), 142. Cf. J. Robson, trans., *Mishkat al-masabih* (Lahore: Ashraf, 1963-66), 341. The hadith continues by providing a parallel description of what happens to the unbeliever. His "evil deeds" appear to him as a man "with an ugly face, ugly garments, and an offensive odor."

9. Ibn al-ʿArabî, *al-Futûhât al-makkiyya* (Beirut: Dâr Sâdir, n.d.), 2:335. 18.

III

DEATH AND AFTERLIFE IN EASTERN RELIGIONS

10

Hindu Views of Death and Afterlife

Thomas J. Hopkins

INTRODUCTION

Death is as close to being universal as anything we know. Sooner or later, like it or not, everyone dies. Every thinking person has always known this, and every culture has had to come to terms with this great inescapable fact of human existence.

Almost as soon as we have evidence of human culture, however, we also have evidence of belief in some kind of afterlife. Carefully equipped burials, deposits of grave goods, or provisions for a journey to another world all attest to an early and sustained assumption that death is not the end of personal existence. Cavemen, pharaohs, classical Greeks, and modern Muslims may not agree on much else, but they share an expectation that life continues in some form after the death of the physical body.

Yet if death is universal and there is early and widespread belief in an afterlife, there is surprisingly little broad agreement on specifics. What is universal about death is the death of the physical body, what we might call biological or physiologic death. This death can be seen, and is seen, more or less the same by everyone. What this death means depends on whether the human person is more than just the body because if so, then the death of the body does not completely describe what happens at the time of death. What happens to the more-than-body, how this happens, and what determines how it happens then become essential issues for defining what death means. How one resolves these issues determines the possibilities and conditions of an afterlife.

Afterlife is an even more complex problem than death because here there is nothing to be observed by ordinary means. The more-than-body also is the not-the-body, and cannot be seen as the body is seen; its circumstances after death are known to the living through concepts and intuitions, not direct experience. Afterlife is a matter of belief and faith, not observation, and its attainment can never be confirmed empirically by those still living.

Afterlife cannot be separated from life, not only because life is the necessary precondition, but also because our views of life and afterlife are always interrelated. The meaning we give to afterlife depends on the meaning we give to life, and vice versa. Life and afterlife represent a continuum, not only in terms of sequence, but also, more important, in terms of concepts and values. Both must fit within the same world view, or else neither has meaning for the other; they must share the same metaphysical assumptions, represent the same beliefs and goals, and rest on faith in the same realities and powers. When world views differ to a significant degree we can expect that the views of death and afterlife also will differ.

These considerations apply at least in theory to all religious traditions, but the issues may remain in the background if the views of death and afterlife are not challenged. In the case of Hinduism metaphysical questions emerged very early—well before 500 B.C.E.—in debates over the nature of human existence: whether there is a permanent component of the individual person, whether and how it survives death, and what happens to it afterward. These issues remained in the foreground from this point on because they were never finally resolved. No single world view won acceptance by all Hindus, and thus no single view of death and afterlife. Instead, there was effectively an agreement to disagree within limits and to allow several different metaphysical viewpoints to coexist.

Three broadly defined alternatives gradually took shape in the course of the first millennium B.C.E., each representing a particular world view and a related view of death and afterlife: the Vedic sacrificial tradition, centered around householder life, which sought an afterlife in the heavenly World of the Fathers; the later Vedic tradition of forest-dwelling seers, who sought release from rebirth and union with the ultimate Reality; and the tradition of devotional theism, which sought an eternal personal relationship with a chosen god or goddess. These three alternative systems, which we will examine in more detail later, represent, respectively, what Hindus call the three *mārgas*, or "paths," to salvation: the path of ritual action *(Karma-mārga)*, the path of knowledge *(Jñāna-mārga)*, and the path of devotion *(Bhakti-mārga)*. Each of these systems has its own metaphysical justification, and each constitutes for its followers a comprehensive means of salvation. Woven together over the centuries, but still preserving their distinctive world views and concepts of afterlife, these systems and their corresponding paths form the mainstream of what we call Hinduism.

HINDUISM AS A RELIGION

It is at this point that most Westerners have a problem with Hinduism as a religion, especially if they use their own monotheistic religions as a standard.

Judaism, Christianity, and Islam strongly disagree on many matters, but they all are based on the worship of one god only, and each assumes a common faith for all its followers. By this monotheistic standard it is almost a minimum requirement for a religion that it defines salvation the same for all believers so that everyone seeks the same goal.

Hinduism clearly is not a religion that fits this monotheistic model, nor would Hindus consider the model valid as a standard. Hinduism is not monotheistic and does not insist on a uniform set of beliefs, for what Hindus consider very good reasons: People are not all the same in background and qualities, and they do not have the same religious needs and interests. Progress toward salvation is not, for most Hindus, a matter of a single lifetime, but a long-term process involving repeated rebirths until one reaches the necessary level of development. Different people at any given time are at different stages of progress toward their goal; they are born into families and communities appropriate to their level, and they need an appropriate religious life as well. This is only possible if there are choices, which are provided by the different *mārgas*, or paths, and their alternative practices and goals.

The development of the three *mārgas* and their different views of death and afterlife was justified rather than produced by religious theory; in origin, all three positions were products of India's historical development. More specifically, the different viewpoints reflected in the three *mārgas* emerged in different historical situations to meet the changing needs of an expanding religious tradition within India. This tradition was not yet "Hinduism" when the various viewpoints emerged in the course of the first millennium B.C.E.; it became "Hinduism" only after the different viewpoints had long been established in Indian culture; that is, Hinduism was a historical fact well before it was known by that collective name.

Given this background, it is not surprising that Hinduism does not fit the religious model of Western monotheism. "Hindu" was at first not even a religious term, but was used by Persians and Greeks in the first millennium B.C.E. as a name for the people east of the Indus River, that is, Indians as a whole. Muslims later borrowed the term "Hindu" to designate the non-Muslim population of India, and the British who governed India in the eighteenth and nineteenth centuries used it in much the same way—excluding in this case Christians, but sometimes including Indian Muslims.

It was not until the late nineteenth century that "Hindu" was given a more precise religious meaning, and even then it was used first by Western scholars and British administrators and only later—more or less in self-defense—by those whom we now call "Hindus." In current usage, further refined by modern scholars, "Hindu" refers to those who follow the mainstream indigenous religious tradition of India and accept—at least nominally—the authority of the ancient priestly scriptures known as the Vedas. Although the definition lacks precision, especially at the boundary with indigenous folk and tribal religions, it does exclude Christians and Muslims (who follow religions of foreign origin) and Buddhists and Jains (who reject Vedic authority). With the same limits, but still with a broad inclusiveness, "Hinduism" has been adopted as the collective name for the religious beliefs and practices of Hindus.

It is clear from this discussion that "Hinduism" is not a religion in the familiar Western sense. It has no specific founder, no clear time of origin, and nothing that corresponds to an institutional church or organizational structure. It is united to some degree by a common acceptance of the Vedic scriptures, but even these are selectively used and often are supplemented by later non-Vedic scriptures. Rather than *a* religion, Hinduism is more accurately described as a long-term accumulation and synthesis of a number of religious viewpoints into a commonly accepted system of complementary means of salvation.

The core of this cumulative tradition, and perhaps its major unifying factor, is the concept of the three *mārgas*. What Hinduism lacks in precise definition it more than makes up for with the variety of insights it offers in these alternative paths to salvation—not least in their views of death and afterlife, where some of the major differences appear. Put simply, each of the three *mārgas* advocates what it considers the best possible life and afterlife. The choices between these positions thus involve value judgments about what is best and metaphysical beliefs about what is possible, both within a person's lifetime and afterward. It is the interactions between these viewpoints over the centuries, evolving but never resolved, that have woven the basic fabric of Hinduism.[1]

DEATH AND AFTERLIFE IN THE THREE *MĀRGAS*

The cultural roots of Hinduism go back to the urban Indus civilization in the third millennium B.C.E., but we know nothing about the concepts of death and afterlife from that early period. It is only with the immigrant Indo-European Aryans in the late second millennium B.C.E. that we have access to Indian *ideas* about death and afterlife as distinct from the mute evidence of earlier burial practices. These ideas, expressed first in relatively obscure references in the earliest Aryan hymn collection, the *Rig Veda,* form the starting point for Hindu speculation about personal salvation.

The theme of the *Rig Veda* references is a simply stated hope that the deceased will obtain a new body and a new home among the Fathers in heaven after death and cremation have consumed the former earthly body. The question of where the new body would come from was not directly addressed in these early hymns, but it was clearly a problem that required solution as part of the larger problem of how one achieved—and maintained—an afterlife in what was called "the World of the Fathers." The task of solving these problems was taken up by the priests who performed the Aryan fire sacrifices, working within the context of their sacrificial rituals and aided by a growing body of ritual materials known collectively as "the Veda." By the early centuries of the first millennium B.C.E. their effort to resolve the issues of death and afterlife had led to the formulation of the earliest Hindu path of salvation, the path of ritual action, which provided the base for both of the later alternatives.

The Path of Ritual Action in the Vedic Ritual Tradition

The starting point for all of the Hindu systems of salvation was the religious tradition of the Indo-European Aryans who migrated into northwestern India as pastoral nomads around 1500 B.C.E. The Aryans who entered India were only one branch of a larger migration of Indo-European tribes from the steppes of eastern Europe into adjacent regions of Europe, the Middle East, and western Asia. Like their distant Greek, Celtic, and Germanic relatives who entered Europe during the same period, they were a warlike patriarchal people with a polytheistic religion and a related oral tradition of mythology and poetry, and they shared with other Indo-European tribes the practice of hospitality rituals to their deities around the household fire. By the time they entered India they had begun to evolve a distinctively Aryan religious tradition out of this common background that provided the base for the later Vedic system.

The central feature of the evolving Aryan religious tradition was the emphasis it gave to fire sacrifices. Starting with the older tradition of household hospitality rituals, the Aryans developed a more complex system of sacrifices involving offerings in three separate fires and the concurrent chanting of formal hymns of praise to the deities, or *devas,* to whom the sacrifices were offered. By around 1200 B.C.E. a collection of the hymns used for these sacrifices was brought together as the *Rig Veda,* the first of the series of ritual texts that was called "the Veda"—the body of knowledge essential for performing sacrificial rituals and, more broadly, for understanding the cosmic order that made the rituals effective.

By the first millennium B.C.E. the increasing complex rituals and their associated Veda had come under the control of a class of priests known as Brāhmans, whose special responsibilities were to perform the rituals correctly and to maintain and transmit the knowledge (i.e., the Veda) required for their proper performance. In pursuit of these responsibilities Brāhmans with different functional roles in the sacrifices assembled new collections of relevant hymns and chants paralleling the earlier *Rig Veda,* and the needed ritual explanations and interpretations for each priestly group were similarly assembled in additional scriptures known as Brāhmaṇas that formed the second major component of the Veda. It was this accumulated body of Vedic teachings that provided the basis for the priestly ritual solution to the problems of death and afterlife.

Two major principles emerged in the Brāhmaṇas as expressions of the priestly understanding of Vedic fire sacrifices: the concepts of ritual knowledge *(veda)* and ritual action *(karma).* The Brāhmaṇas assert the view that fire sacrifices, properly conceived, embody the fundamental dynamic structures of the cosmos; they are microcosmic models of macrocosmic reality. The connection between the two—that is, between the fire sacrifice and the cosmos—is established by proper ritual knowledge *(veda),* which activates the necessary linkages and establishes the identity between microcosm and macrocosm. Once the basic identity has been established, ritual action *(karma)* becomes symbolically and effectively identical with the corresponding cosmic processes. Ritual action thus has cosmic consequences, and proper ritual action can produce desired results at the cosmic level.

The granting of cosmic status to the sacrifice gave extraordinary power to both the ritual and those who performed it. By the time of the late Brāhmaṇas, this power was considered even greater than that of the *devas* to whom earlier sacrifices had been offered. From the perspective of Vedic priests, the sacrifice was effective not because the *devas* chose to grant requests, but because ritual knowledge and action produced results directly. This was true with regard to worldly rewards, and it also was true with regard to the afterlife. Life in the World of the Fathers was thus not a gift of the *devas,* but a product of proper ritual performance. Worldly goods cannot be taken with you, but the effects of ritual action reach beyond the grave—or in this case, beyond the cremation of the earthly body.

In the view of the Vedic ritual tradition cremation returns the physical remains of the deceased to nature as smoke and ashes, but properly performed *karma* establishes the departed in the World of the Fathers. The ritual action required is only partly that of the person before his death. To this early Vedic understanding the developed ritual tradition added the need for a special set of postcremation rituals called the *sapiṇḍīkaraṇa* to complete the transition to the ancestral world.[2] Normally performed by the eldest son of the deceased, these rituals have the function of creating the new body for the departed in the World of the Fathers and ensuring its maintenance, and they in turn are supplemented by later rituals to nourish both the most recently deceased and the generations of prior ancestors. Afterlife is thus not a matter of individual effort alone, but depends on the ritual performances of one's immediate and later descendants to establish and sustain it.

It is evident from this description that afterlife in the Vedic ritual tradition is a corporate family concern. Only a married householder can perform the required rituals for himself and his ancestors, and only a continuing family line can secure the welfare of the departed. From the perspective of this tradition, householder life is therefore not only a means of securing one's own afterlife, but also an obligation owed to one's ancestors, and the debt is only paid—and one's own afterlife maintained—by the procreation of sons to maintain the succession of ritual duties. Despite the appearance of new paths of individual salvation, this responsibility to both past and future generations has remained a central concern of Hindu householders over the ages, just as life in the World of the Fathers has remained the normative goal of afterlife.

The Upaniṣadic Goal of Release from Rebirth

The Vedic ritual tradition reflects the positive view of worldly life and afterlife that characterized the early Aryans and that continues in the later Hindu emphasis on family life and social duties. From the perspective of this tradition, worldly life and afterlife are on a continuum, linked by the process of ritual cause and effect that brings rewards both during and after one's lifetime. Given the values and metaphysical assumptions of the ritual tradition, neither the desirability of worldly rewards nor the goal of life in the World of the Fathers was called into question.

After around 800 B.C.E. the viewpoint and values of the Vedic ritual tradition were challenged by another and seemingly contradictory system of salvation that also emerged within the Vedic tradition: the system set forth in the Vedic scriptures known as the Upaniṣads. Produced between around 800 and 500 B.C.E., the early Upaniṣads reflected the attitudes of teachers—mainly Vedic priests and members of the Aryan ruling class—who had lost confidence in the value of sacrificial rituals and their rewards. The context of this development was the urbanization taking place at that time in the Ganges valley that threatened traditional Aryan society in northern India, but the views of the Upaniṣadic teachers went well beyond a response to historical change. Slowly, but with increasing clarity, they created a new metaphysical system that questioned the permanence not only of this world, but of the World of the Fathers also, and proposed a new conception of afterlife that was apart from both these realms.

The approach of the Upaniṣadic thinkers was to distinguish what is permanent and unchanging from what is transient and impermanent at the levels of both cosmic and personal existence. At the cosmic level they identified the unchanging reality as *Brahman,* the One Being that underlies the transient names and forms of phenomena. As gold is the underlying reality of all objects made of gold, and clay of all objects made of clay, so *Brahman* is the underlying reality and essence of the phenomenal world. At the personal level this same reality is the "self," or *ātman,* the conscious Being that underlies each person and remains unchanging in the midst of activity and change.

The entire phenomenal world is viewed in the Upaniṣads as transient at every level, both personal and cosmic—including the World of the Fathers and even the gods or *devas* themselves. This transient world is not without order, which is provided by the triad of desire, thought, and action *(karma).* It is desire and thought that bring the phenomenal world of activity into existence, and desirous action that perpetuates it. At the personal level it is similarly intentional desirous action that perpetuates individual existence and brings about personal rebirth in the phenomenal world. Like the creative power of the fire sacrifice, the fire of desire and its expression in desirous action create new forms as a vehicle for the *ātman* as long as desire remains unquenched. Life in the World of the Fathers is, in this view, merely one of the many transient forms created to maintain personal existence—lasting for a time, perhaps even a long time, but eventually ending in rebirth back into the world.[3]

The goal of the Upaniṣadic teachers was to escape from this ceaseless cycle of birth, death, and rebirth that they called *samsāra*. *Samsāra* itself as a cosmic process could not be ended, but it was possible for a person to escape from the process by ending personal rebirth. This freedom could not be achieved by ritual sacrifices, which by their basic nature and purpose were based on desire, and life in the World of the Fathers could only be a temporary reprieve from future rebirth. Freedom from rebirth was possible only by giving up all desire and desirous action, and this in turn was only possible if one realized that one's own true self, the *ātman,* was not part of the transient phenomenal world. The self instead was pure consciousness, and its basic nature was identical to the unchanging reality of *Brahman* that underlaid the changing phenomenal world.

The goal of the Upaniṣadic teachers was thus not attainment of what they considered the transient World of the Fathers, but escape from rebirth entirely by means of knowledge, specifically, knowledge of the fundamental identity of the true personal self, or *ātman,* with the Universal Self, or *Brahman*. To achieve this knowledge the Upaniṣadic teachers left their homes and families and their involvement in society and retired to the forest as celibate mendicants so they could pursue their quest without distraction. In contrast to the earlier—but still continuing—path of *karma,* or ritual action, this new path was called the path of knowledge, or *jñāna*.

The Upaniṣadic path of knowledge became an important component of Hinduism alongside the Vedic ritual tradition, despite the differences in values, philosophical assumptions, and goals. The two were in fact brought together in a single system in the early centuries C.E. in what was perhaps the most important Hindu synthesis: the so-called *Varṇāśrama-dharma* system, or the system of duties according to class and stage of life. In this system, which is set forth in texts on duty (Dharma Śāstras) such as the *Laws of Manu,* all of society is arranged in a hierarchy of four classes and a sequence of four stages of life. The three upper classes, or *varṇas,* are entitled to study the Vedic scriptures and learn Vedic ritual, and the male members of these classes are to spend the first stage of their lives as celibate Vedic students, roughly from ages twelve to twenty. At the end of this stage they return home to marry and begin the second stage of their lives as householders. For *Manu* and other Dharma Śāstra texts this is the most important stage of life: the one that produces children to ensure the family line, that ensures the stability of society, and that pays the bills for everyone else, including the Vedic teachers and the forest-dwellers.

The main religious duty of the householder is to perform the necessary rituals for himself, his family, and his departed ancestors in the World of the Fathers. A person has three debts, tradition says: to the Vedic seers, to the gods, and to the ancestors. The first of these he discharges as a celibate student of the Veda, the second is fulfilled by sacrifices to the gods, and the third is paid by having sons who will ensure the family line and maintain the needed offerings to the ancestors. Only when these debts have been satisfied can the householder begin to consider renouncing the world to pursue the path described in the Upaniṣads.

When a householder's hair has turned grey, wrinkles appear on his face, and he has seen the sons of his sons, the *Laws of Manu* states, then he may become a forest-dweller. The third stage in life as a forest-dweller is one of increasing attention to study, meditation, and religious activities such as pilgrimage, retreats, and visits to holy men. The forest-dweller does not leave his family completely, but lives a life of celibacy and detaches himself from family concerns. Most people never pass beyond this stage, and can expect when they die to go to the World of the Fathers and eventually be reborn.

A few pass on into the fourth stage of life, the stage of renunciation, in which the goal of ending rebirth becomes the main focus. Entry into this stage is marked dramatically by a funeral service for the person one once was. At this point a renounced person, or *sannyāsin,* is symbolically dead to his old life: He abandons his family name, he severs all family ties, and he renounces all of his former possessions. In modern India a renounced person is legally dead, and his inheritance is distributed as if he were actually deceased. He now is free to pursue the goal of knowledge for the purpose of release, and if he realizes the identity of his self and *Brahman,* he will pass out of the cycle of rebirth forever.

Sannyāsins do not all follow the same procedures to achieve knowledge and release. Some emphasize study and a more philosophical approach to knowledge, some devote themselves to the practice of yoga and the experience of pure consciousness, and others live a life of increasing austerity and self-denial. The goal for all remains basically the same: not the worldly rewards of Vedic sacrifice or a ritually achieved life in the World of the Fathers, but a final cessation of rebirth by a liberation of the self from all attachment.

The Path of Devotion

Both the system of Vedic rituals and the Upaniṣadic path of knowledge are products of the Vedic tradition. Both rely on the Vedic scriptures for their authority, and are, therefore, heavily influenced by the values and concerns of the Vedic priesthood. Success in either of these paths is largely the result of education and expertise: skill and knowledge to perform the proper rituals and thus control their creative power, and intellect and opportunity to pursue the path to release. Neither path relies on divine assistance, much less divine grace, to attain its goals, since in both cases it is proper human effort or knowledge that ensures results.

The appeal of these paths has, therefore, been mainly confined to the elite social classes, and both in fact deny access to the majority of Hindus who are not qualified by birth for Vedic study. As important as these two paths are in terms of prestige, they thus have never satisfied the religious needs of most

Hindus, especially, though not exclusively, those who are on the lowest rung of the social hierarchy.

By the second century B.C.E. a third path was emerging with both greater popular appeal and greater accessibility. This new path, devotional theism, was based not on Vedic rituals or Vedic knowledge, but on the worship of various popular deities. There had been elements of theism in some of the late Upaniṣads produced between 500 and 200 B.C.E., but the devotional aspect was new and was expounded for the first time in the *Bhagavad Gītā*—not a Vedic text at all, but part of a long popular epic known as the *Mahābhārata* that was accessible to everyone.

Devotional theism expanded rapidly after its first appearance, and by the early centuries C.E. it had become the dominant form of Hinduism in terms of numbers of followers. The elite had their forms of Vedic religion, but the people had their gods and goddesses: Vishnu the protector, with his incarnations as Rāma and as Krisna, the Lord of the *Bhagavad Gītā;* Shiva the destroyer, the divine Yogī and cosmic Lord of dance; and Devī, the goddess in a variety of names and forms. Worshiped with devotion, these deities responded with love and concern for the welfare of their devotees. In contrast to Vedic religion, the goals of their worshipers were not dependent solely on human knowledge and effort, but were aided by divine action. Devotional theism, this third path within Hinduism, was perhaps above all a religion of grace.

The goals of devotional religion also differed from earlier Vedic religion, not least with regard to afterlife. Release from rebirth was no longer a matter of knowledge alone, but also could be a divine gift to faithful devotees. The afterlife sought was not the sterile or abstract World of the Fathers, but a life—or afterlife—of devotion to God. Eternal devotion was not a cliché, but a real and hoped-for possibility. As Krisna promises in the *Bhagavad Gītā:*

> You will be freed from the bonds of action,
> from the fruit of fortune and misfortune;
> armed with the discipline of renunciation,
> yourself liberated, you will join me. . . .
> Keep me in your mind and devotion, sacrifice
> to me, bow to me, discipline yourself to me,
> and you will reach me! (9.28, 34)[4]

These verses express the constant refrain of devotional Hinduism, the hope not only to be "freed from the bonds of action"—that is, to be freed from *karma*-caused rebirth—but to achieve a permanent union with one's personal deity that preserves the devotional relationship. Release from rebirth is important, but not if it means merging with the impersonal *Brahman* in the manner of the Upaniṣadic way of knowledge. The nineteenth-century saint Ramakrishna spoke for all devotees when he said about his own relationship to the goddess: "I want to taste sugar, not become sugar."

As the latest of the three paths of salvation, the path of devotion combined some of the basic features of the two earlier paths. The great majority of devotees were and remained householders, like the followers of the ritual tradition, and it was emphasized from the time of the *Gītā* onward that devotion does not require abandonment of family and society. As is the path of knowledge, however, the goal of life should not be worldly rewards or an afterlife in the World of the Fathers, but relinquishment of the desire and attachment that cause continuing rebirth.

The basis for this new combination of views was the central role of personal deities in devotional theism. In the *Gītā,* the earliest devotional text, the world is affirmed because it not only is created by the Lord, but also is his body. Devotees of Shiva, the other great male deity, likewise view him as the creator of the world, and the goddess often is perceived by her devotees as Nature itself. The world is thus not an impersonal or unreal realm, but the arena of divine activity and divine encounter. Vishnu incarnates himself in the world as Rama and Krisna to save the world from unrighteousness, Shiva manifests himself in the world in theophanies to save his devotees, and the goddess enters the world to defeat demons who threaten its security.

But if devotees need not escape from the world to encounter the divine, they do need to free themselves from desire and attachment to what the *Gītā* calls "the fruits of action," that is, the personal gains that may result from their actions. This is achieved, according to the *Gītā,* not by renouncing actions as in the path of knowledge, but by sacrificing the fruits of action to the Lord in devotion. True renunciation is thus for the *Gītā* renunciation of the fruits of action, not renunciation of actions themselves, and it is this renunciation in devotion that will bring release from rebirth and an afterlife of devotional union with the Lord: "Armed with the discipline of renunciation, your self liberated, you will join me" (*Gītā* 9.28).

The *Gītā* represents only one version of the path of devotion, but its views are broadly typical with respect to both devotion and the afterlife. The issue for all of the Hindu devotional traditions is whether one is attached to the world by selfish desires or attached to one's chosen god or goddess by devotion: If the former, then the karmic effects of desirous actions will bring rebirth; if the latter, the devotee will be freed from rebirth to a permanent union with the object of his or her devotion. All of the devotional traditions agree that neither of the goals of the other paths is sufficient. Life in the World of the Fathers lacks the divine presence, and an impersonal freedom from rebirth is not enough. What the devotee seeks is eternal personal devotion, and only an afterlife that includes this is salvation in the fullest sense.

CONCLUSION

All of the views of afterlife outlined above became part of the continuing Hindu religious tradition, and they and their related systems of salvation—the three *mārgas*—have provided the basic framework of Hinduism for the past 2,000 years. Few Hindus would consider any of these systems or their goals invalid, although most would consider one or the other of them better for themselves. The important point is that the tradition as a whole has not chosen one of them over the others as the exclusive or even the preferred path to salvation or goal of afterlife, but has maintained them all as alternatives.

Although the three paths have preserved their distinctive features over the millennia, there also has been a significant amount of borrowing and blending that has woven them closer together. All Hindus, for example, accept the concept of rebirth as a result of desirous actions, and even followers of the Vedic ritual tradition acknowledge that life in the World of the Fathers is not an eternal afterlife, but only a stage of temporary reward from which one must eventually return. This does not prevent them from seeking that goal or from accepting the responsibility for their ancestors who have sought it, but it does mean that if and when they seek an absolutely final afterlife outside rebirth, they must find it by another path.

This example points out perhaps the most basic feature of the Hindu view of salvation and afterlife: the question of personal choice. The *Gītā,* to cite another example, does not deny that the Upaniṣadic path of knowledge brings release from rebirth and a union with the impersonal *Brahman;* it says instead that this is a difficult path to follow and that the path of devotion is not only easier, but also leads to a more personally rewarding union with the Lord. Which path one chooses is not a matter of right or wrong, but a matter of personal temperament, ability, and opportunity. One chooses the goal and means that fit one's current condition, which realistically is all that one can ever do.

What Hinduism offers with regard to death and afterlife is thus not final decision that must be made in one's present lifetime, but a process that leads through many cycles of death and rebirth until one is able to reach the goal of one's choice. It is not coincidence that there are no massive monuments to the dead in Hinduism, no tombs, sarcophagi, or pyramids to mark the final resting place of the dead, because death is not in any sense a final stopping point. All beings that die will be reborn as long as they are still engaged in the karmic process, so their physical remains are only a transient and insignificant reminder of their passing; and all beings similarly have the possibility of final salvation, although this may be many lifetimes in the future. Any individual death is, therefore, only a transition point in a larger cycle that will present many conditions and opportunities in the course of many lifetimes. What matters is how one uses the circumstances that each life provides to work toward the ultimate afterlife of one's choice.

NOTES

1. For further discussion of these issues and a more detailed presentation of the historical development, see Thomas J. Hopkins, *The Hindu Religious Tradition* (Encino, Calif.: Dickenson Publishing Co., 1971).

2. A detailed discussion of these rituals in the context of the Hindu ritual tradition is provided by David M. Knipe, "*Sapindīkarana:* The Hindu Rite of Entry into Heaven," in Frank E. Reynolds and Earle H. Waugh, eds., *Religious Encounters with Death* (University Park, Pa.: Pennsylvania State University Press, 1977), 111–24.

3. The Hindu view of rebirth or reincarnation is dealt with both directly and in a larger comparative context by J. Bruce Long, "Reincarnation," in *The Encyclopedia of Religion,* 12:265–69, and by R. J. Zwi Werblowsky, "Transmigration," in *The Encyclopedia of Religion,* 15:21–26.

4. Barbara Stoler Miller, trans., *The Bhagavad-Gita* (New York: Bantam Books, 1986).

11

Death as Threat, Death as Achievement: Buddhist Perspectives with Particular Reference to the Theravada Tradition

Frank E. Reynolds

DEATH AND THE CONFRONTATION WITH LIMITS

According to a tradition that I believe to be correct (though I have not been able to locate the text), the European philosopher Ludwig Wittgenstein once noted that death is not an event in life. In so doing he suggested that death is a reality that cannot be dealt with through the kind of categories we ordinarily use to conceptualize, make sense of, and grapple with various aspects of our daily existence. Death, from this point of view, confronts us as a limit that exposes the boundaries and confinements of life as we ordinarily experience it.[1]

For a historian of religions, Wittgenstein's remark has a certain resonance. Many of the religious traditions that we study affirm—at a certain level—notions that are similar to his. But in such cases the otherness of death presents itself in a way that is not as benign as it appears to be in the rather epigrammatic formulation provided by the modern philosopher. In most religious traditions the otherness of death is an otherness that is integrated—at another level—into a larger reality within which—according to the tradition concerned—the limits of death (and in some cases the limits of both life and death) can be overcome or transcended.

Buddhism is one of those religions in which this basic pattern is most evident.[2] Consider, for example, the story that Buddhists recount concerning the future Buddha's first encounter with death, and of the events that followed immediately thereafter. According to the story, the future Buddha had lived his early life in the protected environment of his father's palace. In this context he had experienced all of the various pleasures that life could bring, including those associated with wealth, marriage, and parenthood. One day he ventured outside the palace (or, in some versions, was transported there in a vision) and successively encountered a sick person, an aged person, a corpse, and, finally, a monk who had severed his societal connections and become an ascetic. Soon thereafter the future Buddha himself renounced the pleasures of his own palace life, left his wife and young son, and, like the monk he had seen, took up the life of a wandering mendicant.

The point is clear. Through his venture outside the palace the future Buddha confronted the fundamental facts of life that had previously been hidden from his view. He came face to face with the harsh realities of sickness, of old age, and, most especially, of death. As he did so he recognized, in an immediate and existential way, the inexorable threat that these realities posed to the permanence (and hence to the meaningfulness and value) of the life he had previously been living, and of the pleasures and satisfactions he had previously enjoyed. Thus, through the shock occasioned by the first three sights, the future Buddha was prepared to respond in a positive way to the appearance of the monk. And so he did. Soon after his return to the palace he made his decision to enter the mendicant way, and in that context he began his quest for insight into a larger reality within which the problematics of sickness, old age, and death might be encompassed and resolved.

A similar occurrence is recounted in a famous story reported in the Buddhist scriptures and expanded in the commentaries. In this instance the protagonist is a woman, Kisa Gotami by name, who eventually became an *arhat* (a fully perfected saint). Driven to distraction by the death of her only child, Kisa carried the dead boy on her hip, seeking everywhere for some kind of medicine that would revive him. Finally an old man, recognizing the spiritual character of her malaise, recommended that she visit the Buddha. Following the old man's advice, Kisa approached the Buddha and told him her story. The Buddha's response was to instruct her to go into the village and to bring him a mustard seed from a house in which no death had yet occurred. As she carried on her fruitless search the truth concerning the inexorable universality of death suddenly dawned on her. Shocked by her recognition of the harsh limitations that death imposed on all worldly life, she gave up her hope for finding a medicine that would revive her son. She then went on to renounce her household existence, to enter the Buddhist Order, and to seek, under the Buddha's tutelage, an insight into a larger reality within which the power of death could be domesticated and defeated.

THE DIALECTICS OF DESIRE AND DEATH

According to Buddhist accounts, both the Buddha himself and his disciples such as Kisa Gotami did in fact discover the kind of larger reality that they sought. In the short space of this chapter I cannot hope to describe that larger reality in any full or comprehensive manner. It will be useful, however, to single out several ways in which death appears at this more advanced level of

Buddhist imagery and teaching. It will be especially helpful to look closely at the way Buddhists have come to understand the relationship between death and desire.

Buddhists, in their teachings concerning death, have never relinquished the notion that death is an existential reality that frustrates the desire that drives human beings to grasp after the pleasures and satisfactions of this-worldly life. In their larger vision of reality Buddhists have, however, recognized that the relationship between death and desire is far more complex than this first-level perception would suggest. Probed more deeply, the relationship between death and desire that seemed at first glance to be one of simple opposition, turns out at another, more profound level to be one of intimate association, complimentarity, and interdependence.

Certain crucial aspects of the deep-level affinity between death and desire are made evident in the stories that recount the events through which the future Buddha, following his great renunciation, attained enlightenment. Most colorful in this regard is the report of the great battle that is said to have taken place just before the Enlightenment itself—a battle that pitted the future Buddha against Mara, a god whose name itself signifies death. This battle occurred just after the Buddha had taken his seat on the Enlightenment throne situated under the Bo tree at Bodh Gaya. At that crucial point death, embodied in the figure of Mara, sought, through the attraction provided by his beautiful daughters, to arouse in the future Buddha the desire and the grasping that would bring about his defeat and keep him in bondage. But the future Buddha, in a spectacularly successful response, "called the earth to witness." And what were the events to which the earth bore witness? These events were the great deeds that the future Buddha had performed in his previous lives, deeds of awesome self-denial and self-sacrifice through which his capacity to resist desire had been both demonstrated and perfected. Clearly in this episode, which is one of the best known and most often depicted episodes in all of Buddhist mythology, there is a powerful affirmation of a deep-level alliance between death and desire, on the one hand, and between the victory over death and the victory over desire, on the other.

This deep-level interlocking of death and desire is even more explicitly affirmed in the most crucial insight that Buddhists associate with the Enlightenment itself. According to the accounts, the future Buddha, after his success in routing the forces of Mara, entered into a meditational state in which his actual Enlightenment was accomplished. In the first of the three stages of his attainment he recalled to mind all of his own previous lives. In the second stage of his attainment he envisioned the circulation of all beings in a cosmic round of birth, death, rebirth, and redeath. Finally, in the third stage, which coincided with the coming of the dawn, he achieved a penetrating insight into the central Buddhist truth concerning the codependent origination of all existing realities.

In the early Buddhist scriptures the explicit formulation of this culminating insight concerning the codependent origination of the components that constitute phenomenal reality varies from text to text, and interpretations have differed through the course of Buddhist history. But one of the constant characteristics of this teaching is that along with ignorance, desire and death always appear among the set of basic phenomenal elements that are held to arise co-dependently. What is explicitly stated is the notion that when ignorance and desire arise, then death inevitably arises with them. But at the same time there is a correlated implication that has always played a central role in Buddhist soteriology. The correlated implication is that when ignorance is overcome and desire is quenched, then (the causes having been removed) the demise of death cannot be far behind.

DEATH AS TRANSITION: PROBLEMATICS AND POSSIBILITIES

Within the larger reality that the Buddha and his followers have discerned, this new recognition of a profound affinity between death and desire has been supplemented by a new perception of the way that death functions as a limit or boundary to the extension and meaningfulness of this-worldly existence. From the mythic stories that have already been recounted it can be seen that death in the Buddhist world is no longer understood simply as the end of a single life span that is once-for-all and final. In the story of the future Buddha's encounter with Mara, for example, his act of "calling the earth to witness" vividly demonstrates that he takes his life-at-the-time to be an extension of a series of continuing lives, deaths, and rebirths that stretches far back into the past. In the account of the Buddha's Enlightenment the conception of death as part of an ongoing process of life, death, rebirth, and redeath is made even more explicit and is applied more generally. In the first phase of the Enlightenment process the Buddha remembers his own previous lives. In the second phase he envisions a grand cosmic scenario within which he sees all sentient beings as they proceed through the ongoing series of lives and deaths that constitutes their existence. In the third phase he achieves the culminating insight into the truth of co-dependent origination, and thus he sees, in its essential structure, the process in and through which birth and death, along with ignorance and desire, are continuously being produced and reproduced in a series that—potentially at least—is infinite.

Within this continuing process of birth, death, rebirth, and redeath death continues to function as a limit that calls into question the value of all of the satisfactions and pleasures that can be realized within this-worldly existence. But in the specifically Buddhist context it does so as a transition that poses a limit by virtue of its continuing recurrence rather than by its absolute finality in any given case.

For those who truly understand and appropriate the painful implications of death's continuing recurrence in the ongoing process of life, death, rebirth, and redeath, the only appropriate response is quite obviously the response of the Buddha himself and of the Buddhist saints who follow in his footsteps. In the case of such Noble Beings the impermanent, death-infected, suffering-filled character of phenomenal reality is recognized; as a result, desire is snuffed out, and thus Nibbana (release from the power of death) is attained. When death actually comes to such Noble Beings it simply provides an occasion for culminating and celebrating the triumph over desire and death that has, in principle, already been achieved.[3]

For those who are spiritually less mature (and this includes the great majority of human beings, the great majority of Buddhists, and the great majority of Buddhist monks), any kind of final release from the ongoing process of life, death, rebirth, and redeath is out of the question. In their situations, since at least some remnants of desire and ignorance remain, the continuation of the cycle of death and rebirth is inevitable. Nonetheless, according to Buddhist teaching, such people *can,* by means of their intentions and actions, determine the character of their future lives. Thus they, too, have the possibility of living a life—and dying a death—that has a significant religious meaning.

Within the larger reality that Buddhists have discerned there are some modes of this-worldly existence that, despite their confinement within the limits imposed by the continuing recurrence of death, are relatively advantageous. They are advantageous both in terms of the pleasures and satisfactions that they offer and in terms of the opportunities for further spiritual development that they make available. It is quite possible, for example, to be reborn either in a heavenly realm or in a more privileged position in the human world. On the other hand, there are other, very different modes of this-worldly existence that involve great pain and suffering, and provide little or no possibility for achieving spiritual progress. As a result, it also is quite possible to be reborn in one of any number of Buddhist hells, or in a radically disadvantaged position within human society.

For ordinary Buddhists who face such positive and negative alternatives, the appropriate response obviously is to act in such a way that a better rebirth will be assured. According to Buddhist teaching, this means moderating, as much as possible, the desire that fuels and regulates the process of life, death, rebirth, and redeath. For—so the teaching goes—the more that those who are involved in this process control and moderate their desire, the higher they will rise in the cosmological hierarchy and the closer they will come to attaining the goal of Nibbanic release; the more that they allow their desire to boil and intensify, the lower they will fall in the cosmic hierarchy and the further they will depart from the path that leads to salvation. Expressed in the phrase that Buddhists themselves most often use, those who "make merit"—those who demonstrate and achieve the moderation of their desire by listening to the Buddha's teaching, by adhering to the precepts he laid down, and by giving appropriate gifts—will necessarily be rewarded with a favorable rebirth. Those who engage in immoral activity and fail to make merit will, on the other hand, find themselves reborn in horrible situations in which physical suffering and spiritual hopelessness prevail.[4]

DEATH AS ACHIEVEMENT: THE PARINIBBANA OF THE BUDDHA

Next to the story of the Buddha's Enlightenment, the most important biographical narrative that has been preserved by the Buddhist tradition is the one that recounts his death or (to use the Buddhist term) his Parinibbana. The Buddha's death and the important events that immediately preceded and followed it are described in a widely known and much-quoted text called the Mahaparinibbana Sutta. The importance of several of the most crucial episodes recounted in this text has been both underscored and enhanced through their portrayal in various forms of Buddhist architecture and art.

In discussing the Buddha's Parinibbana the first point that needs to be emphasized is that, for the Theravadins at least, the Buddha's death was very real. Despite the Buddha's prodigious spiritual accomplishments, the basic law of existence—the law that all composite entities are subject to decay and dispersion—could not be abrogated. Quite to the contrary, the coalescence of *skandhas* that had constituted the "person" of the Buddha (a coalescence—a product of past activity driven by ignorance and desire) remained fully subject to the ravages of old age, sickness, and death. Hence, at the age of eighty, the Buddha suffered an attack of food poisoning, and soon thereafter he breathed his last.

But because the Buddha had previously won his victory over Mara, and because he had attained the goal of Enlightenment, death had lost its sting. Through the Buddha's previous efforts he had achieved the Nibbana or release that comes with the elimination of desire and extinction of the defilements *(kilesas);* thus he was able, with the assistance of his disciples, to direct his dying and death so that it became an occasion for a distinctive kind of achievement, both for himself and for them.

At the personal level the mythic account highlights the Buddha's complete equanimity, his complete acceptance of his own demise. According to a fascinating episode that is included in the Mahaparinibbana Sutta, he had it within his power to postpone his death until the end of the present cosmic age. But—so the story goes—his favorite disciple failed to ask him to exercise that option; as a result, he refrained from doing so. Thus he intentionally allowed the process of dying and death to proceed.[5]

According to the story that is told in the Mahaparinibbana Sutta, the Buddha quite self-consciously chose the time and the place of his death. When the proper time had come and he had arrived at the place he had selected he lay down on his right side; he entered into a process of desireless meditation, and then, in a state of complete lucidity and composure, he breathed his last. Thus the Buddha allowed the *skandhas* (the component elements whose coalescence had constituted his identity as a "person") to be dispersed and finally extinguished. In so doing he achieved the ultimate Buddhist goal—the goal of Parinibbana or "Fully Completed Release."[6]

The traditional accounts of the Buddha's Parinibbana also indicate that his death had, in addition to its personal dimension, an important communal dimension. These accounts highlight the belief that the Buddha's death was achieved in a way that was efficacious not only for his own salvation, but also for the maintenance and spiritual well-being of the community he had founded. The stories directly highlight the point that the more communal aspect of the total situation was taken seriously by the Buddha himself. The accounts report, for example, that the Buddha urged his disciples not to be driven to despair by his death, but to recognize that it served as a confirmation of his teaching concerning the impermanence of all composite phenomena. These stories also recount that during the Buddha's last days, he took great care to instruct his followers concerning the way they should act in the new situation that would pertain once his death had occurred.

The Mahaparinibbana narrative also reports that Buddha's disciples, both monastic and lay, were actively involved in the events that surrounded his death. The monks assumed important responsibilities in organizing and presiding at a new kind of funeral that highlighted the purity that the Buddha had achieved and the victory over death that he had won. In playing out their role as monks they both demonstrated and advanced their own practice of the Buddhist Path. The laity, for their part, took charge of his relics; they built stupas to house them, and they initiated rituals of remembrance and veneration. Thus they made their own distinctive contribution to the preservation of continuity in the life of the community, and at the same time, they acquired a supply of merit that enhanced their own soteriological status.

From the perspective of the Buddhist tradition the Parinibbana of the Buddha was distinctive. As the Buddha of the present age, his spiritual achievements, both during his lifetime and at the time of his death, are, in principle, unique within the age. Buddhists also have recognized, however, that in the course of Buddhist history, there do appear figures whose status or attainments closely resemble the status or the attainments of the Founder. These include great Buddhist kings whose exercise of sovereignty leads to a near-identification with the figure of the Buddha. And they include Buddhist saints *(arhats)* whose spiritual attainments are thought to include a similar realization of Nibbanic release. In such cases the deaths (including the events that have immediately preceded and followed them) often have been self-consciously modeled on particular aspects of the Parinibbana of the Buddha. In this regard one need only think of the accounts of the scenarios in which many Buddhist kings and saints are reported to have died.[7] Or of the great cremations and funerary rituals performed for many Buddhist kings and monks.[8] Or of the distribution of relics or relic equivalents that often have followed the deaths of Buddhist saints.[9]

DEATH AS ACHIEVEMENT: THE CASE OF "ORDINARY" BUDDHISTS

For most Buddhists the kind of dying and death that is associated with the Parinibbana of the Buddha is totally out of the question. From the Buddhist perspective, the vast majority of the members of the Buddhist community, including both monks and laypeople, remain entrapped in the ongoing process of life, death, rebirth, and redeath. But it remains the case that according to Buddhist teaching, even ordinary Buddhists who have no pretensions to royal status or sainthood can negotiate death in such a way that it becomes a meaningful soteriological achievement. Consider, in this regard, the process of dying and death as it occurs in communities of ordinary Buddhist practitioners in northern Thailand.[10]

At the personal level serious Buddhists in northern Thailand recognize that, ideally at least, the activities in which they engage throughout their lives should constitute a preparation for the kind of death that will lead them on to a more favorable rebirth. This Buddhist sense of the relationship between all life-activities and the achievement of a good death provides, from the outset, a strong motivation to adhere to Buddhist morality, to become involved in meditative practice, and, most important, to participate in various kinds of merit-making activity. But with the onset of old age these preparations for dying and death become more intense and more focused.[11]

These more intense and focused preparations involve elderly Buddhists in a calculated kind of psychological withdrawal from socially motivated interpersonal involvements, a withdrawal that is expressed and fostered by an increase in meditative and discipline-oriented activity, on the one hand, and by increased merit-making activity, on the other. These preparations do *not* involve—as the preparation for death commonly does in the West—a process of achieving, through memory and confession, a kind of personal "integrity" that has about it the ring of summation and finality.[12] On the contrary, Buddhists in northern Thailand prepare for death by undertaking present-oriented activities that are aimed at achieving psychic detachment from the life they have lived in the past, and at intensifying the practice of the religious path that will lead to the attainment of a more favorable rebirth in their next life and beyond.[13]

In the Buddhist context in northern Thailand members of the surrounding community also play a crucial role in the process of dying and death. The monks who reside at the local temple provide the person facing death with a source of knowledge and supportive guidance, particularly when the actual death-crisis arrives; they also serve as proper recipients for the gifts that an elderly person may give to generate merit intended to assure a more favorable rebirth. For their part relatives and friends engage in activities that generate additional merit that is specifically intended to accrue to the benefit of the one who is dying or deceased. Ideally, the process begins quite early in the life cycle when the younger generation performs various activities (such as spending a rainy season in the monastic order) that earn merit that is transferred to members of the older generation. This process of making merit and transferring its benefits to parents and elders continues right up to the time when death finally arrives. At the funeral the rites that are performed by relatives and friends generate merit, and that merit is dedicated to the cause of the one who has died. In the years that follow still other rituals are performed for the purpose of generating and transferring still more merit in the hope that the rebirth prospects of the deceased will be even further enhanced.[14]

When the death of an ordinary Buddhist is properly achieved the soteriological benefits are not limited to the person who has died. That person has, to be sure, been assured of a favorable rebirth. But, in addition, the other members of the community who have properly participated in the process have accumulated important soteriological gains as well. All of those who were involved have once again confronted, in a direct and vivid way, the basic Buddhist truth concerning the impermanence of all composite realities and the ephemeral character of all purely this-worldly values and pleasures. Thus their soteriological consciousness has been sharpened. In addition, all of the participants have engaged in a merit-making process that has borne soteriological fruit not only for the deceased to whom the merit has been transferred, but also for the participants themselves. For within the Buddhist perspective acts of transferring merit to others (and especially transferring merit to a parent or elder) are, in themselves, acts of selfless giving, and as such they are taken to be acts that generate even more merit (and hence better deaths and better rebirths) for those who perform them.[15]

CONCLUSION

As we have seen, the achievements associated with the Parinibbana of the Buddha and the deaths of great kings and saints who have followed in his footsteps are one thing. And the achievements associated with the deaths of ordinary Buddhists are quite another. But this having been said we should note, in conclusion, that both of these distinctively Buddhist kinds of death-related achievement share at least three aspects in common.

First, both of these Buddhist ways of achieving a good death involve the realization of soteriological progress by the person who undergoes the death. In the case of the Buddha, among others, this is accomplished through the realization of the highest Buddhist goal of fully completed release. In the case of ordinary Buddhists it is accomplished through the more modest attainment of a more favorable rebirth.

Second, both of these Buddhist ways of achieving a good death involve the participation and the maintenance of the surrounding community. In the case of a Buddha or similar figures the community celebrates the Great Attainment, and at the same time the community reclaims the Buddha's legacy, or the legacy of the king or saint, in a new and more lasting way. In the case of the deaths of ordinary Buddhists the community adds its own contribution to the well-being of the deceased and, at the same time, reaffirms the basic structures that undergird its own existence.

Third, both of these ways of achieving a good death create a situation that enables the individual members of the community, by performing the proper roles and rituals that are assigned to them, to attain significant soteriological benefits for themselves.

For Buddhists the bottom line is that within the larger reality they have discerned, death has been encompassed; and that satisfying strategies for overcoming it have been devised for religious virtuosi, on the one hand, and for ordinary Buddhist practitioners, on the other hand. What is more, these strategies have involved the participation of the entire community in ways that—from the Buddhist perspective at least—have redounded to the benefit of all concerned.

NOTES

1. I am appreciative of criticisms and suggestions made by Charles Hallisey, several of which have been incorporated into the text that follows.

2. Given the inexhaustible richness and variety of Buddhist notions and practices related to dying and death, I have chosen to focus my attention on the Theravada tradition. This ancient Buddhist tradition developed in India and spread to Sri Lanka, Burma, Thailand, Cambodia, and Laos, where it continues to hold sway today. Many of the points I will make apply to other forms of Buddhism as well, but the Theravada tradition will provide my primary point of reference.

3. In some Buddhist traditions the quenching of desire is itself referred to as a kind of death. For example, it has been reported that a Zen Master once said, ''Die while alive, and be completely dead, then do whatever you will, all is good.'' See Thomas Kaulis, *Zen Action, Zen Person* (Honolulu: University of Hawaii, 1981), 114.

4. What is involved here is the Buddhist teaching concerning *kamma* (ethically relevant action) and its effects.

5. According to some strands of Buddhist mythology, a number of Buddhist saints *(arhats),* including the Buddha's great disciple Mahakassapa, have taken the option to postpone their deaths until the end of the cosmic age. For a discussion of this theme and its relationship to Buddhist mysticism and eschatology in contemporary Burma see Juliana Schober, *Cosmology and Religious Domains in the Theravada Buddhist Tradition of Upper Burma* (Ph.D. diss., University of Illinois, 1988).

6. Within the Buddhist tradition the question of the continued ''existence'' of the Buddha or of fully realized Buddhist saints after their final death is a vexed one. Generally speaking, the tendency has been (following a teaching attributed to the Buddha himself) to avoid the question on the basis that an answer to it is neither necessary nor helpful for those involved in the practice of the Path.

7. In this regard consider, for example, the description of the last days of King Mongkut, the great Buddhist king who ruled Thailand in the mid-nineteenth century, in Abbot Low Moffat, *Mongkut: King of Siam* (Ithaca, N.Y.: Cornell University Press, 1961), 169–84, and the description of the last days of Acan Man, a twentieth-century

Buddhist saint, provided by Charles Keyes in his excellent paper titled "Death of Two Buddhist Saints in Thailand," in Michael A. Williams, ed., *Charisma and Sacred Biography* (*Journal of the American Academy of Religion Thematic Studies* 48, nos. 3 and 4, American Academy of Religion, 1982), 149–80.

8. For an informative work that deals quite explicitly with this subject see Adhemard Leclere, *Les cremations et les rites funeraires au Cambodge* (Hanoi: F. H. Schneider, 1907), 154.

9. In addition to the Keyes article (op. cit.) see Stanley J. Tambiah's discussion in *The Buddhist Saints of the Forest and the Cult of the Amulets, Cambridge Studies in Anthropology,* no. 49 (Cambridge: Cambridge University Press, 1984), esp. 200–205.

10. I have chosen to focus the discussion on Buddhist communities in northern Thailand both because this is the area of my own field experience and because of the existence of two relevant studies by other scholars. In the discussion that follows I have depended heavily on the research and interpretations of William Delaney, "Socio-Cultural Aspects of Aging in Buddhist Northern Thailand" (Ph.D. diss., University of Illinois, 1977), and Charles Keyes, "From Death to Birth: Ritual Process and Buddhist Meanings in Northern Thailand," *Folk* (Copenhagen) 29 (1987):181–206.

11. In this chapter I attend only to situations in which the death that occurs is what we might call a "natural death." Early or violent deaths (including especially the deaths of mothers in childbirth) are treated as aberrations. In such cases adequate preparation has not occurred, and as a result, the death is considered to be fraught with danger, both for the person who dies and for the community as a whole.

12. I have borrowed the notion of achieving "integrity" from Erik Erickson, a well-known ego psychologist, who has used it to characterize the developmental task that he associates with the imminence of death in the West.

13. According to a view that is widespread in northern Thailand, the deceased (i.e., the *duang winnan,* which serves as the link between the person who dies and the person who is reborn) journeys first of all to a local sacred mountain, and from there is later reborn—in a more or less favorable condition—in a future generation of the same lineage.

14. According to some interpretations, the transfer of merit cannot be reconciled with orthodox Theravada doctrine concerning the role of individuals in generating, through their own deeds, their own *kammic* fate. From canonical times to the present rituals of merit-transference have in fact been performed in Theravada circles, and they play a crucial role in the religiosocial structure of every Theravada society that we know. On this issue see Jean-Michel Agasse, "Le transfert de merite dans le Bouddhisme Pali classique," *Journal Asiatique* 266 (1978):311–22.

15. In the northern Thai case a more mundane benefit also is gained by the community, since the favorable rebirth of the deceased is expected to occur within the lineage group that is performing the rites (see note 13). This is a distinctive aspect of the Buddhist tradition in northern Thailand and is not necessarily characteristic of Theravada traditions in other areas.

12

The Tibetan Tantric View of Death and Afterlife

Elisabeth Benard

INTRODUCTION

Tibetan Tantric Buddhism recognizes the power of an individual and teaches how to harness this internal power. It sees the human body and its inherent energy as an instrument that can be manipulated into focusing and controlling this power to achieve Buddhahood, the ultimate goal of Tibetan Tantra. Tibetan Tantric Buddhism, aware of the relationship between the mind and the body, states that by disciplining the mind, one controls the body. Furthermore the mind likes to develop habits so that these habits become automatic and do not require conscious thought. These habitual tendencies can be beneficial or detrimental in achieving Buddhahood. Tibetan Tantric Buddhism consciously selects to maximize the potential of beneficial habitual tendencies, such as compassion, patience, and transcendental wisdom, and to minimize the potentially negative tendencies, such as hatred, envy, and ignorance. To achieve Buddhahood one must be familiar with the process of death to have control in either becoming liberated or choosing a better rebirth.[1] Tibetan Tantric Buddhist texts abound with teachings and meditations about the death process. They assert that the moment of death is a crucial moment, and it will influence one's afterlife and subsequent rebirth. The present Dalai Lama, Tenzin Gyatso, states: "No matter what has happened in terms of good or bad within this particular lifetime, what happens right around the time of death is particularly powerful. Therefore, it is important to learn about the process of dying and prepare for it."[2]

In the West most of us do not think about our deaths and certainly do not prepare for our deaths. The last person to know that he is dying frequently is the person approaching death. The discussion of death, its process, and possibilities of what occurs after death is shunned in our society. Some of us deny death until confronted with the death of a relative, a close friend, or perhaps a beloved pet. The Tibetan Tantric Buddhists do not shun such discussions because an awareness of death is one of their fundamental teachings.

The major monotheistic religions—Judaism, Christianity, and Islam—all propound the view of one life and a permanent afterlife in either heaven or hell. The Buddhists, on the other hand, believe that one is not born once, but countless times. They believe in cyclical existence—birth, death, intermediate state, and rebirth. One is not reborn always as a human, but may be reborn in any of the six realms of cyclic existence: gods, demigods, humans, animals, hungry ghosts, and hell realms. Existence in any of the six realms is due to one's karma—actions composed of motivation and behavior—and habitual tendencies. When the negative or positive karma that has caused and maintained one's current life is exhausted, one moves on to another rebirth in one of the six realms. Life in any of these six realms is temporary. The Tantric Buddhist goal is liberation from cyclic existence and ultimately the achievement of Buddhahood. Every time a Tibetan Tantric Buddhist dies, he has the special opportunity to be liberated if familiar with the death process. The Dalai Lama states:

> If you believe just in this life and do not accept its continuation, it does not matter much whether you are mindful of death or not. Meditation on death and impermanence is based on the theory of the continuation of consciousness in rebirth—it can only be helpful to prepare for death since, if prepared, you will most likely not be anxious and frightened by the process of dying, not complicating the situation with your own thought.[3]

Thus for Tibetan Tantric Buddhists death is only one aspect of the entire process of cyclic existence and not a finality.

MEDITATIONS ON DEATH AND IMPERMANENCE

Tibetan Tantric Buddhist texts abound on the subject of death and impermanence. The Buddha's first and last teachings emphasized the impermanence of relative existence. The Buddha's final words were: "All composite things must pass away. Strive onward vigilantly." Anything that is born indicates that it is not permanent or eternal, that is, birth implies death. Because death is inevitable, Tibetan Tantric Buddhists are urged to understand the death process. Three reasons to meditate on death are as follows:

1. One should contemplate the inevitability of death. The denial of death is the ultimate delusion, and one should apply its antidote by meditating on the death process.
2. Though one knows that death is certain, one never knows when one will die; therefore, one should prepare for death. "Since there is no certainty whether

tomorrow or the next life will come first, it is proper to strive for the next life rather than striving for tomorrow'' (Udana Varga).

3. At the time of death nothing can help one except religious practices, especially understanding the death process. A great Buddhist scholar, Santideva, said: ''When grasped by death's agents, what value are friends? What value are relatives? At that moment, the only protection is the force of one's own goodness; but this I never cultivated.''[4]

These three reasons—the certainty of death, the uncertainty of the time of death, and the unique help of one's religious practice at the time of death—are reiterated throughout Tibetan Buddhist teachings. The religious teachers, or *lamas,* emphasize the urgency of knowing the death process. The experience of dying is overwhelming, and if one has not meditated on the death process, it is difficult to influence one's release from cyclic existence or rebirth. Conversely, if one is familiar with the death process, one can become less frightened and can gain the expertise to exert influence at this crucial time.

Various meditations on death include the contemplation of impermanence of all composite things. The Buddhists assert that all composite things, including oneself, do not have a permanent intrinsic nature and are subject to constant change. A famous eleventh-century Tibetan *lama,* Ma gCig Labs rGron, told her disciples that at the time of death one should remember one's meditations.

> If you are deluded, you must try to remember and differentiate between dream and reality. . . . You must think that food, wealth, and friends are all impermanent as I am. All compounded things are subject to death. I should have no attachment to anything because all is impermanent. . . . Also you might have fears that you are dying. If you do, then ask yourself why are you afraid? Who am I, who is dying? Realize that there are no causes for dying. So I must realize that there is no birth or death in Ultimate Reality, so how can I be afraid?

This explains the mental attitude one needs to cultivate so as not to fear death and to implement the tremendous power during the death process. Another kind of meditation is the vividly graphic meditation of observing the decomposition of a corpse. One sits by a corpse and observes it decay to bare bones. This meditation demonstrates that the body is not permanent and is composed of the five elements—earth, water, fire, air, and space—that separate and are transformed after death. Another, more difficult meditation is the simulation of the death process—visualizing oneself dying; it is a common daily meditation for the best practitioners. Through this daily practice one becomes familiar with the death process and will not fear it. The present Dalai Lama states: ''In my daily practice, I meditatively pass through the stages of dying six or seven times.''[5] He is not unique among the best practitioners of Tibetan Tantric Buddhism; many practitioners have this experience of simulating the death process daily.

This simulation of the death process is an advanced Tantric practice that involves the manipulation of the subtle winds within the subtle channels to direct the different consciousness.[6] These winds are the foundations of three types of consciousness: coarse, subtle, and very subtle. When one is completely conscious coarse consciousness predominates; when one is semiconscious subtle consciousness predominates; and when one is unconscious very subtle consciousness predominates. At the moment of one's death and during the intermediate state only the very subtle consciousness exists. The Dalai Lama says:

> When we die, at that moment the deepest unconscious level is being experienced. When you start experiencing the deepest level of consciousness through the practice of mental yoga, you are able to control your mind at that level—a very subtle state of mind—and make yourself conscious of a level where generally people are unconscious. So once you have some experiences in these practices, then you can fully control your mind at death.[7]

THE DYING PROCESS

A popular book in Tibet, *The Biography of Ling's Chokyi: A Woman Who Returned from the Bardo,* relates the experiences of a woman named Chokyi from Derge Ling (East Tibet) who had a near-death experience. In the biography Chokyi states that she was sick for sixteen days, and on the sixteenth day she felt dizzy. She felt as if many people were pressing down on her, and this experience scared her. Then she felt as if she were in the middle of the ocean and being pushed in all directions by waves. This also frightened her. After this she heard the crackling of a fire and felt as if her entire body was burning. This burning was painful, and when it ceased she saw a reddish color and heard a thundering sound that bewildered her. After that she could not remember what had occurred, and experienced a quiet happiness. She did not know how she had achieved this calmness. After this calm state she heard a thundering sound all around her, and from the crown of her head a five-colored rainbow emanated. This story illustrates Chokyi's experience of the beginning stages of the death process, when the elements that compose the body dissolve into one another.

When one is dying one's body, composed of the five elements and winds, dissolves in a progressive order. First, the earth element dissolves and is absorbed into the water element, and one feels that everything is falling apart. Then the water element dissolves and is absorbed by the fire element, and one has the sensation that the entire universe has been flooded by water. Successively the fire element dissolves and is absorbed by the air element; this evokes a feeling that everything is burning. Then the air element dissolves and is absorbed by the space element; this gives a sensation that a great windstorm is howling. At this point one stops breathing and one's vital signs are no longer perceptible, but according to the Tibetan Tantric Buddhist teachings, one is not yet dead because one's very subtle consciousness has not separated from the body.

Four more dissolutions must occur that involve the subtle winds in the right and left subtle channels.[8] All the subtle winds gather in the right and left subtle channels, and all subsequently enter into the central channel. Then the winds enter the drop of the heart, where the very subtle life-bearing wind is located. At this point a person becomes unconscious and experiences the Clear Light of death. For the Tibetan Tantric Buddhists this experience of the Clear Light is the moment of death. Most people stay in this Clear Light for three days, but highly accomplished practitioners can remain in the Clear Light for much longer. If one is familiar with the death process, one can become liberated and even attain the final goal of Buddhahood. At this time these highly realized practitioners recognize the Clear Light of death as void of inherent existence and penetrating the true nature of ultimate reality.

DEATH FOR ORDINARY PEOPLE

For many Tibetans the rigorous discipline of meditating on death and impermanence and of simulating the death process daily is too demanding. One may ask, what happens to these people who do not prepare for their death through the prescribed mental practices? Though the Tibetan texts stress the need to be familiar with the death process, there are alternatives. Some people's spiritual teachers perform the ritual known as (Tib. *gzhan po wa*) ''Transferring Others' Consciousness'' for the sake of their disciples. When the disciple dies the teacher is able to transfer the disciple's consciousness to a paradise realm. Another alternative is found in the *Tibetan Book of the Dead.* One's spiritual teachers, relatives, and friends read the book during one's death process. It is a well-known guide for orienting the dying person so that he might hold a proper frame of mind to assure a good future rebirth, or even liberation.

TIBETAN BOOK OF THE DEAD

Some Buddhist schools do not discuss in detail the intermediate state (Tib. *Bardo*) between death and rebirth. The Tibetan Buddhist literature, however, is replete with many sophisticated teachings on the intermediate state—Bardo. As mentioned earlier, the *Tibetan Book of the Dead* (Tib. *Bardo'i thos-grol;* literally ''liberation through hearing in the intermediate state'') is a popular text that describes in detail the death process with particular emphasis on the intermediate state. This book is attributed to Padmasambhava, a famous Indian Tantric master of the eighth century. The purpose of the text is to help people undergo the bewildering death process. It is explained that if one follows the instructions properly, one can be liberated from the cycle of death and rebirth.

Up to the twentieth century the *Tibetan Book of the Dead* was used exclusively by Tibetan Buddhists solely for the purpose of guiding the deceased through the process of death and rebirth. Since the book was translated into English by Lama Kazi Dawa-Samdrup and Evan-Wentz, many new uses for the book have been discovered.[9] The psychologist Carl Jung interpreted the visions described in the *Tibetan Book of the Dead* as archetypes of all human consciousness. By reversing the process in the *Tibetan Book of the Dead,* Jung used the text as a manual describing the process of the human consciousness achieving integration.[10] In the 1960s, during the experimentation with psychedelic drugs, Timothy Leary and others considered the *Tibetan Book of the Dead* as a guide to altered states of consciousness.[11] In the 1970s and 1980s the visions in the *Tibetan Book of the Dead* were compared to accounts of near-death experiences, and similarities were discovered.[12]

Of all Tibetan Buddhist texts, the *Tibetan Book of the Dead* is the most well-known in the West. Now that some Americans and Europeans are becoming Tibetan Buddhists, the traditional use of the *Tibetan Book of the Dead* is being adopted in the West. But some Tibetan lamas caution that the reading of the *Tibetan Book of the Dead* to a deceased person is not useful if the deceased is not familiar with it. A person asked the Dalai Lama if "it is proper or effective for Westerners to use the *Tibetan Book of the Dead,* in translation, for dying persons who have not been instructed about the *Tibetan Book of the Dead.*" The Dalai Lama answered, "In general, without the preparations of initiation, meditation, and so forth, this would be difficult. It is necessary to be familiar with the teachings."[13]

The *Tibetan Book of the Dead* is divided into three sections: the moment of death (Chikai Bardo), the intermediate state between death and rebirth (Chonyid Bardo), and the rebirth process (Sipai Bardo). At each stage the deceased has different experiences and visions. The reading of the *Tibetan Book of the Dead* to the deceased helps him to understand the experiences and reminds him that these visions emanate from his mind and are unsubstantial. These visions are precise to one familiar with the *Tibetan Book of the Dead,* but to one who has never heard it, the images consist of only indistinct forms and colors.[14] Even if one is familiar with the practices of the *Tibetan Book of the Dead,* what one recognizes and how one reacts depend on one's mental training and one's karma.

Ignorance and obscuration prevent most people from recognizing these visions in the intermediate state as illusions. Buddhist texts reiterate the belief in a self that is impermanent and always changing, but few people realize this. The Buddhists believe that the root of all obstacles to the attainment of liberation is based on this misconception about the self. They have developed a highly sophisticated philosophy to help practitioners cultivate the realizations that both the self and phenomena lack a permanent eternal nature and are void of inherent existence. This misconception arises because of the belief that the five aggregates—form, feeling, perception, mental formations, and consciousness—that give a semblance of a self are permanent and independent. As a whole, these aggregates create an illusion of a permanent and independent self. If one applies critical analysis, one can realize that all these aggregates are subject to change and, ultimately, to dissolution. At the point of death these aggregates separate from one another and the dying person experiences fear and bewilderment. The ordinary person cannot recognize the void of inherent existence of the aggregates.

Furthermore our misconceptions with regard to the ultimate nature of reality are caused by many major obscurations that we have held since beginningless time and have nurtured with many negative habits from life to life. Through the cultivation of good habits—for example, compassion and patience—and the diminishment of negative habits—for example, anger and pride—one eventually can attain liberation from cyclic existence. Unfortunately for many people these bad habits are so embedded in our "self" that one believes that these habitual tendencies are one's fundamental nature. Because we have been addicted since beginningless time to these negative habits, they arise frequently and effortlessly. One comes to believe that one needs them to function, and thereby one does not use the antidotes to subdue the arising of these negative tendencies. During the intermediate state (*Chonyid* and *Sipai Bardo*) the negative karma accumulated from the actions of these negative habits is experienced by the deceased. This karma becomes a powerful force that confuses the deceased, prevents him from understanding the visions clearly, and propels him to take rebirth again in one of the six realms of cyclic existence.

THE THREE STATES OF BARDO

Moment of Death *(Chikai Bardo)*

The moment of death begins when one's subtlest consciousness predominates and experiences the Clear Light. The *Tibetan Book of the Dead* states:

> This mind of yours is inseparable luminosity and voidness in the form of a great mass of light, it has no birth or death, therefore it is buddha of Immortal Light. To recognize this is all that is necessary. When you recognize this pure nature of your mind as the buddha, looking into your own mind is resting in the buddhamind.[15]

The person reading this to the deceased should repeat this three or seven times for the person to recognize his consciousness as luminosity and inseparable from the Dharmakaya.[16] Anyone who recognizes this can become liberated; however, most will not recognize this because one's obscuring ignorance and habitual tendencies prevent recognition of Ultimate Reality. For most ordinary people whose bodies were ravaged by sickness or mutilated in an accident this stage can last less than a day. During this time the very subtlest consciousness remains in the body until certain signs indicate that it has departed. The most common signs are a drop of blood and phlegm emerging from the nose or the sexual organ. Thus until these signs appear the body is kept in the house, and it is the custom to pay one's final respects to the deceased on the third day. While the subtlest consciousness remains in the body the deceased is unaware that he has died.

The Intermediate State *(Chonyid Bardo)*

Once the subtlest consciousness departs from the body the deceased begins the actual intermediate state between death and rebirth. While the deceased was in the Clear Light he was unaware of his death. Now he sees his relatives weeping because of his death. He tries to tell them that he is not dead, but they cannot hear or see him. This bewilders the deceased, and he wanders in a confused state. Noticing that he has no shadow or a reflection in the mirror, he realizes that he has died. Now he has only a "mental body," which is indestructible, feeds on odors, and can go everywhere unimpeded. The *Tibetan Book of the Dead* tells the deceased:

> You have what is called a mental body of conscious tendencies, you have no physical body of flesh and blood, so whatever sounds, colors, and rays of light occur, they cannot hurt you and you cannot die. It is enough simply to recognize them as your projections. Know this to be the bardo state.[17]

The deceased may see these illusions as clear visions of Buddhas or as indistinct colors and forms, depending on his mental training and his karma. Each day for six days peaceful manifestations of different Buddhas emanating from different-colored lights appear. Each Buddha represents a particular Buddha-wisdom. Simultaneously, as each Buddha is seen, a soft-colored light of one of the six realms of cyclic existence also is seen. Each of these realms represents a particular poison that prevents one from achieving liberation or even a better rebirth. The *Tibetan Book of the Dead* tells the deceased to seek the particular Buddha and to avoid the soft light of one of the six realms of cyclic existence. If the deceased recognizes the Buddha representing a Buddha-wisdom, he can be liberated. Because of negative karmic tendencies, however, most deceased are attracted to the soft lights of the six realms representing the poisons that prevent liberation (see Table 1). For example, the first day the deceased sees Vairocana Buddha and the female Buddha, Queen of the Vajra Space, emanating a brilliant blue light. If one seeks refuge in Vairocana Buddha and Queen of the Vajra Space, one will achieve the perfect Buddha state. The deceased frequently cannot bear the brilliance of the Buddha's light and seeks refuge in the soft light, which on the first day is the soft white light of the god realm.

Each day for five days the deceased sees another Buddha until the sixth day, when one sees all the five Buddhas together. Moreover, on the sixth day forty-

Table 1
The Intermediate State: *Chonyid Bardo*

Post-mortem Day	Day 1	Day 2	Day 3	Day 4	Day 5
Family	Buddha	Vajra	Jewel	Lotus	Karma
Male Buddha	Vairocana	Aksobhya	Ratnasambhava	Amitabha	Amoghasiddhi
Female Buddha	Vajraspace	Locana	Mamaki	Pandaravasini	Samaya Tara
Wisdom	Dharmadhatu	Mirror-like	Equanimity	Discrimination	All-accomplishing
Bright Light	White Body/ Blue Light	Blue Body/ White Light	Yellow	Red	Green
Soft Light	White	Smoky	Blue	Yellow	Red
Poison	Delusion	Anger	Pride	Greed	Jealousy
Realm	God	Hell	Human	Hungry ghosts	Demigod

two deities in all appear and four of the five Buddha wisdom lights shine brightly. On the sight of any of these visions, if the deceased understands that these are only projections from his mind, he will be liberated. Even if one cannot recognize this but with great devotion appeals to the compassion of the Buddhas, one can become liberated. If one is not liberated, one continues to wander in the Bardo. On the seventh day one sees the "knowledge-holding deities," who have neither peaceful nor wrathful aspects. Likewise, if one recognizes these as illusions or as spiritual friends who will help one become liberated from cyclic existence, one can become free. If it does not happen, one experiences a "small death" and continues to wander in the Bardo.[18]

From the eighth to the twelfth day one has visions of the wrathful manifestations of Buddhas. On the eighth day the *Tibetan Book of the Dead* states that one sees Buddha-Heruka in his wrathful aspects. It states: "He who is called Glorious Great Buddha-Heruka will emerge from within your brain. . . . His body is wine-colored with three heads, six arms, and four legs spread wide apart. . . . His nine eyes gaze into yours with a wrathful expression."[19]

For the next four days these horrifying visions are so terrible that the deceased usually cannot remain calm and reflect that they are emanations of his own mind. The *Tibetan Book of the Dead* continually reiterates not to fear these manifestations; they are projections of one's own mind. If one recognizes this, then one is liberated. During these four days one sees fifty-eight wrathful manifestations of deities; at anytime if one can recognize that these manifestations are only illusory, one can be liberated from cyclic existence. For most of the beings wandering in the Bardo the experience is so terrifying that one seeks only escape from these visions. Without this recognition one enters the third stage of the Bardo—the rebirth process.

The Rebirth Process *(Sipai Bardo)*

At this stage one's past karma will influence one's experience in the rebirth process. If one has accumulated much negative karma, one will be subjected to visions of being attacked by demonic armies, of being in earthquakes, floods, fires, and windstorms. One cannot escape because three precipices obstruct one's path. These precipices are symbols of hatred, desire, and ignorance, which are the three principal poisons that prevent liberation. One who has positive karma will experience bliss, and one who is neither good nor bad will feel indifference. The *Tibetan Book of the Dead* reminds one that whatever one feels one should not be attracted or repelled to these feelings. For one who had no mental training, one's mind cannot remain calm, and this agitation causes pain and restlessness. This suffering becomes unbearable, and one yearns for a new body. The *Tibetan Book of the Dead* tells the deceased that "it is due to one's own karma that you are suffering like this, so you cannot blame anyone else. . . . Supplicate the Three Jewels and they will protect you."[20]

Then one encounters the Lord of Death, who holds up the mirror of karma wherein one sees all one's merits and demerits. One suffers accordingly; one with negative karma will experience the excruciating pain of one's body being cut up and so on. Again, one is reminded that these are illusions, but one usually identifies with the agonizing pain and does not realize that the mental body cannot be affected.

Now the lights of the six realms of cyclic existence appear, and one's body assumes the color of the light in which one will be reborn. Even at this time if one meditates on the light as illusion, one can become liberated. If one has reached this stage in Bardo, however, the chance of being reborn is much greater than that of becoming liberated. Thus the *Tibetan Book of the Dead* cautions the deceased to select the best possible rebirth, which is birth in the human realm in the places where Buddhism is taught. If one is fortunate to be reborn in the human realm, the *Tibetan Book of the Dead* explains that one will be attracted to one's father if one is to be reborn as a female and vice versa.[21] Once the consciousness of the deceased enters in the middle of the uniting ovum and sperm, the rebirth process has been completed. Cyclic existence continues. The entire death process may occur in a day or less, but for most the process lasts for several weeks, up to forty-nine days. The amount of time depends on one's mental training, karma, and place of birth. This concludes the instructions of the *Tibetan Book of the Dead*.

CONCLUSION

The goal of Tibetan Tantric Buddhists, as of all Mahayana Buddhists, is to attain Buddhahood, to help all sentient beings to attain Buddhahood. This attainment of Buddhahood can take as long as three incalculable aeons or as short as one lifetime. A particularly powerful and influential moment in one's life is the moment of death because one experiences directly the void of inherent existence, the Clear Light. Recognizing this Clear Light, one can be liberated from cyclic existence; however, for most beings nonrecognition is a major obstacle to liberation. Because everyone who is born will die and experience the Clear Light at the moment of death, the Tibetan Tantric Buddhists emphasize the importance of being familiar with the death process. Furthermore death is inevitable, but the time of death is uncertain. Thus the Tibetan Tantric Buddhist texts urge one to engage in practices that will familiarize oneself with the death process to be prepared to influence one's rebirth or, ideally, to control one's consciousness in recognizing the Clear Light at the moment of one's death.

Tibetan Tantra offers numerous methods in understanding the death process. Some are philosophically based—for example, analyzing the lack of a permanent eternal self or impermanence; others are physiologically based—for example, simulation of bodily death. These methods are practiced by the individual. Other methods depend on help from others—for example, one's religious teacher transferring one's consciousness or reading the *Tibetan Book of the Dead*.

Any method that is expedient and effective can be used, but the aforementioned ones frequently are implemented. A combination of methods are used for most ordinary people because the deceased is not proficient in the self-reliant methods. In Tibetan Tantra the attainment of Buddhahood by all sentient beings is of utmost importance, and any means that achieves this goal is deemed effective and beneficial.

The reading of the *Tibetan Book of the Dead* is a popular method used by many Tibetans for ordinary people who were not excellent practitioners of Tibetan Buddhism. The book describes clearly and in great detail the process of death, the intermediate state, and rebirth. It describes all the peaceful and wrathful manifestations of deities that one may encounter during the process of death and rebirth. Though these visions are vividly described, it continuously reiterates that these are all projections of one's mind. These do not ultimately exist, nor can one's mental body be affected by these visions. Few have trained their minds to the extent that they recognize these visions as projections of their minds; however, to keep hearing that these are illusions must be helpful to Tibetan Buddhists. The *Tibetan Book of the Dead* is only a guide, and it is one's decision conditioned by karma and habitual tendencies to attempt to follow its instructions. It is interesting to note that Tibetan Tantric Buddhism is one of the few religions that has a guidebook of the death process. This indicates that Tibetan Tantric Buddhists attach special importance to understanding the death process because they believe that by understanding that process, they also can influence and control it. Depending on how one goes through it, the death process can become the opportunity for one's liberation from cyclic existence altogether. Thus the ultimate goal of all Tibetan Buddhists is Buddhahood for all.

NOTES

1. See chapter 11 for general Buddhist beliefs of death and the afterlife.

2. The fourteenth Dalai Lama, Tenzin Gyatso, *Kindness, Clarity, and Insight,* trans. and ed. Jeffery Hopkins (Ithaca, N.Y.: Snow Lion Press, 1984), 170–71.

3. Ibid., 169.

4. The Bodhisattvacaryavatara, cited from Glenn H. Mullin, *Death and Dying: The Tibetan Tradition* (Boston: Arkana, 1986), 65.

5. Gyatso, *Kindness, Clarity, and Insight,* 181.

6. These subtle winds (Tib. *rlung*) and subtle channels (Tib. *rtsa*) are not visible in the body, but Tantric practitioners believe that they exist but are imperceptible. This complex and sophisticated process is clearly explained in Lati Rinbochay and Jeffery Hopkins, *Death, Intermediate State, and Rebirth* (Ithaca, N.Y.: Gabriel/Snow Lion, 1979).

7. Personal interview with Philip Hemley, November 1979.

8. Rinbochay and Hopkins, *Death, Intermediate State, and Rebirth,* 38–48.

9. W. Y. Evan-Wentz, trans. *The Tibetan Book of the Dead* (London: Oxford University Press, 1927).

10. Ibid., xxxv–lii.

11. T. Leary et al., *The Psychedelic Experience: A Manual Based on the* Tibetan Book of the Dead (New York: University Books, 1964).

12. R. Moody, *Life After Death* (New York: Bantam Books, 1975), and M. Sabom, *Recollections of Death: A Medical Investigation* (New York: Harper & Row, 1981).

13. Gyatso, *Kindness, Clarity, and Insight,* 181.

14. Lama Lodro, *Bardo Teachings: The Way of Death and Rebirth* (Ithaca, N.Y.: Snow Lion, 1987).

15. F. Freemantle, trans. *The Tibetan Book of the Dead* (Boulder, Colo.: Shambala, 1975), 37.

16. According to the Mahayana Buddhist tradition, all Buddhas have three bodies: the body of emanation (Nirmanakaya), the body of complete enjoyment (Sambhogakaya), and the transcendent truth body (Dharmakaya).

17. Freemantle, *The Tibetan Book of the Dead,* 41.

18. A person experiences a small death after every seven days in the Bardo, and one can wander in the Bardo for forty-nine days; however, on every seventh day the ritual will be more elaborate because one is experiencing a small death.

19. Freemantle, *The Tibetan Book of the Dead,* 60.

20. Ibid., 76. The Three Jewels are the three supreme refuges—the Buddha, his teachings (the Dharma), and the community who supports the dharma (the Sangha).

21. It is interesting to note the similarities to Freud's Oedipal-Electra complex.

13

Death and Afterlife in Chinese Religions

Judith A. Berling

INTRODUCTION

In most forms of Christianity beliefs about the soul, death, and the afterlife are central religious concerns because they lead directly to the church's message of salvation. Although all religions have to offer some answers to questions about death and afterlife, not all would see those issues as central to their religious message. One of the virtues of the comparative study of religions is that it teaches us how even universal issues are treated very differently in the various religions of the world.

In the case of Chinese religions there is a broad range of beliefs and approaches to the nexus of problems related to death and the afterlife. This chapter offers an overview of Chinese practices and beliefs that are not always easily reconciled. These not only coexisted but were believed and practiced in a variety of combinations. It is too simple to see the differences as based in sectarian or denominational distinctions. In simple terms, sometimes we speak of three great Chinese religious traditions (Confucianism, Buddhism, and Taoism) in their various schools and denominations and a host of folk religions. Such distinctions may reflect in distinctive textual transmissions, some clearly defined groups of religious specialists, the affiliation of a temple at a given point in time, or general cultural perceptions. Historically, the pattern was far more one of confluence and overlapping of these various strands. Chinese religiosity is in part distinct from Western patterns by its nonexclusivity; groups and individuals embraced aspects of more than one "religion" without necessarily reconciling them. There were to be sure some thinkers who pondered how to justify the range of beliefs and practices as a coherent and internally reconciled whole, but most Chinese affirmed a complex and multifaceted loose "system" or body of beliefs and practices that were held together more by patterns of participation than by rational overview. Most Chinese accepted the premise that it was religiously wise to "cover one's bases" by embracing all that seemed promising in the familiar religious world; to put it another way, they rejected or ignored the religious premise, common in the West, that one must choose between religions and denominations to commit to the one right and true faith. The Chinese inclusivistic approach produced a rich body of beliefs and practices that spoke to many levels of religious concern.

Four main themes or leitmotifs loosely organize the variety of views on death and the afterlife. First, Chinese beliefs and practices demonstrated that for them, the boundaries between life and death were relatively porous. That is to say, "existence" on the two sides of this line was not always as radically different as we might expect. There may be "deathlike" experiences in life, and "lifelike" experiences in death. Second, for the Chinese the main religious issue was the health and well-being of the person in this life and beyond; most practices were geared to ensuring and maintaining that vitality. Third, there was a concern with the long-term fate of the person, although it took a variety of forms. Finally, notions of the "end of time" and "eternal salvation" did exist, although they were not as prominent or central to the mainstream Chinese religious traditions as they were in the Western religions.

The beliefs and practices in this chapter are introduced roughly in chronological order, but in such a brief discussion historical developments cannot be treated in detail. It also is important to avoid suggesting a neat linear evolution. Many ancient ideas persisted through history, sometimes in the same form, sometimes altered or in a new context. For all intents and purposes, this panoply of ideas came to coexist and enrich one another in the Chinese religious system.

BOUNDARIES BETWEEN LIFE AND DEATH: THE NOTION OF SOULS

From very ancient times the Chinese had a notion of two souls: (1) the *hun* soul, which might reside in a spirit tablet to receive the commemoration of descendants, but which eventually reverted to "heaven" or the "spirit" in heaven; and (2) the *p'o* soul, which at death and with the decomposition of the body reverted to the earth, resided in the grave, and could become—if angered, disturbed, or maltreated—a *kuei*—ghost, demon, or revenant, depending on one's translation.

These souls inhabited and animated the body; they were the consciousness or life force within it. At death or in deathlike experiences (sleep, coma) the *hun* soul would leave the body in the "breath" and wander about freely. In the case of sleep, for instance, it was believed that dreams were actually the experiences the soul had in its extracorporeal wanderings. If the soul did not return to the body safe and sound, the person could not fully awaken. People with certain kinds of illnesses were thought to be troubled by a prolonged absence, weakening, or muddling of the *hun* soul, which might be adversely affected by its travels or become embroiled in complicated situations. In such a case a spirit medium or special healer with shamanistic powers would have to be called in to restore the soul to its proper place.

Death occurred when the *hun* soul left the body permanently. Given the fact that the *hun* soul moved in and out of the body on a regular basis, it was crucial to distinguish between death and more temporary forms of the soul's absence. Thus it came to be that at the moment of death, people often performed a ceremony called *chao-hun* (or summoning the *hun*). This ceremony formally called back the *hun* soul, giving it a chance to return before the person was officially pronounced dead. The *chao-hun,* which used the garments of the dead to entice back the soul, is ancient, described in the ancient ritual classics.

The *hun* soul also was invited to inhabit ancestral tablets, so that it might receive the commemoration of ancestor worship. Inviting the soul to inhabit the tablet was ritually parallel to inviting a deity *(shen)* to inhabit an image in a temple so that he could receive the prayers of worshipers and supplicants. Ancestor worship or veneration formalized mourning and commemoration of ancestors. It allowed relatives in mourning to pay their respects, express their grief, and to include ancestors in the life and business of the family. In the period immediately after death, food and drink might be set before the tablet to include the deceased symbolically in the most central communal act of the family: meals. At regular intervals the eldest surviving male paid respects and made a formal report on family affairs to the ancestors. This had the effect of making them a continuing presence in family business, an ongoing participant in the life of the clan. As the time after the death increased the attentions to the tablet became less quotidian and intimate and more formal and ceremonial. On high occasions three generations of ancestors were named and included in formal announcements; that would roughly include anyone of whom the living family still had a vivid and specific personal memory. After that they tended to fade into the collectivity of "the ancestors," unless they had been particularly famous or a powerful force in the family.[1]

Not all families could afford the ceremonies and formalities of ancestral worship, although, particularly after the medieval period, it was a goal to which many clans aspired. In early times the common folk had a belief that souls at death went to the "Yellow Springs," a kind of netherworld; because yellow was the color that symbolized the soil, they were in effect absorbed into the earth to participate in this vaguely defined world. The notion of the "Yellow Springs" was later superceded by or elaborated into an underworld that reflected more of the dynamics of the world of the living.[2]

Even in the classic period philosophical thinkers began to reflect on what happened to souls over the long term, when the memory of them had faded or their bodies had entirely decomposed. Chuang Tzu was the thinker who faced head on the issue of the dispersal of the personality of the deceased, assumed in most practices to reside in the souls. He offered a vision of the soul as well as the body absorbed into the ongoing creative processes of nature. His view is captured in the famous story of the death of his wife:

> Chuang Tzu's wife died. When Hui Tzu went to convey his condolences, he found Chuang Tzu sitting with his legs sprawled out, pounding on a tub and singing. "You lived with her, she brought up your children and grew old," said Hui Tzu. "It should be enough simply not to weep at her death. But pounding on a tub and singing—this is going too far, isn't it?"
>
> Chuang Tzu said, "You're wrong. When she first died, do you think I didn't grieve like anyone else? But I looked back to her beginning and the time before she was born. Not only the time before she was born, but the time before she had a body. Not only the time before she had a body, but the time before she had a spirit. In the midst of the jumble of wonder and mystery a change took place and she had a spirit. Another change and she had a body. Another change and she was born. Now there's been another change and she's dead. It's just like the progression of the four seasons, spring, summer, fall, winter."[3]

Chuang Tzu celebrated his wife's passing in a most unconventional manner because he had come to see her death as simply another phase of her existence. There was a time before she was, and like all things, she emerged from the jumble and wonder of the created order; now that she was gone her body and her spirit had both returned to the jumble of creation. In contrast to most Chinese, Chuang Tzu's mourning was not directed to sustaining the presence of her soul or spirit so that he could continue his connection with the person whom he had loved; rather, his reverence is for the natural processes (the Tao) from which she had come and to which she had returned.

We see, then, that although the belief in the two souls was widespread in China, the fate of the souls and the responses to them were quite varied.

HEALTH AND WELL-BEING IN LIFE AND DEATH

Chinese religion is notoriously this-worldly and pragmatic: Its main concerns were health, wealth, and descendants—in other words, good fortune in its various aspects.

From very early in Chinese history we see strains of strong religious interest in the preservation of the body in health *(yang-shen)* and the postponement or avoidance of death (long life and immortality). This combination of practices, motivations, and understandings is far too complex for a simple description, yet this chapter can provide only a brief overview. Concern for health and long life pervades virtually all of Chinese religion in one form or another, but those strands labeled as "Taoist" tended to carry it to its most specialized and refined forms.

Like those of us in the late twentieth century, many Chinese had a strong concern for health, long life, and vigor. They observed ancient and vital religious regimens around various forms of diet, including the macrobiotic diet that many still advocate today, or even extreme forms of fasting, such as living on wind, dew, and sunlight. In addition, there were various forms of exercise for health and longevity; some of these traditions have been incorporated into *tai-chi-ch'uan,* or other traditions of martial arts and religious training. Some adepts recommended regimens of self-massage, and various tonics and treatments, such as acupuncture, which were to assure good health. Some of these practices were absorbed into the medical tradition, with or without their religious contexts and roots. Others were the province of overtly religious (i.e., ritual or meditative) specialists. Finally, various forms of meditation and breath control were related to health and vigor, as were some sexual practices. The interest of the Chinese in health and long life was a major factor in drawing them to religion, and many religious professionals also were healers or directors in the arts of cultivating life.

Healing arts and the cultivation of vitality were religiously tied to the transcendence of human mortality and its limitation. Some of the religious arts strove for more dramatic or extraordinary forms of transcendence: the restoration of youth, the ability to fly or ride the wind, intensified or expanded power of the senses, the liberation and ascendance of the corpse to heaven in broad daylight, and so forth. Once again, Chuang Tzu captures some of the flavor of these practices in his description of a holy man:

> Chien Wu said to Lien Shu, "I was listening to Chieh Yü's talk—big and nothing to back it up, going on and on without turning around. I was completely dumbfounded at his words—no more end than the Milky Way, wild and wide of the mark, never coming near human affairs!"
>
> "What were his words like?" asked Lien Shu.
>
> "He said that there is a Holy Man living faraway on Ku-she Mountain, with skin like ice or snow, and gentle and shy like a young girl. He doesn't eat the five grains, but sucks the wind, drinks the dew, climbs up on the clouds and mist, rides a flying dragon, and wanders beyond the four seas. By concentrating on his spirit, he can protect creatures from sickness and plague and make the harvest plentiful. I thought this was all insane and refused to believe it."
>
> "You would!" said Lien Shu. "We can't expect a blind man to appreciate beautiful patterns or a deaf man to listen to bells and drums. And blindness and deafness are not confined to the body alone—the understanding has them too, as your words just now have shown. This man, with this virtue of his, is about to embrace the ten thousand things and roll them into one. Though the age calls for reform, why should he wear himself out over affairs of the world? There is nothing that can harm this man. Though flood waters pile up to the sky, he will not drown. Though a great drought melts metal and stone and scorches the earth and hills, he will not be burned. From his dust and leavings alone you could mold a Yao or a Shun! Why should he consent to bother about mere things?"[4]

As in the case of the holy man, the impetus for well-being and transcendence could, in some cases, lead to magical or spiritual wonder-working. The miraculous nature of such arts also induced skepticism in the culture, as Chuang Tzu's story vividly suggests. Although these beliefs and practices were not uncontested in Chinese history, they retained a powerful hold on the Chinese religious imagination down to the present day.

In some forms of Taoism the impetus for transcendence was extended to a type of physical immortality in which the deceased was "released from the corpse" and "ascended to heaven in broad daylight." Such a state was attained through the practice of some of the arts described earlier, through knowledge of esoteric rituals and meditative arts that established special relationships with a host of deities, and through a profound realization of certain Taoist tenets. Taoist beliefs in physical immortality, like magical arts, were questioned by some of the cultural elite, but they were nonetheless a powerful and persistent force in Chinese religiosity.

For those who did not achieve physical immortality one of the keys to health and good fortune after death was the preservation of the corpse, since it was seen to be the seat of the *p'o* soul. Once the body had entirely decomposed the soul no longer had a home, and became rootless or depersonalized. Whereas philosophers such as Chuang Tzu could celebrate that possibility, most Chinese felt a strong moral and religious obligation to maintain personal contact with the ancestors not only through the ancestral tablets in the spirit hall, but also by maintaining the presence in the grave. Chinese visited graves, often near the family home, to commune with and pay homage to the souls of the deceased. Many also believed that the satisfied and happy presence of those souls in the grave were vital to the success of the family: that the fertility of their lands, the birth of healthy sons, the welfare of their livestock, the success of major ventures were, to some extent, empowered by the spiritual presence of those souls.

These beliefs led to a strong interest in the care of the corpse, both immediately after death and in the grave. There were elaborate instructions for the care of the corpse at the funeral, stopping up apertures to discourage "leakage" of the *p'o* soul or the entrance into the body of foreign souls seeking a home. From early in Chinese history those with the resources seem to have spent lavishly on elixirs and other treatments that would prevent or slow the process of decay. Families of means invested in watertight and strong coffins to preserve the body as long as possible.

The placement and care of the coffin was important for geomantic reasons. *Feng-shui,* or geomancy, was the science of positioning graves and coffins to ensure that the beneficent spiritual influences of the soul would empower and sustain the health and success of the family. Geomantic specialists were invited to calculate the very best site for the grave.

When inauspicious events or family disasters indicated that the ancestors might not be satisfied with their graves a ritual specialist might be called in to inspect the grave, the coffin, and even the bones. Coffins could be realigned, bones cleaned, rearranged, and even painted to restore the remains to a position of health and comfort.[5] Such tasks were accompanied by prayers and rituals to apologize to the ancestors for their discomfort and pray for good will in the future.

The significance of preserving the body as a means of maintaining a location to pay reverence to the soul and for overcoming the baleful influences of death is perhaps most dramatically illustrated in a rather historically late and Buddhist practice: that of the "meat bodies" *(jou-shen)*. Certain Buddhist monks made a decision to choose the time and manner of their deaths (thereby defeating death's negation of human will) and deliberately to preserve their bodies. They would go into a pit or underground chamber, meditating in solitude and receiving scant food on a signal by rope. After a period they would no longer signal for food and would starve themselves to death in a meditative posture. Wood and branches would be lowered into the pit and burned so as to dry and smoke the body; then the pit would be sealed. After a time the body would be exhumed, wrapped, and lacquered; the body, so treated, was installed in a temple or pagoda as a "flesh buddha" so that the master could be revered by his followers and by pilgrims. These flesh buddhas often were believed to have extraordinary spiritual presence, and were—still are, in a few cases—objects of great devotion.[6]

THE LONG-TERM FATE OF THE SOUL: REALMS OF THE AFTERLIFE

To this point, except for a brief reference to the rather ill-defined Yellow Springs, the story of Chinese religions has been that of the souls of the dead "hanging around" the world of the living as if they had no place to go. In one sense the Chinese were surrounded by the souls of the dead, both beneficent and malign. They also came to have a range of views about otherworldly realms. These views of the netherworld became quite eclectic, eventually composed of many strands so completely interwoven that it is virtually impossible to untangle them. It is a rich and "earthy" view of the nether realms.

First, in conjunction with their search for physical immortality and their beliefs about extraordinary immortals with magical powers, the Chinese cherished a range of beliefs about paradises of immortals. Perhaps the most famous or pervasive was a belief in P'eng-lai or the "isles of the blest," conceived as somewhere out in the ocean or in some far-off realm. Other paradises were envisioned in the mountains, off to the West, for instance. As Wolfgang Bauer has pointed out in his excellent book *China and the Search for Happiness,* the Chinese had a tendency to envision paradises and utopias in those spaces around the "real world" of China, to see those wonderful lands as just beyond the borders, up in the mountains, in the unvisited marshes. They exorcized and idealized the regions around, and populated them with fabulous creatures and immortals.[7]

They also incorporated Buddhist notions of sacred mountains existing in

Buddha realms, usually thought to be in "the West," from whence Buddhism had come; thus there is a growing tendency in Chinese religious history to identify the West, especially mountains in the West, with paradisiacal realms.

After Buddhism's acculturation and its integration with folk and Taoist traditions in China a somewhat more coherent and elaborate version of heaven and hell was added to the looser versions of various paradises. In this later pantheon heaven and hell came to be viewed as paradigms of the real world in the spirit realm. That is, heaven became a bureaucracy similar to the imperial bureaucracy on earth. It had a number of bureaus, palaces, and offices, and worthy people could get an "appointment" in the heavenly courts after their death; this was, to some extent, meshed with Taoist ideas of immortals, so that many immortals were believed to hold official posts in the heavenly bureaus. Mortal emperors embraced this notion, and often added titles to those that heaven had bestowed. Heaven, like the imperial court, watched over the activities of human beings on earth, and took responsibility for maintaining order; human prayers for help often took the form of formal petitions to the officers and armies of heaven.

Heaven could send officers to specific areas of the earth, just as the court sent magistrates. The spiritual counterpart of the human magistrate was the City Wall God, assigned as the local spirit officer. Such gods and many in the pantheon were worthy human beings who, after death, were in effect promoted for their good deeds for an afterlife of official service.

Hell, by contrast, was seen as a model of the judicial and prison system of China. Ghoulish and fierce demon officers played the roles of bailiffs and jailers, carrying out the orders of judges appointed by heaven to mete out punishments to sinners. As in Chinese jails, the sinful "criminals" were tortured to confess, and flogged or otherwise chastised for the wrongs they had committed. As in the Chinese prisons, only bribes of money could lighten punishments or shorten sentences; thus living relatives were pressed to offer spirit moneys to help out their suffering loved ones. In the Chinese religious economy assignment to heaven or hell was not permanent; depending on one's behavior and performance, one could continue to be promoted or demoted, even after death. Thus heaven and hell were centrally about justice and moral retribution.

The Chinese had long put ethics at the center of religion, and they had strong beliefs early on about moral justice and retribution. The Buddhist concept of karma added a new dimension to the beliefs, and led to an elaborate system. Simply stated, karma was a law of ethical cause and effect spanning many lives. One's current circumstances were the result of past actions in this life and past lives; one's future circumstances and future lives were in turn dependent on one's actions in response to the karmically conditioned circumstances. The soul did not live through just one life, but could be reborn indefinitely, living out the result of past acts. Although in one sense the soul lived out its moral retribution in heaven or in hell, in another sense that is too simple. To remain in one's heavenly assignment one had to continue to act in a worthy manner; it was not an eternal reward. Moreover, Chinese popular literature suggests that the deities in heaven had a difficult time maintaining an impeccable level of behavior. A serious misstep could result in rebirth on earth or even demotion to hell.

Hell, on the other hand, usually is seen by the Chinese more as a ghoulish purgatory than a permanent damnation. There one paid for past sins, but then one was sent through the wheel of rebirth into another life. As with prison, there always was the hope of release.

That belief was where the living relatives came in, with an enormous impact on Chinese religious life. Later Buddhism and Taoism incorporated centrally into their religious life the notion that the living could lighten the suffering of their dead ancestors and lead them to an early and pleasant rebirth on earth or in heaven. In Buddhist terms, this was due to the notion of "transfer of merit," according to which one could do religious deeds for the sake of another. In the most formal sense, one did charitable acts, performed religious services, or undertook some religious discipline, and intentionally transferred the merit of that act into an account, as it were, for one's relatives, or for all suffering beings. This notion reinforced the Bodhisattva notion of compassion for all living beings, of seeking not one's own enlightenment, but the salvation of all suffering beings.

In an extension of the impulse Chinese offered masses for the souls of the dead, pacifying rituals for souls, and sent spirit moneys to hell. When the person died and faced the initial journey to hell for the great trial that would determine his assignment in the netherworld, relatives provided all of the amenities: horses, carriages, servants, food, and money. In ancient times some Chinese rulers were buried with horses, servants, and the like. After the classic period these were no longer items of the "real" world, but facsimiles for use in the other world—often paper items. And the money was the famous "spirit money," made of cheap paper and foil, but ritually transmitted to have full value in the other world: It was backed not by bullion, but by the religious merit and ritual prowess of the living.

The journey to hell and the time in purgatory were terrifying to many Chinese. Compassion for the souls suffering in hell was captured in the famous story of Mu-lien, a devout monk who journeyed to the lowest depths of hell to rescue his less-than-virtuous mother from terrible suffering. Mu-lien's journey was celebrated by Chinese in religious dramas, and these dramas often were performed as part of funerals. In some versions the sons themselves would join in part of the drama, going with the actor-priests on a symbolic journey into hell to visit their suffering relatives. When a mother had died, sons who took this ritual journey sometimes were asked to drink a glass of wine, symbolizing a pool of blood in which their mothers were suffering because their mothers' blood had defiled the earth at their birth. That is, the sons take back on themselves the sin and defilement that their mothers suffered in giving them birth, thus releasing them from their suffering in hell. Such rituals have deep symbolic and psychological power.[8]

THE END OF TIME: BEYOND THE REALM OF REBIRTH

None of the views discussed to this point entailed belief in an eternal condition for the soul. There was some impetus in Buddhism to speak of ''final salvation,'' although, ironically, that ''salvation'' would entail the recognition of the nonexistence of the soul, of Nirvana.

Pure Land Buddhists introduced the notion of rebirth not into heaven or hell, but directly in the Pure Land of Bliss established by Amitabha Buddha. This was not a permanent paradise, but a realm devoted to the practice of Buddhism and the nurturance of Buddhist faith. It was the ideal environment in which to achieve Buddhist enlightenment and, eventually, Nirvana. Amitabha established the Pure Land out of his infinite compassion because the world had become an extremely difficult place in which to nurture Buddhist faith and practice. In ''orthodox'' Buddhist terms, as defined by philosophical writings and commentaries, there were two important qualifications on the Pure Land. First, it was not a paradise, but an environment in which to realize that there is ''no soul.'' Nirvana or extinction is the only final release, but there is no more self to enjoy Nirvana; thus a notion of a permanent Buddhist paradise is in conflict with Buddhist philosophy. Second, the Pure Land is merely a skillful means *(fang-pien,* or *upaya)* created by the Buddha to help us aspire to spiritual realization; it does not literally exist. The Pure Land is in one's own pure mind whenever one thinks of Amitabha.[9]

Although both of those qualifications represent the most sophisticated Buddhist doctrine, millions of Chinese believed in the Pure Land as a kind of paradise, and fervently hoped for rebirth there.

In late traditional China millennarian Buddhists came to look for the coming of Maitreya Buddha in the final days at the end of the kalpa, or of this cycle of creation. They believed that the Buddha had sent various emissaries to warn humans that the end was near and that the only hope of salvation was faith. Again, in ''orthodox'' or elite terms the notion of final salvation was a skillful means to support religious aspiration, but in popular terms many people believed themselves to be signing onto the registers of the blest so that they would enjoy bliss and escape damnation.

CONCLUSION

What we have seen in this brief overview is a rich panoply of beliefs and practices that show the Chinese vitally concerned about the well-being of their loved ones in life and in death. There were many unreconciled issues among these various views; that very diversity reflects the nature of Chinese religion. On the other hand, there also were patterns or consistencies at a more general level: (a) the concern for well-being; (b) the strong sense of moral justice; (c) the responsibility of the living not only for themselves but for the ancestors, and vice versa. Perhaps the most profound message of Chinese religion was that of the interconnectedness of souls, of human beings. The living were surrounded by and connected to the dead; the dead influenced and continued to connect with the living. Religion both taught and provided ways for the Chinese to maintain the proper relationships among the living, and between the living and the dead. That was for them the crux of religion and of their views of death and the afterlife.

The central question for the Chinese, then, was not the fate of the soul after death, but rather how to relate properly to the souls of ancestors and of malevolent spirits. As Arthur Wolf has shown in his brilliant essay, there was a pattern to ritual behavior, a cultural code, that defined the treatment of gods, ghosts, and ancestors in patterns not unlike the treatment of rulers, ruffians, and families in the world of the living. Because the dead were very much around the living and the boundaries between life and death were relatively porous, the relationships with the dead and with death form a continuum with relationships with the living.[10]

NOTES

1. The customs of ancestor worship, although theoretically specified by the classic ritual texts, in fact varied considerably by region and social or ethnic group. The description in this chapter is but one fairly typical pattern, useful for limited heuristic purposes. The variations on ancestor worship have produced a voluminous and growing historical and anthropological literature.

2. The later conceptions of the netherworld are discussed in the next section.

3. Chuang Tzu, Sec. 18. Burton Watson, trans., *Chuang Tzu, Basic Writings* (New York: Columbia University Press, 1964), 113. Copyright © 1964 Columbia University Press. Used by permission.

4. Chuang Tzu, Sec. 1. Watson, *Chuang Tzu,* 27–28. Yao and Shun were revered sages of antiquity believed to be responsible for the foundations of much of Chinese civilization.

5. Gary Seaman has produced a number of excellent ethnographic films recording rituals for the care of graves and bones in Taiwan.

6. See Holmes Welch, *The Practice of Chinese Buddhism* (Cambridge, Mass.: Harvard University Press, 1967), 342–45.

7. Wolfgang Bauer, *China and the Search for Happiness,* trans. Michael Shaw (New York: Seabury Press, 1976), esp. chs. 2 and 3.

8. For the information on Mu-lien dramas and funerals, I am deeply indebted to a workshop on Mulien funerary dramas at the University of California, Berkeley, in July 1987.

9. See, for example, *The Platform Sutra of the Sixth Patriarch,* Sec. 35, trans. Philip B. Yampolsky (New York: Columbia University Press, 1967), 156–59.

10. Arthur P. Wolf, "Gods, Ghosts, and Ancestors," in Wolf, ed., *Religion and Ritual in Chinese Society* (Stanford, Calif.: Stanford University Press, 1974), 131–82.

Bibliography: For Further Reading

GENERAL

Eliade, Mircea. "Death, Afterlife and Eschatology." Chap. 3 of *From Primitives to Zen: A Thematic Sourcebook of the History of Religions*. New York: Harper & Row, 1967.

Huntington, Richard, and Peter Metcalf, eds. *Celebrations of Death: The Anthropology of Mortuary Ritual*. Cambridge: Cambridge University Press, 1979.

van der Leeuw, G. *Religion in Essence and Manifestation*. Gloucester, Mass.: Peter Smith, 1967.

Morris, Brian. *Anthropological Studies of Religion*. Cambridge: Cambridge University Press, 1987.

Sharpe, Eric J. *Comparative Religion: A History*. London: Gerald Duckworth, 1975.

Smart, Ninian. *The Religious Experience of Mankind*. New York: Charles Scribner's Sons, 1976.

Sullivan, Lawrence E., ed. *Death, Afterlife and the Soul: Religion, History and Culture Selections from the Encyclopedia of Religion*. New York: Macmillan, 1987.

de Vries, Jan. *The Study of Religion: A Historical Approach*. New York: Harcourt, Brace and World, 1967.

AFRICAN RELIGIONS

Bloch, Maurice. *Placing the Dead*. New York: Seminar Press, 1971.

———. "Death, Women and Power." In *Death and the Regeneration of Life*, edited by M. Bloch and J. Parry, 211–30. New York: Cambridge University Press, 1982.

Bond, George C. *The Politics of Change in a Zambian Community*. Chicago: University of Chicago Press, 1976.

———. "A Prophecy That Failed: The Lumpa Church of Uyombe." In *African Christianity,* edited by George C. Bond, et al. New York: Academic Press, 1979.

———. "Ancestor and Protestants." *American Ethnologist* 14, no. 1 (1987).

Evans-Pritchard, Edward E. *Nuer Religion.* Oxford: Oxford University Press, 1956.

Hofstra, S. "The Ancestral Spirits of the Mende." *Internationales Archiv für Ethnographie* 34, Heft 1–4, 1940.

Little, Kenneth L. *The Mende of Sierra Leone.* London: Routledge & Kegan Paul, 1951.

Woodburn, James. "Social Dimensions of Death in Four African Hunting and Gathering Societies." In *Death and the Regeneration of Life,* edited by M. Bloch and J. Parry, 187–210. New York: Cambridge University Press, 1982.

ANCIENT MESOPOTAMIAN RELIGION

Alster, Bendt, ed. *Death in Mesopotamia.* Papers read at the XXVIe Recontre assyriologique internationale. Mesopotamia. Copenhagen Studies in Assyriology 8. Copenhagen: Akademisk Forlag, 1980.

The Assyrian Dictionary of the Oriental Institute of the University of Chicago. Chicago: Oriental Institute, 1956–.

Bayliss, Miranda. "The Cult of Dead Kin in Assyria and Babylonia." *Iraq* 35 (1973): 115–25.

Cooper, Jerrold S. *Sumerian and Akkadian Royal Inscriptions.* I. Presargonic Inscriptions. American Oriental Society Translation Series I. New Haven, Conn.: American Oriental Society, 1986.

Grayson, A. Kirk. *Assyrian and Babylonian Chronicles.* Texts from Cuneiform Sources, No. 5. Locust Valley, N.Y.: J. J. Augustin, 1975.

Heidel, Alexander. *The Gilgamesh Epic and Old Testament Parallels.* Chicago: University of Chicago Press, 1949.

Kramer, Samuel N. "The Death of Gilgamesh." *Bulletin of the American Schools for Oriental Research* 94 (April 1944):2–12.

———. "Gilgamesh and the Land of the Living." *Journal of Cuneiform Studies* 3 (1947):3–46.

———. "The Death of Ur-Nammu and His Descent to the Netherworld." *Journal of Cuneiform Studies* 21 (1969):104–25.

Lambert, Wilfred G., and Millard, A. R. *Atra-hasis: The Babylonian Story of the Flood.* Oxford: Oxford University Press, 1969.

Oppenheim, A. Leo. *Ancient Mesopotamia. Portrait of a Dead Civilization.* Rev. ed. Chicago: University of Chicago Press, 1977.

Palgi, Phyllis, and Abramovitch, Henry. "Death: A Cross-Cultural Perspective," *Annual Review of Anthropology* 13 (1984):385–417.

Parpola, Simo. *Letters from Assyrian Scholars to the Kings Esarhaddon and Assurbanipal.* Alter Orient und Altes Testament 5/1–2. Kevelaer, Germany: Butzon & Bercker, 1970, 1983.

Pritchard, James B., ed. *Ancient Near Eastern Texts Relating to the Old Testament.* 3rd ed. Princeton, N.J.: Princeton University Press, 1969.

Tigay, Jeffrey H. *The Evolution of the Gilgamesh Epic.* Philadelphia: University of Pennsylvania Press, 1982.

Weiss, Harvey, ed. *Ebla to Damascus. Art and Archaeology of Ancient Syria.* Washington, D.C.: Smithsonian Institution, 1985.

ANCIENT EGYPTIAN RELIGION

Faulkner, Raymond O. *The Ancient Egyptian Pyramid Texts.* Oxford: Clarendon Press, 1969. 2 volumes.

———. *The Ancient Egyptian Coffin Texts.* Warminster: Aris & Phillips, 1973–78. 3 volumes.

———. *The Ancient Egyptian Book of the Dead,* edited by Carol Andrews. London: British Museum Publications, 1985.

Hornung, Erik. *Conceptions of God in Ancient Egypt: The One and the Many,* translated by John Baines. Ithaca, N.Y.: Cornell University Press, 1982.

Kemp, Barry J. *Ancient Egypt: Anatomy of a Civilization.* London: Kegan Paul International, 1989.

Morenz, Siegfried. *Egyptian Religion,* translated by Ann E. Keep. Ithaca, N.Y.: Cornell University Press, 1960.

Spencer, A. J. *Death in Ancient Egypt.* Harmondsworth: Penguin Books, 1982.

Wente, Edward F. "Funerary Beliefs of the Ancient Egyptians." *Expedition* 24, no. 4 (Winter 1982):17–28.

Zandee, J. *Death as an Enemy.* Studies in the History of Religion, Supplements to *Numen* No. 5. Leiden: E. J. Brill, 1960.

ANCIENT GREEK RELIGION

Alexiou, Margaret. *The Ritual Lament in Greek Tradition.* Cambridge: Cambridge University Press, 1974.

Bremmer, Jan. *The Early Greek Concept of the Soul.* Princeton, N.J.: Princeton University Press, 1987.

Claus, David B. *Toward the Soul: An Inquiry into the Meaning of "Psyche" Before Plato.* New Haven, Conn.: Yale University Press, 1981.

Garland, Robert. *The Greek Way of Death.* Ithaca, N.Y.: Cornell University Press, 1985.

Jaeger, Werner. *The Theology of the Early Greek Philosophers,* translated by E. S. Robinson. Oxford: Oxford University Press, 1947, esp. ch. 5.

Kurtz, D. C., and Boardman, John. *Greek Burial Customs.* Ithaca, N.Y.: Cornell University Press, 1971.

Lattimore, Richmond. *Themes in Greek and Latin Epitaphs.* 2nd ed. Urbana: University of Illinois Press, 1962.

MacKenzie, Mary Margaret. *Plato on Punishment.* Berkeley: University of California Press, 1981, esp. ch. 13.

Parker, Robert. *Miasma: Pollution and Purification in Early Greek Religion.* Oxford: Clarendon Press, 1983.

Richardson, N. J. "Early Greek Views About Life After Death." In P. E. Easterling and J. V. Muir. *Greek Religion and Society.* Cambridge: Cambridge University Press, 1985.

Ronde, Erwin. *Psyche: The Cult of Souls and Belief in Immortality.* Originally published in London, 1927; reprinted, New York: Harper & Row, 1966.

Vermeule, Emily D. *Aspects of Death in Early Greek Art and Poetry*. Berkeley: University of California Press, 1979.

OLD TESTAMENT

Brichto, H. C. "Kin, Cult, Land and Afterlife—A Biblical Complex." *Hebrew Union College Annual* 44 (1973):1–54.

Dahood, Mitchell. *Psalms III 101–150,* The Anchor Bible. Garden City, N.Y.: Doubleday, 1970, XLI-LII.

Guillaume, Alfred. *Prophecy and Divination Among the Hebrews and Other Semites*. London: Hodder & Stoughton, 1938.

Hanson, Paul D. *The Dawn of Apocalyptic*. Philadelphia: Fortress Press, 1984.

Hoffner, Harry A., Jr. "Second Millennium Antecedents to the Hebrew '*OB*.' " *Journal of Biblical Literature* 86 (1967):385–401.

Lewis, I. M. *Ecstatic Religion*. Baltimore: Penguin Books, 1971.

Mendenhall, George E. *The Tenth Generation: The Origins of Biblical Tradition*. Baltimore: Johns Hopkins University Press, 1974.

Middleton, John. *Lugbara Religion*. London: Oxford University Press, 1960.

Mowinckel, Sigmund. *The Psalms in Israel's Worship*. A Translation and Revision of *Offersang og Sangoffer,* by D. R. Ap-Thomas, 2 vols. Oxford: Basil Blackwell, 1962.

Smith, Mark S., and Bloch-Smith, Elizabeth M. "Death and Afterlife in Ugarit and Israel." *Journal of American Oriental Society* 108 (1988):277–84.

Spronk, K. *Beatific Afterlife in Ancient Israel and the Ancient Near East*. Alter Orient und Altes Testament 219. Kevelaer, Germany: Butzon & Bercker; Neukirchen-Vluyn: Neukirchener Verlag, 1986.

Tromp, Nicholas J. *Primitive Conceptions of Death and the Nether World in the Old Testament*. Rome: Pontifical Biblical Institute, 1969.

NEW TESTAMENT

Black, C. Clifton. "Pauline Perspectives on Death in Romans 5–8." *Journal of Biblical Literature* 103 (1984):413–33.

Bruce, F. F. "Paul and the Life to Come." In *Paul: Apostle of the Heart Set Free*. Grand Rapids, Mich.: Eerdmans, 1977.

Keck, Leander E. "New Testament Views of Death." In *Perspectives on Death,* edited by L. O. Mills. Nashville: Abingdon Press, 1969.

Rist, Martin. "Millennium." *Interpreter's Dictionary of the Bible,* 3:381–82. Nashville: Abingdon Press, 1962.

Robinson, J.A.T. "Resurrection in the New Testament." *Interpreter's Dictionary of the Bible,* 4:43–53. Nashville: Abingdon Press, 1962.

Schnackenburg, Rudolph. "The Ideas of Life in the Fourth Gospel." In *The Gospel According to John,* 2:352–61. New York: Seabury Press, 1980.

Scott, Ernest F. "Life." In *The Fourth Gospel,* 239–64. Edinburgh: T. & T. Clark, 1906.

Stendall, Krister, ed. *Immortality and Resurrection*. New York: Macmillan, 1965.

JUDAISM

Ganzfield, Solomon. *Code of Jewish Law,* translated by Hyman E. Goldin, 4:84–137. New York: Star Hebrew Publishing Company, 1927.

Lamm, Maurice. *The Jewish Way in Death and Mourning.* New York: Johnathan David Press, 1969.

Lieberman, Saul. "Some Aspects of After Life in Rabbinic Literature." In *Texts and Studies.* New York: Ktav Publishing Co., 1974.

Maimonides, Moses. "The Essay on Resurrection." In *Crisis and Leadership: Epistles of Maimonides,* translated by A. Halkin, 208–92. Philadelphia: Jewish Publication Society of America, 1985.

Moore, George F. *Judaism in the First Centuries of the Christian Era: The Age of the Tannaim.* Esp. 2:279–95. Cambridge, Mass.: Harvard University Press, 1927; repr. 1966.

Rabinowicz, Harry. *A Guide to Life: Jewish Laws and Customs of Mourning.* London: Jewish Chronicle Publications, 1964.

Riemer, Jack. *Jewish Reflections on Death.* New York: Schocken Books, 1975.

Rowley, H. H. *The Faith of Israel.* London: SCM Press, 1956.

Urbach, Ephraim E. *The Sages.* Esp. 1:420–523. Jerusalem: Magnes Press, 1975.

CHRISTIANITY

Augustine. *The City of God,* Book XIII. New York: Modern Library, 1980.

Berdyaev, Nikolai. *The Destiny of Man.* London: G. Bles, 1954.

Hick, John. *Death and Eternal Life.* London: Collins, 1976.

Kung, Hans. *Eternal Life? Life After Death as a Medical, Philosophical, and Theological Problem.* Garden City, N.Y.: Doubleday, 1982.

Mills, Liston O., ed. *Perspectives on Death.* Nashville: Abingdon Press, 1969.

Pelikan, Jaroslav. *The Shape of Death: Life, Death and Immortality in the Early Fathers.* Nashville: Abingdon Press, 1961.

Rahner, Karl. "On the Theology of Death." In *Modern Catholic Thinkers,* edited by A. Robert Caponigri, 138–76. New York: Harper & Brothers, 1960.

Stannard, David. *The Puritan Way of Death: A Study on Religion, Culture and Social Change.* New York: Oxford University Press, 1977.

van de Walle, A. R. *From Darkness to the Dawn.* Mystic, Conn.: Twenty-third Publications, 1984.

ISLAM

Avicenna. *On Theology,* translated by A. J. Arberry. London: John Murray, 1951.

Chittick, W. C. "Eschatology." In *Islamic Spirituality: Foundations,* edited by S. H. Nasr, 378–409. New York: Crossroad, 1987.

Corbin, H. *Spiritual Body and Celestial Earth.* Princeton, N.J.: Princeton University Press, 1977.

Ghazâlî, al-. *The Precious Pearl (al-Durra al-Fakhira),* translated by J. I. Smith. Missoula, Mont.: Scholars Press, 1981.

Morris, J. W. "Lesser and Greater Resurrection." In Ibn ʿArabî. *Les Illuminations de*

La Mecque/The Meccan Illuminations: Textes choisis/Selected Texts. Paris: Sinbad, 1988.

Mullâ Sadrâ. *The Wisdom of the Throne,* translated by J. W. Morris. Princeton, N.J.: Princeton University Press, 1981.

Rahman, F. *Major Themes of the Qur'ân*. Minneapolis: Bibliotheca Islamica, 1980.

Râzî, Najm al-Dîn. *The Path of God's Bondsmen from Origin to Return,* translated by H. Algar. Delmar, N.Y.: Caravan Books, 1982.

Schimmel, A. "Creation and Judgment in the Koran and in Mystico-Poetical Interpretation." In *We Believe in One God,* edited by A. Schimmel and A. Falaturi, 149–77. New York: Seabury, 1979.

Smith, J. I., and Haddad, Y. Y. *The Islamic Understanding of Death and Resurrection*. Albany: State University of New York Press, 1981.

HINDUISM

Bṛhadāraṇyaka Upaniṣad 3.2; Kaṭha Upaniṣad; Kauṣītakī-Brāhmaṇa Upaniṣad 1. In Radhakrishnan, S., trans. *The Principal Upaniṣads,* 215–18, 595–645, 753–60. London: George Allen & Unwin, 1953.

Brown, W. Norman. "The Rigvedic Equivalent for Hell." *Journal of the American Oriental Society* 61 (1941): 76–81.

Knipe, David. "*Sapindīkarana:* The Hindu Rite of Entry into Heaven." In *Religious Encounters with Death,* edited by F. Reynolds and E. Waugh, 111–24. University Park: Pennsylvania State University Press, 1977.

Lincoln, Bruce. "The Lord of the Dead." *History of Religions* 20 (1981): 224–41.

Manu Dharmaśāstra 12. In Bühler, Georg, trans. *The Laws of Manu*. The Sacred Books of the East, 25:483–513. Oxford: Clarendon Press, 1886.

O'Flaherty, Wendy Doniger. *The Origins of Evil in Hindu Mythology*. Berkeley: University of California Press, 1976.

———, ed. *Karma and Rebirth in Classical Indian Tradition*. Berkeley: University of California Press, 1980.

Ṛgveda-saṃhitā. Book 10, Hymns 14, 16, 18, 58, 135, 154. In O'Flaherty, W. D., trans. *The Rig Veda,* 41–58. Hammondsworth: Penguin Books, 1981.

Tull, Herman W. *The Vedic Origins of Karma: Cosmos as Man in Ancient Indian Myth and Ritual*. Albany: State University of New York Press, 1989.

BUDDHISM

Amore, Roy. "The Heterodox Systems." In *Death and Eastern Thought,* edited by Frederick Holck, 114–63. Abingdon Press, 1974.

Bond, George. "Theravada Buddhism's Meditations on Death and the Symbolism of Initiatory Death." *History of Religions* 19 (1980):237–58.

Holt, John. "Assisting the Dead by Venerating the Living." *Numen* 28, no. 1 (1981): 1–28.

Keyes, Charles. "Death of Two Buddhist Saints in Thailand." In *Charisma and Sacred Biography,* edited by Michael A. Williams. *Journal of the American Academy of Religion, Thematic Studies* 48, nos. 3 and 4 (1982):149–80.

———. "From Death to Birth: Ritual Process and Buddhist Meanings in Northern Thailand." In *Folk* (Copenhagen) 29 (1987):181–206.

King, Winston. "Practicing Dying: The Samurai-Zen Death Techniques of Suzuki-Shosan." In *Religious Encounters with Death,* edited by Frank E. Reynolds and Earl H. Waugh, 143–58. University Park: Pennsylvania State University Press, 1976.

LaFleur, William. "Japan." In *Death and Eastern Thought,* edited by Frederick Holck, 226–56. Nashville: Abingdon Press, 1974.

Teiser, Stephen. *The Ghost Festival in Medieval China.* Princeton, N.J.: Princeton University Press, 1987.

Welch, Holmes, *The Practice of Chinese Buddhism: 1900–1950.* Cambridge, Mass.: Harvard University Press, 1967.

TIBETAN TANTRIC RELIGION

Aziz, Barbara. "Reincarnation Reconsidered: The Reincarnate Lama as Shaman." In *Spirit Possession in the Nepal Himalayas,* edited by J. Hitchcock and R. Jones 343–60. New Delhi: Vikas Publishing House, 1976.

Brauen, Martin, and Kvaeme Per. "A Tibetan Death Ceremony." *Temenos* 14 (1978): 9–24.

Evans-Wentz, W. Y., trans. *The Tibetan Book of the Dead.* Oxford: Oxford University Press, 1927.

Freemantle, F., and Chogyam Trungpa, trans. *The Tibetan Book of the Dead.* Boulder, Colo.: Shambala, 1975.

Lama Lodro. *Bardo Teachings: The Way of Death and Rebirth.* Ithaca, N.Y.: Snow Lion, 1987.

Lati Rinbochay and Hopkins, Jeffery. *Death, Intermediate State, and Rebirth.* Ithaca, N.Y.: Gabriel Snow Lion, 1979.

Mumford, Stan Royal. *Himalayan Dialogue, Tibetan Lamas and Gurung Shamans in Nepal.* Madison: University of Wisconsin Press, 1989.

Tenzin Gyatso. *Kindness, Clarity and Insight,* translated and edited by Jeffery Hopkins. Ithaca, N.Y.: Snow Lion Press, 1984.

Tucci, Giuseppe. *The Religions of Tibet.* London: Routledge & Kegan Paul, 1980.

CHINESE RELIGIONS

Ahern, Emily M. *The Cult of the Dead in a Chinese Village.* Stanford, Calif.: Stanford University Press, 1973.

Groot, Jan Jakob M. de. *The Religious System of China.* Book I. *Disposal of the Dead.* Amsterdam, 1892; repr. Taipei: Cheng-wen Publishing, 1969.

Hsü, Francis L. K. *Under the Ancestor's Shadow.* Stanford, Calif.: Stanford University Press, 1967.

Loewe, Michael. *Ways to Paradise. The Chinese Quest for Immortality.* London: Allen & Unwin, 1979.

Reichelt, Karl Ludwig. "The Origin and Development of Masses for the Dead." In *Truth and Tradition in Chinese Buddhism: A Study of Mahayana Buddhism,* translated by Katherine van Wagenen Bugge. Shanghai: Commercial Press, 1927.

Teiser, Stephen F. *The Ghost Festival in Medieval China.* Princeton, N.J.: Princeton University Press, 1988.

Watson, James L. "Of Flesh and Bones. The Management of Death and Pollution in

Cantonese Society.'' In *Death and Regeneration of Life,* edited by M. Bloch and J. Parry, 155–86. Cambridge: Cambridge University Press, 1982.

Watson, James L., and Rawski, Evelyn S., eds. *Death Ritual in Late Imperial and Modern China.* Berkeley: University of California Press, 1988.

Welch, Holmes, and Seidel, Anna, eds. *Facets of Taoism.* New Haven, Conn.: Yale University Press, 1979.

Wolf, Arthur P. ''Gods, Ghosts and Ancestors.'' In *Religion and Ritual in Chinese Society,* edited by A. P. Wolf, 131–82. Stanford, Calif.: Stanford University Press, 1974.

Yü, Ying-shih. ''O Soul, Came Back. A Study of the Changing Conceptions of the Soul and Afterlife in Pre-Buddhist China.'' *Harvard Journal of Asiatic Studies* 47 (1987):363–95.

Index

About the Editor and Contributors

ELISABETH BENARD is visiting assistant professor of Indo-Tibetan Buddhism at the University of Hawaii, Manoa Campus. She is author of *Chinnamasta: The Aweful Buddhist and Hindu Goddess,* which is forthcoming under the Buddhist Tradition Series edited by Alex Wayman. She has published numerous articles, including "The Living Among the Dead: A Comparison of Buddhist and Christian Relics," and has lectured about Tibetan Buddhism and Tibet in the United States, Europe, and India. She is a member of the American Academy of Religion and was the former program chairman of the Society of Women Geographers.

JUDITH A. BERLING is dean and vice-president for Academic Affairs and professor of history of religions at the Graduate Theological Union, Berkeley, also taught for twelve years at Indiana University, and as a visiting professor at Stanford and the University of Chicago Divinity School. She is the author of *The Syncretic Religion of Lin Chao-en* (1980) and numerous articles on Chinese religions, comparative religions, and educational issues. She has been on the board of directors of the Association for Asian Studies, and is currently vice-president of the American Academy of Religion.

GEORGE C. BOND is a professor of applied anthropology at Teachers College, Columbia University. He is the author of *The Politics of Change in a Zambian Community* (Chicago: University of Chicago Press, 1976), coeditor of *African Christianity* (New York: Academic Press, 1979), and the guest editor of a special issue, *African Education and Social Stratification,* of the *Anthropology and Education Quarterly*. He has published articles on topics as diverse as education, kinship, politics, and religion.

WILLIAM C. CHITTICK teaches religious studies at the State University of New York at Stony Brook. Among his books are *A Shi'ite Anthology* (1981), *Fakhruddin Iraqi: Divine Flashes* (1982), *The Sufi Path of Love: The Spiritual Teachings of Rumi* (1983), *The Psalms of Islam* (1988), and *The Sufi Path of Knowledge: Ibn al-ʿArabi's Metaphysics of Imagination* (1989).

JERROLD S. COOPER is professor and chairman of the department of Near Eastern studies at The Johns Hopkins University. He is the author of numerous books and articles on the literature and history of ancient Mesopotamia. He has served as a director of the American Oriental Society, and is a trustee of the American Schools of Oriental Research. He was associate editor of the *Journal of Cuneiform Studies* from 1972 to 1988, and currently edits the monograph series Mesopotamian Civilizations.

ROBERT GOLDENBERG is associate professor of Judaic studies and chair of the department of comparative studies at the State University of New York at Stony Brook. He holds degrees from Cornell and Brown universities, as well as rabbinic ordination from the Jewish Theological Seminary of America. Dr. Goldenberg is especially interested in the transition from the temple-based Judaism of prerabbinic times to the period of rabbinic leadership, and has published several studies relating to the thought, literature, and early history of rabbinic Judaism. His current research concerns the nature and basis of rabbinic authority in the Jewish community and the question of ancient Jewish attitudes toward the religions of other people.

THOMAS J. HOPKINS is professor of religious studies at Franklin and Marshall College. He is the author of *The Hindu Religious Tradition* (1971) and coauthor of *Guide to Hindu Religion* (1981), and has published a variety of articles on Indian religious history, ranging from the earliest developments in the Indus valley to nineteenth- and twentieth-century Hindu devotional movements. He is a member of the American Society for the Study of Religion and the American Academy of Religion, where he served from 1982 to 1988 as cochair of the comparative studies in religion section.

LEANDER E. KECK is Winkley professor of biblical theology at Yale Divinity School, where he also served as dean from 1979 to 1989. Before coming to Yale he was professor of New Testament at Emory University and Vanderbilt University. Among his books are *A Future for the Historical Jesus, The Bible in the Pulpit,* and *Paul and His Letters*. He has lectured at many universities and divinity schools in the United States, Canada, and Australia.

GEORGE E. MENDENHALL is professor of ancient and biblical studies at the University of Michigan since 1952, retired in 1986, and since 1987 has been part-time visiting professor at the Institute of Archaeology and Anthropology, Yarmouk University, Irbid, Jordan. He was director of the American School of Oriental Research in Arab Jerusalem in 1965–66, and of the American Center of Oriental Research in Amman, Jordan, in 1975. He was visiting research professor at the American University of Beirut in 1971, and visiting professor at the Pontifical Biblical Institute in Rome in 1985. He is author of *Law and Covenant in Israel and the Ancient Near East* (1955), *The Tenth Generation: The Origins of the Biblical Tradition* (1973), and *The Syllabic Inscriptions from Byblos* (1985).

WILLIAM J. MURNANE is associate professor of history at Memphis State University and author of numerous articles and reviews on ancient Egyptian history. His books include *The Penguin Guide to Ancient Egypt* (1985) and *The Road to Kadesh* (2nd ed., 1990). He is field director of the El-Amarna Boundary Stelae Project and the ongoing program of publishing the reliefs and inscriptions of the Great Hypostyle Hall at Karnak.

HELEN F. NORTH is centennial professor of classics, Swarthmore College, and is the author of *Sophrosyne: Self-Knowledge and Self-Restraint in Greek Literature* and *From Myth to Icon: Reflections of Greek Ethical Doctrine in Literature and Art.* She is editor of *Interpretations of Plato: A Swarthmore Symposium* and coeditor of *Of Eloquence: Studies in Ancient and Mediaeval Rhetoric,* by Harry Caplan. She has served as president as well as on many of the committees of the American Philological Association.

HIROSHI OBAYASHI is professor and former chairman of the department of religion at Rutgers University. He is the author of books and articles both in English and in Japanese. Books include *Ernst Troeltsch and Theology of Our Own Times* (1972) and *Agape and History* (1981), and numerous scholarly articles have appeared in Japan, Scandinavia, and Canada, as well as in the United States. He has served on the board of directors of the American Academy of Religion and as the president of its mid-Atlantic region. He also has lectured at universities and theological seminaries in the United States, Japan, and Israel.

FRANK E. REYNOLDS is professor of history of religions and Buddhist studies at the University of Chicago. He is an author, editor, and translator of ten books, including *Religious Encounters with Death, Three Worlds of King Ruang: A Thai Buddhist Cosmology,* and *Cosmogony and Ethical Order.* He currently is serving as a director of two major projects—a five-year series of institutes for college and university teachers on ''Religious Studies and Liberal Education: Opportunities and New Directions'' (sponsored by the National Endowment for the Humanities) and a six-year project on ''Religion(s) in Culture and History,'' sponsored by the Institute for the Advanced Study of Religion at the Divinity School, University of Chicago.